SOLDIER IN WHITE

Soldier in White

THE LIFE OF GENERAL GEORGE MILLER STERNBERG

John M. Gibson

DUKE UNIVERSITY PRESS · Durham, N. C. 1958

Printed in the United States of America
The Seeman Printery, Inc., Durham, N. C.

To MISS LOUISE PATTISON *and the late* MRS. CLARENCE B. MILLER, *nieces of General and Mrs. Sternberg, who were most helpful in furnishing many personal letters, records, and other valuable material on their distinguished kinsman.*

Contents

SOLDIER IN WHITE

Farewell to Peace

QUEEN VICTORIA always remembered 1838 as the year of her coronation. The people of London and Liverpool and the communities in between remembered it as the year the railroad connecting those two cities was opened. Frenchmen still remember it as the year Talleyrand died. To Samuel F. B. Morse it was memorable as the year he demonstrated the practical workability of the electric telegraph. And to the Rev. Levi Sternberg 1838 had three excellent reasons for standing out as a red-letter year: He received his Master's degree from Union College after a hard struggle. He was ordained to the Lutheran ministry, to which he had long aspired. And, most important of all, he and Margaret Levering Miller Sternberg became—on June 8—the parents of their first baby.

That baby's most distinguished living relative was his maternal grandfather, the Rev. George B. Miller, who had been principal of Hartwick Seminary, a small but influential institution in upstate New York, since 1830. So the first of the new generation of Sternbergs—there were to be eight babies in all—was named George Miller.

The elder Sternberg had been teaching at Hartwick Seminary for some time when these three important events occurred, and he remained there for some time afterward. But his heart was set on the ministry, and he made the break from teacher to preacher as soon as he could. For eleven years, from 1839 to 1850, he devoted his full time and his vast energies to churches—Lutheran churches, of course—in Danville, Buffalo, and Middleburg. Then his aged father-in-law, wearying of the heavy responsibilities of the principalship, asked the trustees to name someone else, younger, stronger, and better able to carry the heavy burden, to take charge. The choice fell upon the Rev. Levi Sternberg.

But young George did not return to Hartwick Seminary (which was a post office and municipality, as well as a college) with his parents. He was already there. The climate at Buffalo, where his father was then pastor of the First English Evangelical Lutheran Church, had been extremely severe. There had been disturbing signs that it was affecting the child's health and might even wreck it. So, in 1846, when he was eight, his maternal grandmother had prevailed upon his parents to let him go and live with her and his grandfather. He had been there about four years when his own parents moved back to the college community. During that time he had developed a warm attachment to both of his grandparents, although not at the expense of his devotion to his father and mother.

Thus it was that Hartwick Seminary came to be George Sternberg's childhood home, as well as the place of his birth. In spite of a number of absences, some of them extended, he was to regard it as home until after he reached early manhood. And he never ceased to remember it with deep and even sentimental affection. At his seventieth birthday banquet, near the end of a long and distinguished career which had given him few opportunities to revisit it, he pictured the Hartwick Seminary community as "a quiet valley among the hills of Otsego County, New York, made famous by the writings of Fenimore Cooper." He remembered it, as have many others, as a place of surpassing, though rugged, beauty. Here, as another aging son of Otsego County once said, "nature has scattered her gifts with generous profusion." Along those first few miles of its course from Otsego Lake to the Chesapeake, the Susquehanna was "as bright and beautiful as river can be." Along those beginning miles it raced then, as it does today, in a vivaciously leaping current between lofty hills. Otsego Lake itself, small as lakes go, rests placidly on upland nearly a quarter of a mile above sea level. And strongly burned into George Sternberg's boyhood memories were the thick woods stretching in a dazzling succession of hills and valleys in nearly all directions from the lake's very banks. He remembered, too, how those thick forests had come alive with a multitude of birds, wild, swift, noisy at times, but always fascinating to an eager youngster who kept wondering what the world was like beyond those singing, swinging forests.

He also remembered, and remembered with pride and thankfulness, what his father and mother and others of the community told him about his ancestors and the ancestors of most of his boyhood friends and neighbors. Like many another youngster who has grown up in Hartwick Seminary, Cooperstown, and those other Otsego County neighborhoods, he learned early about the religious migration which started in the German Palatinate in the early 1700's and ended in various parts of America, including, of course, Otsego County, some forty years later.

During those four decades some ponderous mechanism seemed to be holding open a huge gate against which powerful forces had been pressing for a long, long time, and through that vast gateway flowed a steady stream of religious refugees, irresistibly drawn to the New World. From its starting point in south Germany that stream flooded westward to Holland and England. There it broke up into smaller streams, some leading to Pennsylvania, some to North Carolina, some to New Jersey, and some to upstate New York. Nearly three thousand of those liberty-loving Palatines landed in New York City within a six-week period in June and July, 1710. Never before had so many new Americans reached our shores in such a short time. Never again, until long after the Revolutionary War, would anything like so many do so.

Among those emigrating Palatines and their descendants, young George was told, were many as eager to fight for freedom as they were to go far in search of it. They had volunteered, not a handful at a time, but in entire companies for French and Indian wars. They had taken up arms in even greater numbers and with even greater fervor in the Revolutionary War. There was no way for him to find out how many Sternbergs had borne arms in those wars, for the records were, and are, extremely skimpy. But Levi Sternberg could tell him that his own father and three of his uncles had seen military service during the Revolution.

The elder Sternberg also told him a great deal about himself: how he had always been extraordinarily fond of reading and studying; how he had become interested in religion as a child; how that interest had grown and developed into a determination to become a teacher and, if possible, a Lutheran minister; how that dream of entering the Lutheran ministry had become a virtual passion; how at nineteen he had entered Union College and had received the Bachelor of Arts degree there at the age of twenty-one, after winning membership in Phi Beta Kappa; how he had studied theology at Hartwick Seminary for three years, earning expense money by teaching at the same institution; and how, at the age of twenty-four, the three important events had occurred which had made 1838 a red-letter year for him—winning his Master's degree, being ordained a Lutheran minister, and becoming a father for the first time.

Hartwick Seminary, which was to figure importantly in the shaping of George Sternberg's thinking, conduct, and career, was no ordinary college. A church school at a time when the Christian denominations wielded a far stronger influence upon the institutions they supported than they do now, this first Lutheran institution of higher learning to be established in the New World naturally stressed high moral conduct and religion. But it went far beyond that. Its founder, the Rev. Joseph Christopher Hartwick, was like no other minister of his own or our time. He held extraordinarily strong religious views, and these he sternly imposed upon the administration of the college. His will, under which it was established, was one of the very few, if indeed not the only one, to name Jesus Christ as the chief beneficiary. It not only stipulated in not-to-be-misunderstood terms that Hartwick Seminary students would have to meet the strictest standards of personal morality. It also closed the institution's doors to everyone whose mind had been "warped and formed by heretical, Sectarian, Philosophical Opinions, which, if early imbibed, unqualifieth men for the pure and simple Religion of the Gospel." A majority of the trustees had to be Lutheran clergymen or laymen. Full-time professors in the Theological Department were required to sign the following declaration: "I solemnly declare in the presence of God and the Trustees of this Seminary that I do *ex animo* believe the Scriptures of the Old and New Testaments to be the inspired Word of God and the only perfect rule of faith and practice. I believe the Augsburg Confession to be a summary and just exhibition of the fundamental doctrines of the Word of God. I declare that I approve of the general principles of church government adopted by the Lutheran Church in this Country and believe them to be consistent with the word of God. And I do solemnly promise not to teach anything, either directly or by insinuation, which shall appear to me to contradict or to be, in any degree more or less remote, inconsistent with the doctrine or principles avowed in those declarations. On the contrary, I promise, by the aid of God, to vindicate and inculcate those doctrines and principles in opposition to the views of Atheists, Deists, Jews, Socinians, Unitarians, Calvinists, Arians, Universalists, Pelagians, Antimonians, and all other errorists, while I remain a professor in this Seminary."

Such was the academic atmosphere in which George Sternberg grew up. Stern as it was, he liked it, and for Hartwick Seminary he developed a warm devotion. Although his wealth did not keep pace with his fame, he made generous donations to his alma mater while he lived and left it a considerable bequest in his will.

Hartwick Seminary, in its turn, took great pride in him as its most distinguished alumnus. It paid him a particularly great honor by choosing him as princpal speaker when the time came for it to celebrate its hundredth birthday.

The firm religious discipline to which George Sternberg was subjected as a student at Hartwick Seminary carried over to his home life, for the Rev. Levi Sternberg was as stern a parent as he was a teacher. Moreover, he was by no means the only strait-laced minister who played a part in the child's upbringing. At one time there were no fewer than nine minister-members of the Hartwick Seminary faculty who were also members of the Sternberg clan by blood or by marriage. All of this emphasis upon religion at home, as well as at school, had its effect. Someone who knew him in his later years said of him: "His fame never robbed him of the Christian character he inherited. He was always a gentle, unassuming individual, full of reverence for the things of the Lord, and he was strongly Christian in all his relationships."

Hartwick Seminary's records of that period have long since been destroyed, so there is no way of telling how many years he was a student there. For the same reason, we may only presume that he was a good student. (There is sound, off-the-record reason to think he was.) As has already been pointed out, there is no question whatsoever about his having been a loyal and devoted alumnus.

Hartwick Seminary's nearness to Cooperstown entitled it to a share in the renown which came to all Otsego County as the home of James Fenimore Cooper. The famous novelist's bitter quarrels with his Cooperstown neighbors, his libel suits against local newspapers, and the other evidences of his personal weaknesses detracted only slightly from these people's pride in him. The "Chalet," the Cooper farm, where the author spent—with little to show for it—much of the fortune he had won from his writing, was a showplace. So was the mansion he had inherited from his father, contentious, conniving, sharp-dealing old John Cooper. And, after James Fenimore Cooper's death, which occurred in the year after the elder Sternberg moved back to Hartwick Seminary, George joined the literary-minded tourists from near and far who began visiting the grave at Cooperstown's Christ Church.

As a youth, as well as later, George showed how greatly he was influenced by his parents. From Margaret Levering Miller Sternberg, who learned languages with no trouble at all, he inherited the ability to pick up German and French with little effort. From her too, he inherited, or acquired, a quiet, philosophical nature, which kept him from becoming too greatly concerned over problems and controversies that marked his childhood and particularly the much larger ones that plagued him later in life. He was also an unusually affectionate child, in this, too, being more like his mother than his father, who tended to inspire great respect and admiration, in a rigid, stern sort of way, but few demonstrations of affection. From her, too, he inherited his compassionate brown eyes and hair that was strikingly dark until, later in life, it became progressively thin and white. From Levi Sternberg he learned the stern obligation to keep his promises and do his duty at all times, even when that involved severe inconvenience or rugged sacrifice. His broad nose, high forehead, and certain other facial features were like his father's. From both Margaret and Levi he acquired a strong sense of family loyalty and love and ambition to make the most of his opportunities.

Hartwick Seminary was chronically hard-pressed financially, in spite of the generous endowment, mostly in land, which it had received from John Christopher Hartwick. And the school's poverty extended to its faculty. It was a never-ending struggle in the Sternberg household to keep expenses on a level with income. Nor was the economic stringency eased materially those eleven years when the father gave up teaching for the ministry, nor yet when he returned to the institution to become its principal. From beginning to end, the struggle was a grim one.

George seized the first opportunity to help out. In nearby Cooperstown there was a bookstore well known throughout that part of New York State. Founded by Elihu Phinney in 1795, it was then being operated by his sons, Henry and Elihu. The business had grown so much that they needed someone to help them. In 1850, George, then twelve, applied for the job and got it. He made good on it too.

His subsequent firsthand knowledge of the business showed him why it was so well known and so successful. For it was like no other bookstore he had ever seen or heard of. The two Phinney brothers had their own ideas about persuading people to read —and buy—books and were vigorously putting them into practice. Soon after George Sternberg went to work for them, *Blake's Biographical Dictionary* said of them: "No house out of our largest cities, and but few in them at that period, evinced greater or more efficient enterprise in the book trade than these gentlemen."

Like the two Phinney brothers, George Sternberg helped carry wagonloads of books from that Cooperstown store to customers in other towns and isolated rural communities. Later the enterprising Phinneys bought a boat and fitted it out as a floating bookstore, which became a familiar and welcome visitor to any number of communities along the Erie Canal, its visits being looked forward to as eagerly by readers as the overnight stops of the show boats were by amusement-hungry people along the Mississippi and Ohio. On those slow runs between stops the youngster, who had tasted the delights of reading before taking this job, found a made-to-order opportunity to explore those delights to the fullest. Indeed, during those bookselling excursions, with a small-scale world of books all around him, he developed that avid hunger for reading that was to leave its mark upon his mind, his writing, and his conversation as long as he lived.

As pleasant as that bookstore job was, however, George Sternberg had no idea of making it permanent. He had his eyes on better things. So, upon the earnest urging of his mother, he gave it up after about a year and returned to his studies. Like her, and with considerable encouragement from her, he showed that pronounced interest in foreign languages which was to evidence itself so conspicuously later. But he also had a distinct flair for chemistry, mathematics, and the natural sciences.

The financial pressure became more acute about this time, and George decided to do something about it, if possible. The logical thing to do was to get another job. There was a vacancy in a small school about a dozen miles from Hartwick Seminary. Being that close, he could frequently visit his parents and grandparents on weekends, if he could get that job. He did, in spite of being only sixteen.

His salary was ten dollars a month, plus board. Later he taught in another school at twenty dollars a month, presumably without board. This was increased in a series of small boosts until it reached a hundred dollars a quarter. Small as such salaries seem by modern standards, he was able to save money.

He was as successful as a school teacher as he had been as a book salesman. His treatment of his students, some of whom were pretty rowdy and hard to manage, has been described as "a quiet reign." As both teacher and school administrator (he had to be both in those small rural schools) he won golden opinions from the school boards and the communities generally. His "quiet reign" was marked by "thoroughness, general good will and regret at his departure."

With a comfortable nest egg saved, he became a student again in the institution which his father was now heading. During the years that had intervened since his son quit the classroom Levi Sternberg had launched several of the important innovations that were to make his administration notable. Hartwick Seminary had become coeducational, one of the first educational institutions —if not the first—in the country to open its doors indiscriminately to both women and men. Its first woman faculty member, also one of the first on any college faculty, had been appointed. A normal department for the training of teachers, eventually to be emulated by other and better-known colleges and universities all over the country, had been established.

Soon after resuming his studies at Hartwick Seminary George also resumed teaching, this time at the college. The subjects he taught were those favorites of his, mathematics, chemistry, and the natural sciences.

After about two years as teacher-student he reached a decision that had been slowly forming in his mind for a long time. He decided he was going to be a doctor. How he would be able to do so, he had very little idea. For, in 1857 as today, although not to the same extent perhaps, the road to a medical career was long, slow, uncertain, and frighteningly expensive.

He began as ambition-fired youths had been doing for generations, by reading medical texts and getting practical instruction and experience in the office of an older physician. It was his unusual good fortune to be able to work under Dr. Horace Lathrop, Jr., one of the outstanding practitioners of that section. An alumnus of Hartwick Seminary, Hamilton College, and the Jefferson Medical College, Dr. Lathrop had been practicing in Cooperstown since 1852. The *Biographical Review of Otsego County,* published in 1893, calls him "one of the prominent men of the county in many respects." It mentions his "always taking an active interest in whatever tends to benefit the community and elevate his fellowman." This was especially the case, that anonymous author wrote, "in educational and religious matters, as is indicated by his long service on the school board of Cooperstown." A member of the American Academy of Science, as well as the Otsego County Medical Society, Dr. Lathrop was an excellent teacher, inspirer, and guide for an earnest young man on his way to becoming a doctor.

But even an exceptional doctor-teacher like Horace Lathrop could take the young medical student only so far. Formal instruction in one of the medical colleges would have to follow, and here young George Sternberg came face to face with the toughest financial crisis of his life. Medical school tuition would call for a great deal of money, far more than he and his parents could hope to get together.

There was an answer to their problem, however. An uncle on his mother's side was a person of considerable means. Equally important, he was willing to spend a substantial portion of his savings upon a bright young man who showed promise and ambition. George was not interested in a gift. All he wanted was a loan, enough to keep him going until he could finish college and begin practicing. A loan having been arranged—and a loan it definitely was, at his insistence—he entered the Western College School of Medicine in Buffalo, now a part of the University of Buffalo. Later, in the fall of 1859, he transferred to Columbia University's College of Physicians and Surgeons in New York City. He was graduated with the degree of M.D. in 1860.

To Dr. George M. Sternberg, still a trifle self-conscious about that new title of Doctor, a medical career was no pathway to either wealth or fame. As he said years later, "When I graduated in medicine from the College of Physicians and Surgeons, my ambition did not extend beyond the hope of securing a living practice in the country."

Such a hope was certainly modest enough. But it appeared for a while that even it was too ambitious for realization, for his hard-won medical career did not begin at all auspiciously. In fact it began disastrously:

> My first venture was a little town on Long Island, where a vacancy was supposed to exist owing to the recent death of an old and highly respected physician. Apparently I was not able to fill this vacancy, for my professional shingle was displayed for months and I did not receive a single professional call.

This "conservative community" was obviously not the place for him. He decided to try his luck elsewhere, choosing Elizabeth City (now Elizabeth), New Jersey. He did better there.

Meanwhile, stirring and tragic events had been occurring. The nation had been racing madly toward intersectional war. Those on both sides who saw the tragedy and the madness of it were shouted down by those who saw, or thought they saw, the glory and the triumph of it. And finally, in that tragic and momentous April of 1861, the dam broke at Fort Sumter. Another vast floodgate was swung open, different from that which had opened wide to his ancestors and those others of the Palatinate a century and a half earlier. It released no new stream of migrants in the name of religious freedom. It released, instead, an overpowering flood of dammed-up hatred and bitterness that has not entirely dried up to this day.

Dr. Sternberg was just beginning to enjoy "a little practice" in his new home in New Jersey when the war began. The war fever was running high, as it always does at a time like that, and the army was calling for doctors. He decided that his duty to his country far outweighed his need to continue the gradual upbuilding of his practice. That could wait until after victory. The wait would not be long, just a few weeks or months at most—he, like practically everybody else, was sure of that.

The best way a young doctor could serve was as a medical officer in the army. Dr. Sternberg was sure he could make good as an assistant surgeon. But he would have to pass a stiff examination. It was not easy even to get permission to take that examination. Aspirants for appointments had to show they were potential officer material before they were admitted to the examination rooms. Their personal qualities, as well as their professional capabilities, were carefully looked into. Recommendations and endorsements by prominent people were always helpful.

There was just one person of national reputation in the Hartwick Seminary-Cooperstown community after James Fenimore Cooper's death, Justice Samuel Nelson of the United States Supreme Court. He and Levi Sternberg had been friends for years, and the famed jurist had been watching George's progress over the years with interest and admiration. When the young doctor asked him for a letter of recommendation, he was glad to help. He wrote Secretary of War Simeon Cameron:

> He is a young man of a most respectable family and of good education, character and habits and fairly entitled to the place he seeks. I cordially recommend him to the kindness of the board.

Dr. Sternberg considered such a recommendation from such an influential person all he needed. "I am desirous," he wrote on April 14, "of obtaining a situation as assistant surgeon in the Army. Thinking that the enclosed letter from Judge Nelson would be as satisfactory as any I could present, I have not endeavored to obtain any others." His letter ended with a brief summary of his education and experience as a physician.

Secretary Cameron was impressed by Judge Nelson's endorsement and the young man's record. He wrote Dr. Sternberg on April 22 that he would be admitted to the next examinations, scheduled for May 1, in New York City.

The young doctor from Elizabeth City found twenty others in the examination room when he showed up, eager, anxious and full of fears about the outcome. All twenty-one passed. Dr. Sternberg ranked twenty-first. In first place was Dr. William A. Hammond. Like Dr. Sternberg, he was in time to become Surgeon General of the Army.

Dr. Sternberg was appointed an assistant surgeon on May 22. While awaiting his call to active duty he completed arrangements for closing his office for those few weeks or months he expected to be away. It was understood when he asked his patients to call other doctors in his absence that they would return to him after his return. He would have been greatly surprised had someone told him that the war would not last just a few weeks or months but four years and longer. He would have been even more surprised had anyone told him that he was actually leaving the regular practice of medicine for good, that he would never again examine or treat a sick or injured person except as a medical officer of the United States Army.

CHAPTER II

Battlefield Doctor

AT 2:30 o'clock Sunday morning, July 21, Assistant Surgeon Sternberg of the Third U. S. Infantry, Army of the Potomac, encamped at Centreville, Virginia, was awakened by ominous drum beats. Fighting off the weariness that let go only stubbornly, he finally grasped the meaning of the order which the drummer was tapping out in the nearby company street: "Prepare to march."

The moon was ablaze with placid light as he and his comrades prepared to break camp for the march which they had good reason to think would lead to the first major battle of the war. Breakfast was cooked and eaten in a hurry. They received two days' rations, which they carefully stowed away in their haversacks.*

The new day was beginning when the long blue columns started moving. Some thirty-five thousand Union troops were on their way toward Manassas Junction, where forty thousand Confederates had taken up strong positions on the road to Richmond. The weather was terrifically hot. That long march in such heat took something out of them that they would need very much before the day was over.

Those thirty-five thousand troops under General Irvin Mc-Dowell were not the only people who started moving toward Manassas Junction that bright and beautiful and hot Sunday morning. A major battle somewhere along the road to Richmond had been regarded as a certainty ever since those five divisions

---

* This account of the events on the eve of the battle of Bull Run, based upon Dr. Sternberg's letters, differs somewhat from others, which state the Union troops had no breakfast the day of the battle.

had marched out of Washington five days earlier. When the news
got back that McDowell and his men were on the march again,
civilians of all ranks and stations were seized with a desire to see
that stirring spectacle of battle. Members of Congress, leaders
in Washington society, office workers, officials of the various
governmental agencies—just about everybody who could get
transportation for the thirty-mile trip—poured across the long
Potomac bridge and headed toward Manassas Junction. A quick
but thrilling victory was taken for granted. After the Confederates had been routed and the march on Richmond resumed, they
would leave their grandstand seats on the rolling hillsides and return to their Washington homes.

For some time it appeared that that day's gay excursion would
end as anticipated. For, as any schoolboy knows, the battle went
favorably for the Federals at first. Those hillside watchers shouted excitedly as the Confederates yielded one position after another and signs of gathering weakness appeared. But, as any
schoolboy also knows, the tide turned disastrously later on, as
the tired troops from the South received powerful reinforcements
when they were most needed. Those men who had marched so
confidently toward Bull Run that morning, or most of them, fled
in panic toward Washington in the late afternoon, demoralized
and stunned, with no more fight left in them. Equally stunned
and no less anxious to get back to the safety of the Washington
defenses were those frivolous civilians who had come to watch a
battle as people come nowadays to watch a football game. What
they had seen from their safely distant hillsides and what those
disorganized, undisciplined troops had participated in was one of
the most overwhelming battlefield defeats ever suffered by a great
nation.

Although unwounded, Assistant Surgeon Sternberg had been
in some of the most furious fighting. His regiment had crossed
Bull Run about ten o'clock after a long march under the broiling sun and had gone into action immediately. His first duty as
a medical officer had been to the commanding officer of his division, Col. David Hunter, who had been wounded in the neck,
though not seriously. Then, as the battle boiled into furious ac-

tion, he had begun treating the wounded of all ranks from both armies.

When it was over—that battle which had begun so auspiciously and ended so disastrously—he watched that wild, disorganized surge up the road to Washington and tried to grasp what had happened and why. He had some questions about the latter but none whatsoever about the former. The evidence was too plain. It was, he said later, "a complete rout." The troops who had been so confident and apparently invincible a few short hours before "would make no attempt to rally." Many "threw away their muskets and cartridge boxes, everything in fact, each one seeming to think of nothing but personal safety."

But there were exceptions. Some did themselves great credit, even in the face of approaching defeat. He was especially proud of his own battalion. It "covered the retreat on the right in good order."

As soon as it became apparent that the Federal army had been soundly defeated and that nothing could be gained by staying where he was, Dr. Sternberg* hurried to the place where he had tied his horse just before the battle. But it was not there. Either it had been frightened by the cannonading and broken loose or (much more likely) someone had stolen it. There was nothing left to do but to join that confused, dispirited mob making its frightened way up the road toward Washington and spilling over into the nearby fields and woods.

He did not go far, however. He soon came to a church, in and around which there were many wounded. They had been there, most of them lying on improvised cots and on the bare floor, for several hours, and not a doctor or nurse was anywhere around. The fleeing soldier became the practicing man of medicine once more. He stepped out of that swift-moving current. His action set a good example. Several other doctors stepped aside too, and he soon had six or seven able assistants. They put up a white flag to protect themselves and their patients against being fired upon by the advancing Confederates. Then they went to

* Army physicians were often referred to by their medical title of Doctor, as well as by their military titles. This was believed to promote a higher professional spirit among them.

work. They did not have much to work with but were able to
do much with instruments and medicines they managed to find
and improvise. Dr. Sternberg himself performed several amputations after deciding it was better for the men to give up their
arms and legs than their lives. Years later, after aseptic surgery
had revolutionized the treatment of wounds, he wondered how
so many had survived. He recalled especially his and other battlefield doctors' "infecting gun-shot wounds with dirty fingers and
unsterilized cold water dressings."

They had been working away with those "dirty fingers and
unsterilized cold water dressings" for less than an hour when a
company of Confederate cavalry pulled up in front of the church.
The captain had no objection to their continuing their care of
the wounded. But he wanted it made clear that they were prisoners of war. Would they give their word that they would not try to
escape if they were allowed to keep on with their work? They
readily promised. Then the troops rode off, and they returned to
their patients.

The next day was blue Monday, as rainy and generally disagreeable as the day before had been sunshiny and pleasant. The
church was too small to accommodate all the wounded, number-
ing about two hundred and eighty, and a good many had been
kept outside. That was certainly no place for them in a rainstorm.
They needed shelter badly, and Dr. Sternberg set about seeing
that they got it. The cavalry company which had made that un-
resisted capture the afternoon before was encamped nearby, and
he asked the captain for enough men to build a shack of some
kind. Under his direction they put up a crude affair with blankets for a roof. But it kept off the rain, after a fashion. The
wounded were in no mood to be critical, and the doctors were
able to work more efficiently and in greater comfort. The Confederate captain watched the operations with a great deal of interest and the air of one deeply absorbed in something about
which he knew nothing at all.

That evening the captain had news for Dr. Sternberg. He
had been ordered, he said, to send him and the other doctors to
Manassas. The others made the trip in ambulances, but Dr.
Sternberg rode a horse furnished him by the captain. The rain,

which had been coming down depressingly all day, was falling in drenching showers when he left, and the weather had turned sharply cold. Riding horseback on such a night was inevitably an extremely disagreeable experience, and he envied his more fortunate fellows traveling in ambulances. Moreover, he was suffering from extreme physical weakness, brought on by hunger. Something had happened to those two days' rations supplied him just before he started out the day before on the march to Bull Run; except for a cup of corn meal gruel someone had given him during a lull in his work at the church, he had eaten nothing since starting out on that long, hot march. By the time he arrived in Manassas, cold, rain-soaked, half-sick, and ravenously hungry, he was having a great deal of trouble staying on the horse.

It was still raining dismally, and the air was disagreeably cold. His captors were in no hurry to make things more pleasant for him either. It took them two hours to decide what to do with their prisoners. Meanwhile, he had to stay out in the rain, hungry, wet, weak, and dispirited. Eventually it was decided to take the whole party to the guardhouse, a barn before the war. It already contained a number of other prisoners who had been rounded up after the battle and taken there directly from the battlefield, woods, and highways.

The old barn was unheated, of course, and the men had only their blankets and wet clothing between them and the cold night. Dr. Sternberg at first had only his wet clothing; for, like the other members of his outfit, he had left his blanket behind when his regiment joined in the battle. Fortunately, however, one of his fellow prisoners had three and gave him one. Numbed by its embracing warmth, he did not think too much about his empty stomach and soggy clothing. A few minutes after he climbed to the loft and stretched out on the rough plank floor, deep, overwhelming sleep seized him.

In spite of his hunger, the drafty barn, and his wet clothes, he slept well through the night. Early the next morning his nostrils gave him a pleasant sensation indeed—the smell of meat. It was not a choice delicacy but a hunk of salt bacon which had been sent to the stockade on a piece of planking. Nevertheless, after going forty-eight hours or longer virtually without eating, he was neither choosy nor fastidious. He ate his none-too-generous portion with consummate enjoyment. So did the others, for they had not had any food to speak of since before the battle either.

A colonel made the rounds soon after breakfast with a handful of handwritten forms. Those who signed them, he said, would be virtually free from all restraint and could come and go pretty much as they pleased. But the act of signing was a pledge not to escape or do anything to help the Federal government. A few of the prisoner-doctors—"four or five," Dr. Sternberg said—signed. But not he: already planning to escape and return to his outfit, he had no idea of assuming such an obligation.

Those who had signed returned to the church and resumed their care of the wounded. Dr. Sternberg and the others, as resolutely determined against signing as ever, nevertheless begged to be allowed to go back there too, or somewhere else where they were badly needed.

A compromise was reached. The colonel told them they could go back to work if they would sign a pledge not to try to escape or give any information to Federal troops for five days. That was not so bad. A five-day parole might delay but need not seriously interfere with escape plans. Dr. Sternberg signed, and so did the others. They left at once, not for the church but for another place, a shed near the railroad, where there were many wounded. Some had just arrived from the battlefield, where they had lain nearly two days and nights, part of the time in that driving, cold rain.

These men certainly needed doctors. Mass infection had already set in. Many wounds were alive with maggots, which these physicians, like others of their day, thought should be kept away from wounds at all costs. (It was some time afterward that medical opinion reversed itself, regarding maggots as a great help in bringing about the healing of wounds.) Dr. Sternberg and the others found it extremely difficult to get them out of damaged areas and even harder to keep them out. They would work over a wound and think they had it just as they wanted it. Then, when time came to change the dressing, they would find as many maggots as before. That uphill battle against those tiny organisms and the infection responsible for them was pretty discouraging. But they kept on and eventually managed to keep the wounds, or most of them at any rate, fairly maggot-free. Like the other experiences he underwent during those few days after Bull Run, this one burned itself deeply in the Sternberg memory. He particularly remembered those men's suffering. Their condition he called "most pitiable."

A train of several cars was standing on a siding near the shed. One of the Confederate officers told him and the other doctors to dress the wounds as well as they could and load the wounded on the cars. Some were to be taken to Culpeper and some to Charlotte. There were supposed to be good hospitals at both places.

The loading of the wounded was a tedious and difficult task, for they were short of help. But it was completed before nightfall, and the train was scheduled to pull out immediately. Their day's work done, Dr. Sternberg and the other doctors went back to the dreary barn where they had spent the night before. When they got up the next morning and got ready to plunge into another hard day of battling maggots and performing amputations, they spoke of their patients of the day before and wondered how they were faring. They soon found out. When they went back to the shed, there was a surprise for them. Those wounded men were not resting under clean sheets in comfortable hospital beds in Culpeper and Charlotte at all. They were right there in Manassas—the train had not moved a foot. They had been without medical care of any kind throughout the night. That was not Dr. Sternberg's idea of the proper way to treat wounded men, and he said so. He was even more indignant when hour after hour passed and not a wheel turned. Actually, the train did not pull out until Wednesday night, more than twenty-four hours after it was supposed to.

These men's cots there under the shed did not remain empty long. Wounded troops were constantly arriving to take their places and keep Dr. Sternberg and the other doctors as busy as they had been the day before. The pressure did not let up. The battle against maggots, suppuration, and death went on without a break and practically without rest.

On Thursday evening Dr. Sternberg and a friend of his, a Dr. Taylor, were told to get ready to move. Battle casualties had been piling up at Centreville, and they were needed there. This looked like an extraordinarily lucky break, for these two friends had been planning to escape together. At Centreville they would not be under the strict supervision that might have complicated their escape from Manassas. Afraid to trust their knowledge of Virginia geography, they looked for and found an atlas, ancient, battered, but dependable. From its dog-eared pages Dr. Sternberg tore a map of that state. From that map, kept carefully folded and hidden in an inside pocket, they learned where they were in relation to other places. Washington, they found, was northeast. The escape route they decided upon led north several miles, then turned east, crossed the Potomac, and continued straight to the capital. It seemed the one likely to get them most quickly out of Confederate-occupied territory. That settled, the two men waited with such patience as they could command for the expiration of their five-day paroles. Dr. Sternberg's would expire Sunday at noon, Dr. Taylor's two days later.

Then, just when everything seemed ready for the break, all their careful planning appeared to have netted them nothing. On Sunday morning Dr. Taylor was taken back to Manassas. Both men were sure the authorities had made a mistake and taken the wrong man. They could see no sense in bringing back under close supervision a prisoner whose parole still had two days to go and leaving virtually at liberty one whose parole would expire in a few hours.

This mistake, if mistake it was, turned out to be fortunate for Dr. Sternberg, although a bad break for his friend. As they had no idea when they would be together again, if ever, the former decided to go it alone, leaving about forty-eight hours earlier than planned. That meant his departure was just two or three hours away.

When noon came, freeing him from his parole, he was practically ready. Not quite; it would be unwise to start out on an empty stomach, for, once under way, he probably would get something to eat only at the risk of his life, or at least of recapture. He ate a hearty lunch, then made a final visit to the hospital and bantered briefly with some of his patients. Finding some crackers lying handily near, he slipped half a dozen into his pocket. Now he was ready to make the break.

He might arouse suspicion if he should head directly for the woods from the hospital without some sort of explanation or excuse. So, as casually as he could, he asked the sentinels where he could find some red oak, to be used (he hoped they would think) in making up some medicine for his patients. Neither of the other men became in the least suspicious. One told him exactly what he was hoping to be told: that there was plenty of red oak in the woods across the way. Dr. Sternberg had considerable difficulty maintaining his leisurely, indifferent-appearing pace for the half mile to where the woods began, but managed to do so. Once out of sight, he got away as fast as he could, hoping it would be hours before his disappearance would be discovered.

After half-walking, half-running about two miles due north, he reached a stream which he supposed to be Bull Run. Removing his shoes and hose, he forded it with little trouble. Then, in accordance with the decision he and Dr. Taylor had reached about the route, he continued straight north until late in the afternoon. Then the bright sun, which had served him so well in keeping him going in the right direction, disappeared under dark, angry clouds. When they started emptying he was caught in a wooded area full of second growth pines so close together he could barely wedge between them. But he slogged along as best he could, fighting those obstacles in his path along with the driving rain. After about an hour of this tough, slow going, he reached a small clearing containing a dilapidated house and stable, the latter made of logs. Here was shelter—but here was also the risk of being captured if he availed himself of it. Tired to the point of exhaustion and his clothing soaked, he decided to take the risk, and made a run for the old barn. What a blessed relief it was to be under a roof once more, hearing and seeing the rain, but not being drenched by it!

The storm finally ended, and the sun reappeared. He then

made a distressing discovery: he had wandered considerably off
his course while the sun was not there to guide him. Instead of
continuing directly northward, he had borne sharply to the south.
Had he not found out in time, he would have wandered back into the general area from which he was fleeing. Fortunately, the
thick pines and the pelting rain had slowed him up considerably,
and actually he had not gone very far southward.

But that experience taught him a lesson. From then on, he
resolved, he would travel only when he could see the sun, the
moon, or the north star. He could then see neither, for the sun
had reappeared only briefly after the storm. That house in the
clearing looked like a good place to spend the night, provided it
was unoccupied or occupied by people who would be friendly.
As far as he could tell, there was nobody in it, but he wanted to
take no chances. Making a gingerly examination that began some
distance away and ended at the entrance, he found that it really
was completely empty except for a barrel and a door which had
been removed from its hinges and laid on the floor.

His anxiety concerning his personal safety now at rest, he became conscious of hunger. That heavy meal he had eaten just
before his escape had served him well, but now it was time to eat
again. To make his small stock of crackers last as long as possible, he ate only one, leaving five to stay the pangs of future hunger. He had one cigar left and smoked it. Then he stretched out
on the unhinged door, which he found more comfortable than
the floor. A thick blanket of utter physical exhaustion fell upon
him. In almost no time he was sound asleep.

He did not sleep long, however. He woke with a frightened
start when he thought he heard someone calling him. He was
still alone. That voice had spoken only in a dream. Going to a
window, he found the weather had again turned fair, and the
moon had just risen. He had no idea what time it was or how
long he had slept. But he was ready to start out again, guided
by the moon. Bright enough to keep him traveling northward,
it nevertheless was not bright enough to light his pathway, and
he found the going through the thick underbrush exasperatingly
slow and difficult. When he had struggled on for another hour or
two, the clouds again covered the moon, leaving him without

guidance. Sticking to his resolve to take no chances on repeating his error of the previous afternoon, he dropped to the ground completely exhausted. Once again he was soon smothered in sleep.

This second nap of the night, like the first, did not last long. When his eyes opened, the upper rim of the sun was edging flamingly over the horizon. It was time to start moving again, this time toward that rising disk, for he decided he had gone as far north as he needed to and now needed to head straight eastward to Washington. He ate as he walked, picking blackberries to satisfy the hunger that could not be quieted by those five crackers he had left.

About noon, from the protective thickness of the forests in which he had kept almost constantly since his escape, he saw a man working in a field. He was almost certain he was not far from Washington. But he could not be sure, and he needed to know exactly where he was, lest his travels and privations of the past twenty-four hours be for nought. Gambling his liberty on his belief that he was in, or at least near, Northern territory and his hope that this man was a Northern sympathizer, he emerged from the woods and approached him. To his vast relief, he found him not only friendly but glad to help.

The Potomac was about a mile and a half to the east, the man told him: Washington was about twelve miles beyond the river. Was it safe to travel those thirteen and a half miles in the daytime?

The man was fairly certain it was safe if he stayed in the woods. But the highway, which the fugitive would have to cross, was under constant patrol by troops from a South Carolina regiment. Once across, he should not have any particular trouble keeping out of sight.

The escapee strained his eyes as he had never strained them before, peering up and down the road for those South Carolinians. Seeing none, he hurried across. He felt a blessed sense of relief when that sea of trees closed in behind him.

At the river he remembered the many times he had swum the Susquehanna as a youth, his clothing tied in a tight knot held aloft with one hand while he swam with the other. He decided he would cross the Potomac in the same way. But, when he undressed, he found his clothing so wet it made a much heavier bundle than he had expected. It would be dangerous to try to take it across as he had planned. Should it become too heavy in midstream for him to carry farther, he would reach the other bank a conspicious, not to say shocking, target for suspicion and questioning. Putting his clothes on again, he started walking down the river bank in search of some material with which to build a raft to take him across. Collecting pieces of timber here and there, he almost had enough when he found he did not need a raft after all. There ahead of him was a boat, old but entirely serviceable, which someone had tied up at an improvised pier. This was indeed a lucky break for a person utterly fagged out from many hours of tramping through thick forests with little sleep. To float downstream toward Washington with nothing more exhausting to do than watching the passing scenery was unspeakable luxury. His only fear was that it would not last long enough.

It didn't. After drifting in this delightful, effortless fashion for three or four hours, he saw a dam straight ahead, with a sharp drop over the falls. To try to get past them would be to wreck the boat and risk his own life. By this time he almost certainly was in Federal territory, so it should be safe to land and tell people who he was.

The satisfaction of his hunger supplied by those five crackers and the wild blackberries had ended hours ago. Now, ravenous, he headed for the first house he saw. The door was opened by an Irishman, whose manner was friendly. When Dr. Sternberg explained that he was an escaped Federal officer on his way back to Washington and very, very hungry, that householder also became one of the most hospitable of Irishmen. He did not have much to eat in the house, and its variety was limited. But, such as it was, it was his to eat and take with him. Two large bowls of milk, bread and yellow pats of butter were delicacies of the highest order to the famished traveler.

But Dr. Sternberg was hungry for information as well as for nourishment. While he enjoyed that delicious food, "the best, I think, I ever ate," he shot question after question at his host. He

was in Maryland, the other man told him. Washington was about
five miles away. And of course he was well inside the Federal
lines. The danger of recapture was definitely over.

But his troubles were not.

Refreshed and strengthened by that good food, he thanked
that friendly Irishman and started out on what he confidently expected to be the brief final lap of his journey. Up the road a bit
he fell in with some soldiers from a Maine regiment. Deciding he
had walked enough, he inquired of them where he could hire a
horse. Their camp was nearby, they told him. If he would go
with them, the colonel would certainly provide transportation to
the city.

The colonel promised to do so. But just then a soldier
showed up and started eyeing Dr. Sternberg with considerable interest and later with active, militant suspicion. That man was
positive, he told the colonel, that this disreputable-looking fellow
—and Dr. Sternberg realized that, after all his trials and tramping, he did look a great deal more like a tramp or deserter than
an officer trying to get back to his outfit—was the one who had
spent the night before in the guardhouse. Four others who happened to be present were equally positive. With all this overwhelming weight of evidence, even Dr. Sternberg "almost began
to believe it myself." Fortunately for him, one of those who had
seen the guardhouse prisoner began to have some doubts. After
taking another look at this man in the Weary Willie clothes—
this time standing up—he admitted that the guardhouse inmate
was at least a head taller.

This should have ended the matter. The misadventure should
have been only a passing incident in a trying experience, nothing
more than a slight delay in Dr. Sternberg's Odyssey. But it
wasn't. Even though apparently convinced that this disreputable-
looking man and the one in the guardhouse had nothing else in
common, the colonel showed no more interest in him. His former cordial, sympathetic manner did not return, and he did
nothing to carry out his promise to get him to the city.

Two hours of fruitless waiting were followed by rain, and a
five-mile walk on muddy roads in a pelting storm through thick
darkness did not appeal to the weary traveler. One of the officers,

a captain, had an extra cot in his tent and offered it to him. Thanks to this soldierly hospitality, he got that night far more sleep than he had had since two nights before the battle of Bull Run. But it ended early: he was walking toward Washington a little after five o'clock.

His tired legs served him well now as before. About seven o'clock the countryside dropped behind him and he began to recognize familiar streets and buildings. He had been away fourteen days.

Before starting out on the campaign, he had left a trunk at the home of a Mrs. Boyle. There he went first. After he had had a bath that made all the difference in the world in his feelings, the trunk yielded up all he needed for a complete new outfit. The softness of everything, the crispness of everything, the freshness of everything, and especially the dryness of everything, after hours and days in rain-soaked clothing, were like the coming true of a long-dreamed dream.

Properly attired and refreshed, he began looking up old friends. These reunions were not always happy occasions, for he learned then of the death and capture of many of his comrades. He was surprised to find that, to many of those who had survived, his arrival was in the nature of an escape from the grave. For they had heard a report—which he was glad to refute in the most convincing way—that he had been killed by a cannon ball while administering first aid to a wounded man on the battlefield. That report had found quick, though reluctant, credence as a result of his failure to rejoin his outfit after the battle.

Next he reported to the aged and decrepit General Winfield Scott, then under heavy fire from newspapers and politicians for his order to begin the march toward Richmond before the Army was ready. That visit took place in the general's home. Scott received him warmly, did not appear too unhappy over the criticism, and asked him many questions about his experiences.

Next came a visit to Surgeon General Clement A. Finley. He also asked many questions. As the two men sat there in pleasant conversation, it never once occurred to the younger one that he might be sitting in the Surgeon General's chair—and bearing up as best he could under the Surgeon General's responsibilities and public criticism—in the nation's next major war.

Dr. Sternberg's regiment, reorganized and restored to full strength after its terrific mauling at Bull Run, was then encamped at Arlington Heights. His absence from duty ended officially when he reported there. General McDowell, field commander at Bull Run, was as eager as the others to get a full account of his experiences.

Dr. Sternberg's Army career was much less exciting during the next several months. The day after his return to his regiment his battalion was ordered back into the city to serve as a police force. There it remained until the opening of the Peninsular Campaign in April, 1862.

His first major battle in that campaign and his second of the war occurred on June 27 at Gaines Mill. As at Bull Run some eleven months earlier, the timely arrival of reinforcements at a critical moment gave General Lee his first victory, though at a fearful loss of more than eight thousand killed and wounded. Dr. Sternberg served under his old commander, Brigadier General (then Major) George Sykes.

His next big battle was at Malvern Hill. Attacking while General George B. McClellan was away on an inspection trip, the enemy began an artillery barrage in the early afternoon of July 1 preparatory to a strong infantry advance. It was rendered ineffective by an overpowering counter barrage which was aided powerfully by the inability of the Confederates to understand and carry out orders. Lacking the protection they should have received from their own heavy guns, the enemy infantry moved grimly forward, suffering steadily mounting casualties as they slowly narrowed the gap between the lines. Whether they could have won a victory in that fearfully unequal struggle between human flesh and concentrated artillery fire will never be known for sure, though there has been vast speculation about it. The struggle did not last long enough for a decision. It had to be called off when night came, with that gap still unclosed. The weary Confederates withdrew to the protection of the nearby forests, leaving behind their dead and wounded, the latter crying piteously for relief from their suffering.

This was admittedly a defensive victory, but it was a major
one, nevertheless. Indeed many authorities on history's great
"if's" are convinced that it was a battle that might have assured
the immediate winning of the war. For, they are sure, the weakened and demoralized condition in which it left the Confederates
actually opened up the road to Richmond, just as Bull Run, at
about that time the year before, had opened up the road to Washington. That this advantage was not promptly and energetically
followed up has been blamed upon General McClellan. His over-
caution and lack of initiative, many say, lengthened the war by
three years.

Fortunately for his admirers and the welfare of the wounded,
Dr. Sternberg conducted himself much more creditably in the bat-
tles of Gaines Mill and Malvern Hill than those higher up. The
War of the Rebellion Records contain this tribute from General
Sykes: "Dr. Sternberg [in the Peninsular Campaign] added large-
ly to the reputation already acquired on the disastrous field of
Bull Run."

Others who saw him working with the wounded have paid
him more personal tributes. One, Colonel (later Brigadier General) William H. H. Penrose, wrote: "It gives me much pleasure
to bear witness to your coolness and bravery under fire at the
Battle of Malvern Hill, Va., 1862; . . . you made an amputation
of the arm of one of our men; . . . at the time you were in an
exposed position and under heavy fire from the enemy. Your
conduct on that occasion showed a remarkable coolness under
most trying and dangerous circumstances and elicited most complimentary comments from all who witnessed it."

General McClellan had his own reason, sound or unsound,
for not following up the advantage gained at Malvern Hill. (Most
historians say it was quite unsound.) While that battle was being fought he had been at Harrison's Landing, some distance
down the James River, studying its potentialities as a military
encampment. They had impressed him most favorably. There,
he decided, not realizing the extent to which Lee's army had been
weakened, his own troops should take up strong defensive positions after the battle instead of making another major drive immediately. In selecting Harrison's Landing he took little—cer-

tainly insufficient—account of the extremely unfavorable health
conditions in that area. A more capable commander would have
known better. Thanks to his ignorance, his indifference, or his
stubborn unwillingness to listen to those who argued vigorously
against the Harrison Landing move, the toll of fifteen thousand
men he had lost since May 28 grew rapidly as more and more
of his troops fell victims to typhoid, malaria, and the many other
infectious diseases that find such areas ideal breeding places. Dr.
Sternberg was one of those who found those fever-ridden James
River banks too much for them. He became dangerously ill with
typhoid in August. Taken to a more healthful environment, he
was fortunate enough to recover in about a month. He was then
ordered to Portsmouth Grove, Rhode Island, as executive officer
of an army hospital containing some twenty-two hundred beds.

That assignment, lasting about three months, gave him his
first experience in leading a battle against a major epidemic, although, of course, he had helped others fight outbreaks of disease
at Harrison Landing and other places. The form of illness against
which he fought at Portsmouth Grove is now all but unheard of,
but outbreaks of hospital gangrene were commonplace in 1862,
especially in military hospitals crowded with the wounded. Inevitably, his experience made a deep and lasting impression on
him. He called it "a lesson never to be forgotten."

Two wards had been set aside for surgical patients, and their
current occupants were battle casualties from the Army of the
Potomac. About half of the men had received simple flesh wounds
and were improving satisfactorily. The others had been more
seriously wounded, and their wounds contained a great deal of
pus. No physician or hospital attendant in his right mind would
do such a thing nowadays, but the doctor in charge of those
wards—not Dr. Sternberg, of course—did not consider it necessary to use a fresh dressing in cleaning each man's wound. A
single dressing was used on patient after patient, some slightly
wounded, some near death. The result Dr. Sternberg called "a
conflagration." Wounds that theretofore had been free of pus and
well on their way to complete healing became inflamed and angry looking. The pain the men suffered was almost unbearable.
Inflamed areas became greatly enlarged. Huge hunks of flesh,

some as large as a man's hand, separated from the rest of the body and sloughed off. Nor was this loss of tissue confined to surface areas: it extended "deeply among the muscles" and far inside ordinary tissue. This was all a pretty tough experience for a young army physician just beginning a career of personal war against germs. But it was excellent training for what lay ahead.

Dr. Sternberg and the other physicians on the staff attacked the outbreak as soon as they realized its nature and extent. The trouble was traced to its source—the reuse of dressings—and this was ordered discontinued. Those whose wounds had not become infected or pussy were removed to other wards. The whole place underwent a vigorous clean-up. Walls were scrubbed to shiningness and whitewashed. These measures proved effective: the chain of infection was broken. Dr. Sternberg had conquered his first epidemic.

Meanwhile, President Lincoln and his military advisers had been laying plans for an attack upon the South from a new direction. An expedition against New Orleans was organized in the fall of 1862 under the command of Major General N. P. Banks. Dr. Sternberg, now completely recovered from the typhoid attack which had made him "very sick," and fully capable of standing up under the strain of active campaigning, was assigned to that expedition. After the fall of New Orleans he became assistant medical director of the Department of the Gulf. During that assignment, which lasted until early in 1864, he accompanied General Banks on several inland expeditions, including those to Brownsville, Texas, and into the Teche country of Louisiana. Later, he was on the staff of the medical director of the army's Northern Department. His final assignment of the war took him to Cleveland, Ohio, to become surgeon-in-charge of a large general hospital. He was there when the war ended.

CHAPTER III

Twice a Husband

A HAPPY EVENT took Dr. Sternberg back to his boyhood community in mid-October, 1865. There, in Cooperstown, he was married on October 19 to Miss Maria Louisa Russell, member of a prominent Cooperstown family and only daughter of one of the town's leading merchants. The Rev. Levi Sternberg, still pioneering in higher education at nearby Hartwick Seminary, assisted the pastor of the local Presbyterian Church in the ceremony. The marriage made the bridegroom a relative of Supreme Court Justice Samuel Nelson, whose support at the outbreak of the war had given him his chance to become a medical officer in the army.

The younger Sternberg was stationed at the time at Jefferson Barracks, Missouri, and at the expiration of his leave the happy couple, looking forward to a long lifetime together, took up their residence in the army community, headquarters of the Thirteenth Infantry.

In April of the following year, about seven months after their marriage, he was ordered to Fort Harker, Kansas. The refinements of living which they had enjoyed at Jefferson Barracks, they learned, were not to be had at the new post, and the latest move brought troublesome problems to the young couple. These were complicated by the state of Mrs. Sternberg's health, which had not been robust for a long time and was then teetering on the thin edge of physical collapse. Fearing a breakdown under the stress of the hard living conditions at Fort Harker, they faced a cruel decision between a temporary separation dictated by her health and a permanent separation by death. She therefore returned to Cooperstown instead of accompanying him to Fort Harker. They hoped the separation would be brief, and he worked hard to that end, trying to arrange living quarters that would be suitable to her weakened condition. But that separation was not brief; it dragged on for a year or more. It was not until the spring of 1867 that she made the long trip to Kansas, her health apparently improved.

A few weeks later, at three o'clock on the morning of June 28, an acting assistant surgeon was called to the quarters of a civilian employee working as a herder and butcher. When he arrived the patient was in a state of collapse. His stomach and bowels were discharging a bad-looking liquid of "rice water" appearance. He was suffering severe cramps. His fingers were bony and shriveled. He told the doctor he had had diarrhea for two days. About twelve hours later he died, a victim, the doctors said, of Asiatic cholera.

At seven o'clock that same day a soldier became seriously ill, with orthodox cholera symptoms. He died in the post hospital at eleven o'clock the next morning.

These cases were only the beginning. An hour before that second victim died a young child developed the disease. Two hours later the child's mother also did so, and, early the next afternoon, the father showed those characteristic symptoms. The mother and child died the day after they became sick, but the father recovered. A sixth person, a soldier, developed cholera some hours before the father did so. Other cases and other deaths followed these in terrifying succession. During the next few weeks Dr. Sternberg and the other doctors battled one of the worst cholera epidemics ever to appear in the New World.

Dr. Sternberg reported to Army Surgeon General Joseph K. Barnes some of the conditions he had found which he considered responsible, at least in part, for the outbreak. Policing of the camp was "not good." Some of the company sinks (latrines) were "in wretched condition." There were "several offensive holes about the post where slops and garbage from the kitchen had been thrown." To a sanitation-minded man like Dr. Sternberg such conditions were intolerable. He instituted a strict system of policing. The camps were moved to new ground. Disinfectants were applied liberally and vigorously. The men were taken out of the wedge tents where they had been sleeping two to four to the tent, and a special tent was attached to each company for use of patients with slight diarrhea and similar disturbances. The seriously sick were treated in hospital tents pitched about fifty yards from the post hospital. Cholera cases were kept isolated from others. Special attention was devoted to disinfection of the body discharges of all patients. The men were warned against river water, which was regarded as the primary source of the outbreak. He likewise warned against impure food, also regarded as a primary contributor to the illness and deaths.

Eventually these measures and others he instituted were successful. Like the storm at sea, the fury of battle, and the raging forest fire, the epidemic slowed and stopped. But not until it had done vast damage: Dr. Sternberg reported to the Surgeon General that forty-seven cases among military personnel had come under his personal supervision between June 28 and August 1. Thirty-two of them—about two-thirds—had proved fatal. As four companies of Kansas militia then on duty at Fort Harker had their independent medical commands, many of their cases were not included in the Sternberg totals. Too, these totals did not include civilian employees, some of whom had been treated by army doctors. Moreover, as Dr. Sternberg pointed out in his report, "many cases, that I am now satisfied were mild cases of cholera, were diagnosed as choleric diarrhea." The truth is, nobody knows to this day how many cholera cases and deaths actually occurred. However, both the statements of those who lived through the outbreak and the official and unofficial records, incomplete as they are, leave no doubt that the totals were staggering.

Dr. Sternberg also made a number of other observations regarding the epidemic and events occurring just prior to it. These he passed on to Surgeon General Barnes. The Smoky Hill River had overflowed its banks "to an unusual extent" a few weeks before the outbreak, and "the lowlands near it were extensively flooded." There was "an unusual amount of moisture in the atmosphere" from April through July. There was also "a great deal of rain for this section of the country." Decomposition of animal and vegetable matter "has taken place with unusual rapidity." The air, which normally was "so pure and dry that a piece of meat, cut thin, will dry when hung in the air without becoming tainted," had not been like that this summer. There had been "an unusual number of flies and mosquitoes." Houses in and near the post "have been infected with a large fly which differs from the common house fly." During the epidemic, although it was midsummer, the nights were cool, "and often almost cold." There were considerably more deaths on the abnormally cold nights than on others. Cases had decreased sharply after a thunderstorm. They had occurred predominantly among new arrivals at the post. All of these observations were to be brought up and considered later when he and other disease-fighters toiled in laboratory and sickroom to find answers to cholera's deadly secrets.

Dr. Sternberg's report to Surgeon General Barnes ended with this sentence: "One of the ladies of the garrison died of cholera on the fifteenth of July." The report did not identify her. But she was his bride of less than two years. Still frail in spite of her long visit with her family, she had been able to put up only feeble resistance to the infection. She had been ill less than twelve hours.

Understandably enough, Dr. Sternberg, now a captain and assistant surgeon, did not find Fort Harker a pleasant or happy place to live after his wife's death. Everywhere he turned he saw reminders of their cruelly shortened married life, reminders that set aflame the hurt that burned inside. He wanted to get away. He wanted to begin again somewhere else, away from those symbols of happiness that had turned into tokens of death. As soon as the epidemic was over, he asked for and obtained a leave of absence, leaving in August, almost exactly a month after her death.

During the next few months he visited his family and friends in the East. Gradually the acute pain of his bereavement eased somewhat. As time went on, absorption in his work, aided by his unusual common sense which made him see the folly of letting grief shape his life, restored him to his former, normal, cheerful, congenial self. Those who knew him during those months of bereavement and overpowering loneliness, as well as at other times, were drawn to him by his strong personal charm at the same time that they admired his well-disciplined mind and his devotion to the cause of medicine.

Upon expiration of his leave, in December, 1867, he was ordered to Fort Riley, where he became post surgeon and served on court-martial duty. Soon afterward he had several brushes with hostile Indians while accompanying the Tenth Cavalry from Fort Riley to Fort Hays, Kansas. He saw more Indian fighting the following September as chief medical officer of Colonel A. Silley's expedition to Arkansas, Kansas, and Indian territory.

His assignment to Major General Philip H. Sheridan's command, also operating in Indian territory, gave him a new interest, geology. Spending a great deal of time on the march, he saw much of the country at first hand and had opportunities to study the geologic formations along the way. During this assignment he also became interested in Indian relics. Both interests were to give him much pleasure throughout his life. He took in good spirit the good-natured ribbing of fellow officers, who pretended to a great deal of concern lest he meet injury or death from the arrows of live Indians while exploring the relics left behind by dead ones.

His collection proved more useful than most hobbies do. Some of his specimens he sent to the well-known Philadelphia naturalist, Professor Joseph Leidy, who mentioned them in one of his reports on *The Vertebrates of the West*. Other items from the Sternberg collection, for the most part the skulls of Indians, animals, and birds, rated a letter of appreciation from the Army Medical Museum.

On February 22, 1869, President Andrew Johnson named Captain Sternberg for promotion to Major and Surgeon. Routine Senate confirmation was taken for granted, but one thing after another delayed the vote, and before it was taken both houses of Congress passed the new army appropriation bill and the President signed it. To the extreme discomfiture of Dr. Sternberg and two other medical officers whose promotions were also awaiting Senate confirmation, the new measure was found to contain a proviso forbidding all army appointments and promotions except as provided for by subsequent legislative acts. These three

men and their friends were indignant. The proviso should properly apply, they conceded, to those nominated after the law became effective, but they argued that it should not apply to men
whose promotion had been recommended by the President before the new measure was passed. Nevertheless, the official rul-
ing was that, unfair or not, it applied to them as well. Captain
Sternberg remained Captain Sternberg for more than six years
longer. That seemed shabby treatment for an officer who had
been breveted a captain and major for "faithful and meritorious
services during the war."

He was greatly disappointed of course. He considered it extremely unfair to punish him and those others for the Senate's
dilatoriness. But he did not mope, nor allow his disappointment
and sense of injustice to affect his pleasant relationships with his
fellow officers and his official superiors or to diminish his enthusiasm for his work.

That enthusiasm covered everything he had to do—but it
applied particularly to work he did not have to do. He had found
a particular delight in research, which definitely lay outside his
official duties. The quest for knowledge which might add to
man's weapons against disease had a fascination for him. Every
minute he could spare from his regular duties found him hard at
work in improvised laboratories. The work was carried on under
great difficulties, including a complete lack of interest or encouragement on the part of his official superiors. If he or some
other officer chose to spend tedious hours bent over a microscope,
that was his own affair and privilege. But he could expect no pat
on the back. And he certainly must not run up any bills for the
government to pay.

"When I commenced my research work I had to provide my
own microscope and material of all kinds," he said years later.
"There not only was no bacteriological laboratory or apparatus
at any military post, but so far as I am informed none at any
medical school or university in the country." He did receive
a measure of encouragement, however. One of his superior officers, Colonel Jack S. Hamilton, began noticing that he appeared
only infrequently at officers' clubs and could be found almost anytime he was not on duty in his makeshift hideaway, his eyes

trained on a microscope lense or trying to get the right light for a test tube experiment. Thinking such labor beyond the call of duty ought to be encouraged, Colonel Hamilton wrote to the Surgeon General about it:

I am very much pleased with Sternberg. He is, like myself a dabbler in natural science. He is a photographer and is getting up microscopic photographs. He tells me that he applied last year under the General Order for a microscope. I also hear that his turn for relief comes this year—fall. Could it be staved off till next spring, and couldn't you send him a microscope? He works hard every day and, I think, should be encouraged. He spends all his loose change in science. Tell me what you can do in the matter.

Colonel Hamilton's reference to Captain Sternberg's interest in photography pointed to another scientific hobby which had aroused his enthusiasm. The kind of picture-taking in which he had become interested was the new science of photomicrography —making photographs through the lens of a microscope. While it was invented by someone else, he certainly was one of the pioneers, and no bacteriologist ever used it to better advantage. A few years later he was to use the new technique to excellent and startling advantage in bringing important scientific truths to the attention of fellow scientists and even school children.

The records do not show whether Colonel Hamilton's plea for a new microscope was effective. However, the army's interest in scientific medical development being what it was, it seems safe to assume that Dr. Sternberg had to keep on getting along as best he could with crude equipment he had managed to provide at his own expense. As it happened, however, that did not matter quite as much as it would have earlier or later. For just about that time medical research began to have a rival for his enthusiasm. Letter writing and visits to Indianapolis left him less time for his microscope and test tubes. The person responsible for that change was Miss Martha L. Pattison, whom he had met some time before.

The hard-working army doctor and the small, vivacious, and attractive young woman from Indianapolis found they shared many interests and enthusiasms, particularly an interest in science, modern languages, and amateur archeology. When they could not be together, which was much oftener and much longer than either of them wished, they made up for the loss as best they could with long, earnest letters.

Among the many things they had in common were liberty-loving forebears. Just as he was descended from freedom-seeking Palatines, so she was only two generations removed from stern-opinioned ministers of the Gospel who held as strong convictions against human slavery as any emigrating Palatine ever held against religious persecution. Neither her father's father nor her mother's father had been able to reconcile his religious faith with slave-holding. When slavery became a legally recognized institution in Kentucky, where they were shepherding their small flocks, they faced a cruel choice: to live with the hated business or get out of the state. They chose to get out. Before doing so they wiped their hands clean by returning to their parents the slaves given them as wedding gifts. Then they moved, with their small families, to Indiana, a free state, where they would not have to wrestle with their consciences over the slavery issue. There Martha Pattison was born.

Thus it came about that Captain George M. Sternberg went to Indianapolis to be married the second time. The wedding occurred on September 1, 1869. The union was a most congenial and happy one. On more than one public occasion, and in innumerable private conversations, he spoke in the warmest terms of Martha Sternberg's devotion, her encouragement in his work, her cheerful prodding when failure piled on failure, her great ambition for him, her eagerness to see that he received the recognition she was sure he deserved, her sympathy when sympathy was called for, her willingness to endure great hardships to accompany him on difficult and even dangerous assignments, and her help and inspiration in many other ways.

Captain Sternberg was a busy man, and their honeymoon was necessarily brief. Much of it was spent in earnest discussions of his work and the part she hoped to play in it. There was also much talk about the new home they were about to set up on the Kansas prairies, how she would adjust herself to the social life at an army post, how they would budget his comparatively small salary and innumerable other matters of commanding interest to a couple very much in love and just starting out on the great adventure of marriage. After the honeymoon there was an even briefer visit with Martha Sternberg's family in Indianapolis. Then began the long, tedious trip to Fort Riley. Dr. Sternberg's fellow officers had prepared for their arrival. As they left the train they saw an army ambulance pulled by four spirited mules. This, they were told, had been sent to take them the rest of the way to their new home. At the top of the steep hill that took about all the strength the puffing mules possessed, Martha Sternberg saw a cluster of pleasant-looking buildings—barracks, officers' quarters, the hospital where her husband had spent many weary but happy hours, the stables and the many other structures that add up to an army camp. Everything was made of stone. Not a wooden building was in sight. That puzzled her at first. Her husband, who had been there long enough to know why, explained: there was a stone quarry nearby, and this cream-colored stone was cheaper and easier to use than anything else.

There were the customary social amenities to be observed, somewhat frightening to a young bride far from her old home. Dr. Sternberg's friends had to meet her; they were guests of honor at a few simple parties; there were callers and calls to be returned. At last they settled down, with considerable relief, to their new life as man and wife.

They found it all they had dreamed of. Dr. Sternberg, weary of loneliness and the absence of a woman companion and counsellor, found a new zest for life. Gone, he hoped forever, were the comfortable but solitary unmarried officers' quarters where he had been living. Now there was something to come home to. His overtime work with his microscope and test tubes had a strong rival for his prime attention. But this was a friendly rivalry, as far as she was concerned. There was no jealousy. Martha Sternberg was as eager for him to toil for his advancement in his profession as he was, and she knew she would have to share him generously with his work if the success she considered his destiny was to come. She did not complain when supper grew cold while she waited for his arrival and his arrival waited for the completion of an exciting experiment or the finishing of a chapter in a scientific textbook. She learned almost at the start that the man she had married was little interested in social life and would gladly sacrifice it for a chance to explore the far frontiers of medicine and bacteriology. She had had a great deal of social life in the gay Indianapolis set in which she had grown up, and she had liked it very much. But she was willing to give it up, either completely (if that should be the price of her husband's success) or to as large an extent as might be called for by a wise compromise between too much work and too much play. The friends this friendly young woman readily made in the army community—the people whom she had worried about fitting in with before she was married—learned from her, if they had not found it out for themselves, that Captain Sternberg was a different kind of army officer: he worked as hard, and often as long, after he was supposed to stop work as he did when everybody at the post was supposed to be hard at it. Nevertheless, in spite of his preoccupation with his work, the Sternberg home became a popular place. And even Captain Sternberg's long hours of off-duty toil did not make him a social recluse by any means. There were occasional times when he was able to pull himself, with Martha Sternberg's help, away from his laboratory. And, whenever he did, he enjoyed himself immensely.

But he enjoyed most the hours he and Martha spent alone. Usually on duty early at the post hospital, he either got a simple breakfast for himself while she slept or ate the one she insisted upon getting up and preparing for him. Later in the morning, his first burst of activity over, he would return home for a real breakfast. There was no hurry about either cooking or eating this one. While she got together the bacon and eggs and whatever else she thought he would most enjoy and put them on to cook, he would attend to odd jobs about the place. Or perhaps he would put on a kitchen apron and help her. Or he might read—a newspaper, a magazine or, just as likely as not, a heavy scientific volume. The kitchen, and indeed the whole place, had a cheerful air of congenial contentment.

Both were active devotees of the outdoors. Both found relaxation in physical exercise. Both particularly enjoyed horseback riding: they rode for miles across the hot prairies in all directions. They became ardent pickers of the wild flowers that struggled valiantly against the arid sand. Attracted at first by their beauty, they became interested in their botanic classification and pored over whatever books on botany they could lay their hands on. And on special occasions they would ride in their newly bought phaeton to Junction City, some two and a half miles away. Those infrequent trips were particular treats. Their friends there were different from those at Fort Riley. Junction City was a civilian community, with a liberal sprinkling of doctors, lawyers, and others in the learned professions. A sizable number of graduates of some of the leading colleges and universities in the East were living there. There they encountered none of the rigid social stratification found in military communities. They heard little talk of military matters and campaigns—a great relief for two young people whose lives were steeped in military thinking and military talking. In brief, they found there, and delighted in, an easy-going way of life that seemed remote and unreal at an army post. All this was for Martha Sternberg a delightful taste of the sort of life she had known and loved back in Indiana.

For some time after their marriage she wondered why they had been assigned to the quarters they were occupying. Not that it mattered a great deal, but she could not understand why her husband rated a less desirable house than any of the other officers, including those junior to him. Then she found out. A lieutenant had been assigned to a modest structure known as the sutler's house, while a much nicer place had been assigned to the Sternbergs. But that junior officer was in poor health, and living in the sutler's house would involve long walks to and from his work. So the sympathetic Captain Sternberg had offered to exchange with him. The latter had interposed some polite objections but was grateful.

CHAPTER IV

Battle in the Harbor

Soon after the Sternbergs got settled in the sutler's house another interest began competing with his wife and his laboratory for first attention. He became interested in invention. That rambling old building, with all its shortcomings, had one great virtue: it was large, one of the largest dwellings on the post. There was plenty of room for tinkering. With considerable help from Martha, he rigged up a workshop near the laboratory. Thereafter, whenever his mind would tire of bacteriological experiments, he would turn to his slide rule, his electrical wiring, and the other gadgets that he bought and made.

Ever since coming to Fort Riley and, before that, at other stations, he had been devoting considerable time to weather observations. As in the case of other medical officers, the keeping of weather records was one of his official duties. As long ago as April 2, 1814, long before there was anything like an official weather agency, the Surgeon General of the Army, Dr. James Tilton, had ordered hospital surgeons all over the country to become weather record keepers and weather reporters. Somewhat later another Surgeon General, Dr. Joseph Lovell, had put into effect a general expansion of the army's meteorological service. His instructions were that every army physician above a certain rank must keep a journal describing the weather in his area, "as the influence of the weather and climate upon diseases, especially epidemics, is perfectly well known." Every collaborating surgeon was furnished a weather thermometer, and, in addition to keeping a diary of the weather, was required to "note everything relative to the topography of his station, the climate, complaints prevalent in the vicinity, etc., that may tend to discover the causes of diseases, to the promotion of health, and the improvement of medical science."

After several years as a part-time weather observer, Captain Sternberg naturally explored the weather as a possible field for invention. His interest centered upon the anemometer, an instrument which makes a continuous record of the direction and force of the wind. He was sure that this instrument, which had not been materially changed in decades, could be improved; so he got busy working on it. After much painstaking work he was confident that he had made a substantial contribution to the science of weather observation. Then he set out for Washington with his drawings to obtain a patent for his invention.

Unfortunately, his enthusiasm was not shared by the officials of the Patent Office, especially after they had searched the records. They found that the type of anemometer he had developed was nothing new. It had been invented more than a hundred years earlier by a native of Holland. But that was not all, or the worst. The Sternberg contribution of which he had been most proud—what he called the "eccentric"—had been described in a Latin book published in Germany in 1720. His application for a patent was, of course, rejected.

Disappointed he certainly was. But he refused to be too much so. There was a cheerful side which he looked for and found.

The old saying, "There is nothing new under the sun," certainly applies to my anemometer [he said in his letter to Mrs. Sternberg giving her the bad news]. Well, I am not greatly disappointed. It has been no great expense, has furnished me profitable employment, and I had not expected to make money out of it. It has at any rate helped to develop and show my inventive powers.

He had better luck with another invention. During the Civil War and since, he had noticed the effect of sudden weather changes upon the sick. At Fort Riley especially, where a shifting of the wind off the prairies frequently brought sharp drops in the temperature, he was sure many patients had not made satisfactory progress because of these changes. What a boon it would be, he thought, to have the sickroom kept at a constant temperature, defiant of weather changes outside! How much this would mean to the comfort of invalids and the well alike!

Crude efforts had long been made to that end. Stoves and open fireplaces were kept hot in cold weather and allowed to cool off, or go out entirely, in warm. But those changes in room temperature always followed outside weather changes some time after they occurred. There was no way to make immediate changes of this kind.

What the sick needed—and many other people too, for that matter—was some form of heat regulation that would respond immediately to temperature changes. And what responds more quickly than a column of mercury in a thermometer? That thought drove him to his workshop to spend weeks trying to turn thermometers into heat regulators.

There were many heart-breaking disappointments and false starts. But he was sure his principle was sound. All he needed to do was to put it to work. The eventual fruit of all his toil and frustration was simplicity itself. He wondered afterward why he had managed to overlook it in the maze of complicated designs he tried out and had to discard. His device consisted of a thermometer from which extended two small wires. One ended inside the bulb containing the mercury. The other entered the mercury column from the top and ended at a prearranged position, that position being determined of course by the temperature which it was desired to maintain constantly in the room. The two wires were connected at their other ends to a heat-making apparatus. Whenever the mercury would rise to the designated point, it would make contact with the top wire and complete an electrical circuit. That would actuate the device shutting off the heating apparatus. Immediately after that happened, the room temperature would drop. The mercury column would fall. Then that electrical contact inside the column would be broken, and the heating apparatus would again go into action. Then, of course, the previously described sequence would occur, ending with the cutting off of the heat-furnishing apparatus and the beginning of another cycle. Thus a remarkable degree of uniformity of room temperature would be maintained.

This time he was not bothered with patent troubles. The

Patent Office research staff could find no record of an earlier invention of this kind.

The device had obvious commercial possibilities, and businessmen looking for new products to put on the market became interested. One group wished not only to market the Sternberg heat regulator but also to enlist the Sternberg promotional capabilities. That, of course, would have necessitated his resigning his commission, which he was not willing to do. So the matter was not pushed at that time. Later another firm showed considerable interest, and offered him five thousand dollars for his patent. He considered it worth more but realized how difficult it probably would be to obtain a better offer without going to a great deal of expense and spending a great deal of time looking for a buyer. Having no superfluity of either time or money, he accepted the offer and left for Washington to arrange a transfer of the patent. He had hardly left the house when another prospect called. That man told Mrs. Sternberg he would pay ten thousand dollars. The other deal had not been consummated, of course, and was not legally binding. But both he and Mrs. Sternberg considered it morally binding: the new offer was turned down.

There have been many improvements and refinements in heat regulation, of course, but the basic idea embodied in that first Sternberg patent is essentially the same as that found in the apparatus which keeps apartment buildings, residences, factories, stores, etc. evenly heated today.

Captain Sternberg's interest in automatic heat regulation was by no means confined to keeping room temperatures at predetermined levels. In another invention conceived in his questing brain and born in his cluttered workshop, he made it possible to keep laboratory compounds—or any other kind—at any desired heat by harnessing thermometers to gas burners. Still other adaptations of the central idea were put to still other practical uses.

The company organized to manufacture and market the Sternberg heat regulator lost no time in getting started. One of its first moves was to issue an attractively printed and handsomely illustrated booklet with the dual purpose of selling stock and attracting users. The booklet dismissed any idea that the regulator

was of less than revolutionary importance. It "is not to be classed
with the churns, washing machines, &c. (valuable in their way),"
its anonymous author proclaimed. Rather, it "claims a place beside the electric telegraph and inventions of like importance and
value to the world."

The publication listed four important uses to which, it
claimed, the Sternberg Electromagnetic Regulator was well
adapted. The most important, of course, was "the regulation of
the temperature of public buildings, factories, school-houses,
dwelling-houses, malt-houses, drying-houses, &c., &c. to any point
desired." Its other recommended uses were for the regulation of
the temperature of any liquid undergoing evaporation or dis-
tillation, steam pressure, and the height of liquid in a reservoir,
including "the height of water in a steam boiler." With the Sternberg regulator, that promotional leaflet went on, "the physician
in charge of a hospital may be enabled to say, 'I will have this
ward kept at a temperature of 60 degrees, and this one at 70 degrees.' He may in a moment adjust the regulator for himself, secure it by lock and key, if necessary, and go away with the assurance that no carelessness of nurses can allow the temperature to exceed the point he has fixed."

And how about controlling the temperature of one's own
home or apartment? That would be easy too:

A gentleman of intelligence desires to have his house kept at such
a temperature as is most conducive to the health and comfort of himself
and family. A regulating thermometer hangs in his sitting-room or par-
lor; wires descend to the cellar where they are connected with the me-
chanical apparatus governing the damper on the furnace. He adjusts the
wire in the tube of his thermometer to 65 degrees, and his servants cannot waste his fuel, render him uncomfortable, or endanger the health of
his family by heating the room to 100 degrees.

Another leaflet, also intended to promote the sale of stock,
listed Dr. Sternberg as a trustee of the Automatic Heat Regulating and Ventilating Company, capitalized at half a million dollars and incorporated under the laws of the State of New York.
It pointed out that the Sternberg regulator had won the highest
award at the American Institute Fair. Moreover, it had been
"noticed in most complimentary terms by Professor Silliman in
his address at the close of the Fair." It had also been "noticed in

a most favorable manner by several scientific journals" and had been publicly indorsed by a number of well known scientists. The New York *Telegraph* called it "one of the most ingenious and useful inventions on exhibition" at the American Institute Fair, and the *Scientific American* commented: "We have carefully inspected the operation of this arrangement in a number of its different applications and consider it in every respect an unqualified success. Every electrician and expert who has seen it has been at once impressed with its entire simplicity and perfect adaptation to the purposes for which it was designed."

Nevertheless, in spite of the many enthusiastic indorsements it received, the public did not take readily to automatic temperature control at that time. It remained for later men of the Sternberg turn of mind, and an America more conscious of its need for such a contrivance, to make automatic heat control a near-necessity in the properly equipped home. But those who had better success than he and that company in "selling" it to the American public are indebted to him and to it for taking a long and important step in that direction.

Martha Sternberg's extended visits with her family in Indianapolis made her husband an extremely lonely man, but they did give him more time to work on his inventions and in his laboratory. Those two rooms in the rambling, barnlike sutler's house which had been dedicated to invention and research were in almost constant use while he was off duty. His letters told her of his loneliness; they told also of his activities and accomplishments. "I spend most of my time now with the microscope" and "Today I have been busy reading and working with my microscope" are typical sentences from those frequent husbandly missives.

As trying as his loneliness often was, he preferred it to gay parties. With all his liking for the army, he never liked that side of army life. "I don't like Army parties," he wrote her, "because one meets so many silly, flirting married women and because the officers generally have to drink too much whiskey to make them pleasant companions for those who do not drink with them." However, "a nice party, where you are among friends and relatives and a nice dance in which all join with spirit and

pleasure, I enjoy as much as anyone would." In another letter
he told her about a "grand blow-out" given by one of their neighbors. He did not go and was certainly glad later he hadn't, for
"they kept up the dancing all night and were a seedy looking set
in the morning."

Other letters told about business matters, visiting some of
the neighbors (he was not a social hermit, after all), and having
"nothing to read." That last, referring to reading of a general, or
popular, nature, did not especially bother him, for "I have my
botany and microscope and manage to get along without getting
too blue."

In June, 1870, the Sternbergs were ordered to pack up and
ship "my botany and my microscope" and their other personal
possessions to Governors Island, in New York Harbor. This
post, headquarters of the Department of the East, a collection
center for recruits and an ordnance depot, they found much more
active than Fort Riley.

They had been there about three months when Captain Sternberg returned home one morning from the hospital at the usual
time. There was an unusual look on his face—a look of anxiety,
worry, and fatigue—which did not escape his solicitous wife.
She asked him what was the matter. One of the men had developed a strange illness, he told her. He had been watching the
case at the hospital for several hours and didn't like what he had
seen. It looked like yellow fever, and it made him sick to think
what might happen if there should be a serious outbreak within
sight of the nation's largest city.

Other men at the post soon began falling victims to that
strange, malignant malady. Many succumbed quickly, unable to
put up any kind of fight against the overpowering infection. Dr.
Sternberg consulted frequently with the senior medical officer,
and both of them watched the rising tide of illness and death
with rising anxiety. The look on Dr. Sternberg's face became
more troubled. He feared the epidemic would get completely out
of hand. Physicians on the staffs of the New York and Brooklyn
health departments were called into consultation, as was a surgeon on duty at West Point who had treated yellow fever cases
in Mexico. The latter removed all doubt as to the nature of the

outbreak. Dr. Sternberg, who was soon to become a battle-scarred veteran of the war against yellow fever, was getting his baptism of fire.

New York quickly clamped down a quarantine against Governors Island. Under the whiplash of fear a frantic effort was made to seal off the post in the hope that nonintercourse would keep the epidemic confined to that small area. Governors Island authorities also moved energetically to keep the outbreak under control. Arrangements were made to transfer the eighty yellow fever patients to what was known as the West Bank Quarantine Hospital, far down the bay. Paying no attention to the fact that he had never had yellow fever and was therefore a nonimmune, Dr. Sternberg's official superiors ordered him to take charge of the transfer and look after the patients afterward.

He was thoroughly steeped in the army tradition of unquestioning obedience to every order. He certainly had no thought except to get those sick men to the West Bank Quarantine Hospital as comfortably and safely as possible and to do everything he could for them there. Nevertheless, the assignment was an extremely unwelcome and distasteful one. The first Mrs. Sternberg had succumbed to cholera less than two years after their marriage. And now, just about a year after his second marriage, he had been ordered to leave his wife, as unprotected against yellow fever as himself, in a yellow fever epidemic center while he fought the disease in a particularly malignant outbreak some distance away.

Hiding his anxiety, he went forward with preparations for the mass transfer. Under his direction attendants covered each yellow fever patient with a sheet and carefully pushed his bed down the long corridor to the outside entrance. There it and its occupant were carried to the waiting boat. After the last bed had been made fast, he ordered the helmsman to wait a few minutes before shoving off. He was not quite ready. While the stout rope kept the craft alongside the small pier, he hurried off to one of the most difficult farewells of his life. Martha Sternberg, who had been watching the loading operations from a distance, broke down and wept when she realized that the moment of parting, possibly a final parting, was at last at hand. He had little heart for cheering up her or anybody else. But he did his best under a mask of lighthearted cheerfulness. She was not to worry about him. He would come through all right. She must keep herself in good spirits. He would get messages through to her as often as he could. And it would not be so very long (he hoped) before they would be together again. "Be a brave little woman," he pleaded as he tore himself away from her arms.

She promised she would do her best. With that promise echoing in his memory, he was away, hurrying toward the dock. As she stood there and, through the dim mist of her tears, saw the craft begin slipping away from its anchorage, she thought of a second-story window in their home that afforded an excellent view of the harbor and Brooklyn. Hurrying home and running up the stairs like an excited schoolgirl, her steps echoing through the depressingly quiet house, she looked out. There he was, standing with soldierly dignity in the bow as the boat rapidly gathered speed. He saw her too and waved. They waved at each other until the boat shrank to a tiny spot lost in the labyrinth of harbor traffic.

Unfortunately, the removal of those yellow fever patients did not bring an end of the disease on Governors Island. Other cases developed, many of them, and all were sent to Dr. Sternberg's West Bank Quarantine Hospital except those ending with death or recovery before they could be transferred.

Returning home a few weeks after the outbreak of the epidemic from a visit to the seriously sick wife of the post surgeon, Mrs. Sternberg found a visitor, a distinguished visitor, at her house. Seeing the commanding officer of the post frightened her. The only reason she could think of for such a visit was bad— perhaps terrible—news from her husband. Had he developed yellow fever?

But the C. O.'s news was not bad. Dr. Sternberg was all right, but very much worried about her. He was not satisfied to have her stay any longer at the post. She needed to be with relatives, he thought. He had been in touch with a cousin of his in Newark, a businessman, who wanted her to make an extended visit with him and his family. The C. O. told her a boat was waiting at the pier for her reply.

She found herself struggling in a dizzy whirlpool of impulses and conflicts. She would certainly find living in Newark much more pleasant than here in this epidemic-ridden army post. There would be a partial easing of the crushing loneliness that was depressing her more than she would ever admit. She would no longer have to spend weary, dragged-out hours in that house that echoed with emptiness. A nonimmune, she was exposed to yellow fever as long as she remained so close to so many cases. All these considerations strongly inclined her to leave, but others made her hesitate. She wanted to be as near her husband as she could, and Governors Island was much nearer than Newark. Even more important, she wanted to be where she could hear from him often, and that she had been able to do, since a boat made a round trip every day between the post and the West Bank Quarantine Hospital. She would be miserable if she had to wait days on end for letters that did not come or took too long to come. This last consideration tipped the scales in her mind. She decided to stay where she was.

Nevertheless, the C. O. thought she ought to go. He reminded her that her husband wanted her to do so. She would undoubtedly be much safer in Newark, and that would greatly relieve his mind, burdened with the care of a colony of sick men. He would be driven almost to distraction if she should get yellow fever. That certainly was a ponderous argument. After all, it was her husband's peace of mind, next to his physical health, that meant most to her. She began seeing it their way. Perhaps she ought to do as they wanted her to.

There was a difficulty neither had yet brought up—the New York quarantine. How could she get through the city on her way to Newark? How embarrassing it would be for a medical officer's wife to be arrested for deliberately violating the quarantine rules!

Her visitor had thought of that: so had her husband. The former's barge would take her and her maid to the Battery late that night. They would disembark quietly. Dr. Sternberg's cousin would be there with a carriage to convey her across the river to Newark as quickly as possible. There was very little danger of their being stopped and questioned; there was practically none of their giving yellow fever to anyone in either New York or Newark.

Then another problem bobbed in her mind. What would she do with the house? The arrangements awaiting her approval called for her to leave that very night, in just a few hours. There was not enough time to find a renter, make arrangements for the care of the furniture, and see to all the other matters that needed attending to before she left for an indefinite stay. The C. O. had an answer to that, too. She could turn everything over to him. He would take complete charge.

That settled it. She would go. Her visitor, pleased that he had won his point, hurried with her message to the waiting boat.

At eleven o'clock that night a young woman with mind awhirl accompanied by her maid stepped ashore from a small shadow-hidden boat at the Battery. All was quiet. They could see nothing disturbing as they looked in every direction for an inquisitive policeman or quarantine officer. Nearby they saw a carriage in which was a man whom she recognized as her cousin-by-marriage. They spoke softly and as little as possible. In a few minutes they were lost in the big city's traffic. They reached Newark without arousing suspicion in the early hours of the morning.

Mrs. Sternberg had unquestionably been guilty of a clear violation of the quarantine regulations and was worried, now that she had more time to think about it, lest her hosts become involved in legal difficulties for having become parties to it. To protect them as far as possible and also to minimize the risk of introducing yellow fever in the community, she and her maid kept to their rooms for some time. As both dangers diminished and finally disappeared, their self-imposed isolation ended. The maid left to visit relatives, and Mrs. Sternberg took part more freely in family and community activities.

Dr. Sternberg showed in his letters how relieved he was that she was no longer in the epidemic center. Although their exchange of mail was not as easy or as frequent as before, they managed to hear from each other fairly frequently. His missives, often written hurriedly, kept her informed regarding his work and the progress of the epidemic.

He wrote to her on October 2, assuring her that he was well

and comfortable, and was looking forward to seeing her "before very long." The place where he was working was "a fine hospital with every convenience and in an exceedingly healthy location." Another doctor had arrived to help him; a third was expected soon. Three days later he wrote that he was "still well." He was hoping to see her "before very long, perhaps in seven or eight days." Meanwhile, his mind was much more at ease about her: "You can not think what a relief it is to my mind that you are at Cousin Watson's. I am very glad and grateful that he insisted upon taking you and that you consented to go." The boat from Governors Island had brought five patients the night before. Two deaths had occurred during the night, and he expected more the next night. But the situation was improving: "A good many that I brought here are now out of bed and helping take care of the sick." Most of the patients "are now in a fair way to recover." He told her about another death in his letter of October 6. The victim was somebody they both knew, "the little drummer in the band," for whom "I have done my best"—unfortunately, not enough. Another patient was expected to die soon. Most of the others were "doing well." He hoped "we may not be called upon to report many more deaths." There had been no arrivals the day before. That was a good sign.

One of his letters had especially interesting news for her. It told about a visit he had made to their home on Governors Island. He was there only long enough to get some clean clothing, about fifteen minutes in all. He found everything in good order. But "it looked very lonely there." "Much as I would have liked to see my wife," he wrote, "yet I was very glad to think she was safe and among kind friends, rather than by herself in our house, lonely and weeping."

The patients then at the West Bank Quarantine Hospital, he wrote her about the same time, "will all be well or dead in a few days." Unless there should be some more arrivals, he hoped to be relieved in a week or ten days. He was feeling "quite well" and not working as hard as at first. There was just one death during the next twenty-four hours. He hoped, he said in his letter of October 7, he "will not have any more to report." His work by this time had eased greatly, for many of his patients had improved

so much that they could relieve him of numerous light but time-
consuming tasks. Too, he had "a very good assistant," presumably the doctor he had mentioned earlier. No longer a slave to
his work, he was looking forward to making a short trip to Newark in two or three days. Everything depended upon there being no more arrivals from Governors Island.

But that was not to be. That flow of new yellow fever cases
had not yet dried up. Instead of making the trip to Newark
which he had looked forward to, he was kept busy looking after
them. On October 13 he took courage and a certain amount of
hope from what the calendar told him—that "the month of October is nearly half gone." Colder weather and its frosts had
for centuries ended yellow fever epidemics that had mocked man's
best efforts. Referring to the latest two arrivals, he said: "I hope
and trust they may be the last."

But they were not. He had to tell her on October 25 of the
arrival of three new patients, one of whom had died the night before. They "have disarranged all my plans," and "I can't say
positively what day I can see you again." That day-to-day post-
ponement of their reunion was exasperating. At last, however,
it came to pass. He needed to make an official trip to New York,
and Newark and his waiting wife were too close for him to miss
this opportunity. But the reunion was not the enjoyable experience she had hoped it would be: she was shocked to see how
cruelly the past several weeks at the West Bank Quarantine Hospital had borne down upon him. He had lost much weight, the
ruddy color had gone from his cheeks, leaving them pallid and
careworn, his step had lost much of its accustomed spring. There
was a noticeable droop to his shoulders. His eyes looked tired.

She was upset over him all through his visit. And, the more
she thought about it, the more strongly she was convinced that
he needed her badly, that she ought to go back with him. When
she mentioned it, he would not listen to her. Her place, he insisted, was right where she was. The epidemic was not yet over,
and it would be foolishly risky to go to a place like that unless
you had to or were needed to care for the sick. Life at the West
Bank Quarantine Hospital was hard: she might overtax her
strength and contract some other disease, if not yellow fever.

But her mind was made up, and when Martha Sternberg made up her mind, it was a mind to contend with. She would not listen to him. She knew he really wanted her with him, that he was only thinking of what he regarded as best for her. In the end, she won her point and started packing.

Captain Sternberg had long ago become accustomed to the depressing atmosphere at the West Bank Quarantine Hospital, but it struck his wife like a body blow even before she got there. As the boat approached the dock, this sensitive, observant woman noticed and was saddened by emaciated, weak-looking men in the convalescent stages of their tough bouts with Yellow Jack. She saw how careworn their faces were as they sat around the boat landing or performed simple tasks, how slow their steps, how pale their faces, how dispirited their manner. And she also noticed the row upon row of coffins neatly piled there on the pier, grim reminders of yellow fever's ruthless sweep.

She had not been there long before she found that now it was her turn to endure loneliness. For her husband was still away from home for many weary hours at a time. The battle at the hospital was now going better, but it had not yet been won. There was still much more mork for him to do than any one man should have to do. And that was not all; after his official daily stint was over there was the call of the microscope, which he still answered as often, and for as long, as he could. He had had to give up most, but not all of this outside research during the worst part of the epidemic. Now that the pressure had eased he was working nearly as hard as ever, the difference being that he was spending less time at the hospital and more in his laboratory.

Martha Sternberg was finding other difficulties piled on top of loneliness. In fact she was finding it a particularly trying business being the wife of a man dedicated with zealous passion to the pursuit of scientific knowledge. Such devotion of a man to his work is never conducive to companionship or a full family life or, for that matter, anything approaching normal living. Meals were eaten haphazardly, mealtime being dependent upon the volume of work at the hospital and the intensity of his interest in experiments currently under way. They were seldom able to plan anything ahead. But Martha Sternberg was still an under-

standing, as well as devoted, wife. She did not complain of her
loneliness, her disarranged mode of living. She considered them
her share of the price they were having to pay for the success
and fame which she considered certain if they would only per-
severe and keep their health.

That frost which Dr. Sternberg had expected in mid-October—the one he was depending upon to stop the epidemic—
did not come for about another two weeks. When it did come,
the flow of yellow fever patients from Governors Island slowed
to a trickle and then dried up entirely. The West Bank Quarantine Hospital was closed, and the Sternbergs began packing for
the long-delayed trip back to their Governors Island home. When
he made out his final report he found that he and the other medical officers had treated 152 yellow fever patients. That figure
included those treated at Governors Island before the opening
of the West Bank Quarantine Hospital and also those who died
or recovered there before they could be moved. About a third
of these cases had ended fatally.

The return to Governors Island was not an altogether happy
one. Many of their friends were no longer there. Some, like
"the little drummer in the band," had succumbed to yellow fever.
Others had been so weakened by it that they had been sent away
to rebuild their strength and health. Still others had left under
happier circumstances, in obedience to routine army orders sending them to other posts. Even their home would never be the
same: every mattress, every blanket, every sheet, every pillow
case, every rug, and everything else about the place that, the
authorities believed, might be harboring yellow fever germs had
been ruthlessly put to the torch. The returning Sternbergs found
only stark, naked places where those cherished household articles
had stood, the emptiness a thousand times more noticeable than
the things themselves had been. It was painful to give up those
simple objects which had been their close companions during all
their brief married life. They resolved that one of their first tasks
would be to fill those gaping pools of emptiness and make their
home look like a home again. That sadness and depression stayed
on with them, even after those empty spaces disappeared. The
place had undergone a change more fundamental than missing

household articles. So they were glad when another army order came, sending them away, only a short distance, it is true, but far enough to be another place. The move, which came in the spring of 1871, was to Fort Hamilton, also in New York's expansive, busy, and beautiful harbor. There they could make new friends without too much missing the old ones.

Their stay at Fort Hamilton, however, was quite brief, just two months. Then they were off again, this time to Fort Warren, in Boston Harbor. They arrived there on the last day of June, 1871.

The wandering Sternbergs found much at their new station to like and a few things they did not like at all. Fellow officers and their families were hospitable, friendly, and neighborly. Boston, a pleasant place to be near, was only nine miles away. The hospital was well equipped. And there was considerable leisure time for Dr. Sternberg to spend with his beloved microscope. But they missed, so very much, their pleasant home, in its own building, at Governors Island . Like other officers' families, they were quartered, not in individual houses or even apartments but in casemates. These had not been built or designed as living quarters at all but as emplacements for heavy guns. Their tiny openings admitted only meager sunlight. Their masonry construction made them feel and look like prison cells. They were cold and cheerless. The heavy moisture liquified into streamlets that trickled down the walls unless fires were kept going to heat the surfaces somewhat. Kitchenware, knives, and indeed almost everything else made of metal rusted from the cancerous dampness far sooner than they could wear out in use. Unheated mirrors were constantly covered with thick films of moisture that would start dripping after reaching the saturation point, ruining whatever happened to be underneath. That perpetual dampness softened the plastered walls and even dripped from the ceiling. Many a medical officer stationed briefly and unhappily at Fort Warren had complained bitterly about requiring army personnel and their families to live in such quarters, but their protests had been politely ignored, as were Dr. Sternberg's and those of his successors for a long time. It did not relieve their discomfort to know that Jefferson Davis had spent several months cooped up

like a caged eagle in the damp, dreary, cold casemates at Fort
Monroe, Virginia, nor did it help any to know that their own
quarters had once served as prison cells for high-ranking officers
of the Confederate Army.

The hospital was in the casemates too, so Captain Sternberg was cold, damp, and sunshine-starved practically all through
the day and night, except for brief escapes that gave him the ex-
hilarating feeling which comes to the briefly liberated dungeon
denizen.

Nevertheless, the dampness, the scanty sunshine, and the raw
New England cold could not smother all social intercourse. Social life, it is true, was limited. The garrison was quite small at
the time, consisting of a single company, plus some engineering
troops engaged in repairing and renovating some of the structures. Mrs. Sternberg had only two neighbors of her own sex,
both officers' wives. But the bachelor officers were jolly, friendly,
and strongly opposed to anybody's getting too lonely. The Sternbergs dined with them from time to time and had them as their
guests. They also participated with enthusiasm in the impromptu
musicales that got going whenever music-lovers got together,
usually sparked by a piano-playing lieutenant. Some time before, Dr. Sternberg had managed to drag himself away from his
hospitals, his laboratories, and his workshops long enough to
learn to play the flute—"well," his wife boasted, probably not
without prejudice. Martha Sternberg, for her part, was profi-
cient on the Spanish guitar her mother had given her.

The Sternbergs and their fellow prisoners of the casemates
were able to escape into the great outdoors after spring came.
There was sunshine out on the parapets, if you could stand the
cold, and, after being cooped up like that, you certainly were
willing to try. On Sunday afternoons and at other times when he
was not tied to his work, they would go out there to read. From
their lofty perch they could see the stately ship parade moving
in solemn grandeur to and from the city, here a big liner off for
Europe or the Orient, here a rusty tramp putting in from the
Far East, here a tiny coastwiser carrying New England textiles
and shoes to Mobile or New Orleans. If they did not care to eat
with the gay bachelor officers or make music with them or read

on the parapet or watch the ships, they could go fishing, and occasionally they did—there were some excellent places not far away. Sitting out in the bright sunshine with a pole in hand proved relaxing to the hard-working medical man who still showed the effects of his long stay at the West Bank Quarantine Hospital and needed all the sunshine he could get.

They also found relaxation, sunshine, and fresh air in boating. As a youngster Captain Sternberg had spent much time on the Susquehanna, where he had learned to handle almost any small craft. With a fellow officer, he now bought a small sailboat, and he and Martha Sternberg used it on many excursions to the various seaside resorts within easy sailing distance of the fort. Later, with another officer-friend as co-owner, he bought a larger boat. Soon both husband and wife had healthy coats of tan.

In July, 1872, they exchanged, without too many regrets, the dank, depressing casemates of Fort Warren for the cheerful, stimulating sunshine of New Orleans. This, however, was a temorary assignment to enable another medical officer to take a short leave. Dr. Sternberg wondered how much the city had changed since he was there with the army during the war.

It was some time before he was able to find out. Almost the first news he got after reporting for duty was that he had another yellow fever epidemic on his hands. Fortunately, it did not prove serious, and he was able to handle it without much trouble.

CHAPTER V

Doctor in Bed

As THEY HAD ANTICIPATED, the Sternbergs' stay in New Orleans was short, lasting only about six weeks. At its end they moved to Fort Barrancas, Florida, arriving on September 2. They felt that they would be there much longer. The first few months were pleasant enough. There was no yellow fever to speak of nearer than New Orleans. The post itself had had no cases in nearly twenty years, and Pensacola, up the bay, had been free of the disease for six years or longer. This looked like a good place to carry on normal official duties, enjoy as much social life as one cared to participate in, and, of particular importance to Dr. Sternberg, have lots of time for research.

They spent a great deal of time improving the ugly frame house assigned them for their quarters, which was "neither well planned nor well built," in Mrs. Sternberg's words. The "burr grass" that grew everywhere became a great nuisance and gave the place a desolate look. They particularly disliked it and decided to do something about it, if they could. Finding that no other kind of grass would grow in that soil, they arranged with a schooner captain to bring them some soil which would support other vegetation. They were delighted to find that it enabled them to grow blooming plants and even fruit trees, to the considerable envy of their neighbors. From time to time they would attend parties on board "dying" ironclad warships of the Civil War period which were being towed to their final anchorages before being broken up for scrap. On another brief relief assignment in New Orleans, during which Mrs. Sternberg stayed at home, Dr. Sternberg bought a horse and phaeton, which he gallantly presented to her upon his return. As if to prove that the bitterness of the war had been completely forgotten, as far as they were concerned, they named the frisky, friendly animal Robert E. Lee. There were frequent opportunities to refresh their knowledge of botany on excursions into the woods and swamps. They acquired—by borrowing from the contractor who kept the post supplied with beef—a cow and a calf, which rebelled loudly and angrily at the idea of sharing its mother's milk with human beings. All in all, this was a pleasant life. Peace and quiet, it seemed, had come to the Sternberg home in greater measure than they had ever known, except for brief intervals. And this pleasant existence apparently was to continue indefinitely.

But, as at Governors Island about two years before, Dr. Sternberg returned home one morning from the hospital looking troubled and anxious. Mrs. Sternberg asked him what the trouble was. "I have a very sick patient at the hospital," he told her. "I am very much concerned about him. It looks like a case of yellow fever." He couldn't quite make up his mind about it at the time. Nor was he able to during the rest of the day, although there was increasing evidence that his tentative diagnosis had been correct. The next morning he was about to hurry off to the hospital without any breakfast, but Martha Sternberg objected.

"You mustn't go off without at least a cup of coffee," she urged. "Wait a minute. I'll get you some." When she went into the kitchen the cook told her about being up all night with her two sick children and asked if Dr. Sternberg would go by to see them. He promised he would after seeing his patients at the hospital. When he returned home about two hours later, he told his wife and the children's mother that he had examined the youngsters and was sure they had yellow fever. He advised the mother to go home as soon as she could and look after them.

Those three cases—the first now definitely diagnosed as yellow fever—were soon followed by others. As soon as the first positive diagnosis was made, Dr. Sternberg urged upon his official superiors the wisdom of removing the entire encampment across the bay to a camp near Fort Pickens, and the order was issued immediately. The navy helped by loaning a vessel from the navy yard at nearby Pensacola, and the transfer was completed before nightfall. All the Fort Barrancas personnel were moved except the commanding officer, who had had yellow fever and was therefore immune to it, the Sternbergs, both of whom were nonimmune, of course, an officer with a slight case of typhoid, whose removal was considered inadvisable, the nurses on duty at the hospital, the hospital steward, and some enlisted men needed to look after the animals. This prompt action prevented the epidemic from getting out of hand, but, unfortunately, did not end it at once. There were twelve cases in all. Three of the victims—the cook's children and that man whose condition had sent Dr. Sternberg home with the worried look on his face—died. The troops stayed away until a light frost fell in early November.

His cook's children were only two of the many nonmilitary patients Dr. Sternberg was called upon to treat. In accordance with a custom which had been followed so long as to have the effect of unofficial law, army doctors were expected to do their best to cure the illnesses and heal the injuries of almost anyone living within a wide radius of an army camp. In theory, patients not legally entitled to this service were expected to pay for it. In practice, only a tiny fraction of them were able to do so, and an even tinier fraction were both able and willing to do so. Therefore, Dr. Sternberg and his fellow medical officers spent a considerable portion of their time, much of it off-duty time, as unpaid general practitioners, lancing angry boils, treating a multitude of illnesses, setting broken bones, and performing other feats of medical magic. Occasionally, however, they were compensated in vastly more satisfying and more pleasant ways than by monetary payment.

There was, for example, the case of the poor colored woman threatened by creeping blindness. Dr. Sternberg knew he would never get a dime from her when she asked him to treat her faltering eyes, but that fact did not diminish in the least his interest in the case or his desire to help her. His examination showed she had a cataract, and, at her request, he operated. Her dimming vision became clear again, and the gloomy threat of economic dependency vanished. Her benefactor would have quickly forgotten the incident as a passing episode in a busy day. But the humble old woman, too poor to pay in cash, paid lavishly in gratitude and appreciation. As long as he was at Fort Barrancas she never saw him without seizing his hand and kissing it. He was embarrassed but pleased.

Dr. Sternberg, who by this time had earned a considerable reputation as an authority on yellow fever, was called to Pensacola in the late summer of 1874 to examine some suspicious cases among the naval personnel. In company with the surgeon on duty at the navy yard, he visited the hospital and also went to see some officers who were sick in their quarters. The naval surgeon was strongly inclined to attribute the outbreak to Chagres fever, since a vessel had recently arrived at the navy yard from the Isthmus of Panama, where this highly malignant form of malaria was widely prevalent. But Dr. Sternberg did not agree with him. His diagnosis was that these men were all suffering from yellow fever. He was positive of it.

The naval doctor, unwilling to accept his diagnosis, nevertheless agreed to go with him to the admiral in command of the navy yard. To that high-ranking officer Dr. Sternberg was as positive as he had been to the medical officer that a yellow fever epidemic had broken out at the yard. Explaining how the quick transfer of the well to other camps had prevented the recent Fort Barrancas outbreak and others from getting out of control, he urged that the same be done with the unaffected personnel at the navy yard. The admiral listened with great courtesy, but was unconvinced. In the first place, he was not certain the cases were yellow fever at all. And, even if they should be, he did not see why their presence at the navy yard called for such drastic action. Still completely courteous, he refused to order the transfer.

Dr. Sternberg's diagnosis had been correct. That the cases were yellow fever, even the urbane but highly opinionated admiral was obliged to concede in time. Unfortunately, the conviction reached him too late. He was among the first to develop the disease and one of the 354 who succumbed to it. Others who did so were that naval surgeon who was also reluctant to accept the Sternberg diagnosis, and his wife, whose children were doubly orphaned in just a few days. Another navy couple—a captain and his wife—also left suddenly orphaned children. The paymaster and his wife narrowly missed doing so but managed to recover after a long and trying convalescence. There undoubtedly would have been many more deaths had not nearly two thousand frightened people fled from the accursed area.

Dr. Sternberg's task was not completed with his diagnosis of those early cases. When its correctness was established in that terrible way, he was called upon to help put out the fire which those others had refused to see. He bore no resentment, of course. He did not even pay any attention to the fact that he was still a nonimmune. He simply volunteered his services to the navy medical officers and toiled shoulder to shoulder with them in trying to control the conflagration.

In one respect at least he was better off than he had been during the early stages of that outbreak on Governors Island. Mrs. Sternberg was out of the yellow fever area. She had gone back to Indiana to visit her relatives and was still there when those few early cases exploded into a grave epidemic, so that he did not have to worry about her. Or rather, he did not until she began insisting upon rejoining him. To that he was strongly and vigorously opposed, as he made plain in letter after letter.

In any number of letters written early in September,1874, she kept saying she felt she ought to get back home immediately and asking him to set a date for her to do so. But that he resolutely refused to do. He called her return "impossible at present."

"I cannot think of allowing you to come until all danger from yellow fever is over," he wrote on September 11. One of their friends had died the day before. Another was at the point of death. Two companies from the post were getting away to Baton Rouge to stay until the Pensacola epidemic should end. Others had gone back to Fort Pickens to wait out the storm. "Submit, my dear, to the inevitable as well as possible," he pleaded with her. "I know how great your disappointment will be at not being allowed to come home. Perhaps after a while I can get a leave and come after you."

She kept up her pleading. It was her duty to be with him, she insisted. But he was as unyielding as ever; he wrote her on

September 13 about "quite a number" of yellow fever cases and several deaths at the navy yard and in nearby communities, and added: "You will see that it is impossible for you to come home before the frost."

To ease her mind and make her less insistent about returning, he promised to telegraph her at once, or have someone else to do so, if he should get yellow fever. And, should he do so, he assured her that the other medical officers at the post would see that he had the very best of medical care. Even his own illness, if it should eventuate, should not cause her to return:

In such a case, you must not think of coming here. I forbid it, my dear. I will have telegrams sent to you frequently and will conceal nothing from you in case I am taken, but you must stay at home. It is a disease of such short duration that I would be convalescent or beyond help before you could reach me and after a fatiguing journey you would be sure to have the disease. . . . I want to see you very much, my dear wife, but we must both exercise the virtue of patience.

She was still not convinced, persisting in her wish to return to Fort Barrancas at once. He persisted in his determination to prevent her from doing so, if possible, though he was seriously handicapped in his campaign of persuasion by the quarantine slapped upon the epidemic area by the frightened officials of nearby cities and towns and others not so near but situated on railroads leading to that area. Those quarantines interfered greatly with the northbound mails and sometimes stopped them altogether. Dr. Sternberg complained a number of times that his letters, urgently pleading with her to stay away, had been piling up at a small junction point. Hers to him went through freely.

His letter of September 7, like the others, was full of reasons why she should stay where she was until the danger was over. A "Mr. Cora, the watchmaker," had died the day before; all but twenty enlisted men at Fort Barrancas had been ordered away; an illness suffered by "Lieut. Ingals," about which he and the other doctors had been in some doubt, "turns out to be yellow fever after all"; "Captain Franklin and his little boy" were down with the fever; Mrs. Franklin and another of the couple's children had had it for some time. (All four cases were to prove fatal.) Dr. Sternberg was receiving reports every day from the medical officer at the navy yard, telling about cases and deaths there.

> You can not think, my dear little wife, how happy I will be when you are with me again and everything goes on at our home as it did before you went away [he wrote her about that same time]. It is now a whole month since we parted. A little more than a month must pass before I can let you come back, but that will soon pass away, and then, my dear, we will be as happy as possible. So let us look forward to the 1st of Nov. as the time when we are to meet.

Dr. Sternberg won his point, finally convincing her that it would be unwise, even foolhardy, to leave the safety of her Indianapolis home while the epidemic still raged in the Pensacola-Fort Barrancas area. The last case was reported on November 9, almost simultaneously with the arrival of the first frost of the season, that traditional ender of yellow fever outbreaks. With the danger definitely over at last, the stern, duty-dictated man of medicine yielded to the lonely, devoted husband. A message went out over the wires asking her to let him know when he should meet her train.

That, however, she was not able to do. Railroad travel in that part of the country was still in a chaotic state. Connections were uncertain. Travel schedules had to be revised almost hourly. Three times he went up the bay to meet her at Pensacola. Twice he found when he got there that she would not arrive until later. But the loneliness of the past few months and the opportunity to end it at last made such temporary disappointments only minor irritants leading up to the happy climax of a long-delayed reunion. When they were at last in each other's arms, they fervently hoped no later epidemic or anything else would ever keep them away from each other for such a long time again. It was well for their enjoyment of that reunion that they did not know how soon Yellow Jack was going to strike once more or how cruelly his striking would affect them.

Dr. Sternberg's successful handling of the Fort Barrancas phase of the Barrancas-Pensacola outbreak and his valuable assistance to the medical officers at the navy yard had added substantially to his standing as an authority on yellow fever; and his extensive research in that field, which he had still been carrying on in his makeshift laboratory in spite of his greatly increased duties, had reached the eyes and ears of medical men in many parts of the country. Having learned a great deal about the disease from treating many cases and even more from his persistent delving into its baffling secrets by means of the microscope and the test tube, he wondered if medical journal editors would not be willing to publish some scientific papers of his if he should write them. The only way to find out, obviously, was to try his hand at medical writing. He found breaking into the new field of medical authorship difficult at first. Selecting just the right words and phrases to express what he wanted to say posed some troublesome problems, as it does to most beginning writers. The going was easier after a while; he found he had a natural flair for writing which developed rapidly with practice. It gave him a kind of satisfaction nothing else ever had. The idea of sharing the fruits of his studies with other doctors and, through them, perhaps helping to improve the outlook for millions of sick people appealed to him greatly. Nor was he unaware of the prestige which would come from having his writings widely published.

At last he finished an article that satisfied his ideas of what such a paper ought to be: he was sure it contained a great deal of information that would prove interesting to his fellow physicians, and was well pleased with the manner in which he had presented his material. The leading medical publication of the South at that time was the *New Orleans Medical and Surgical Journal*. So, aiming high, he sent that first paper to it. The editor not only liked it and promised to publish it in an early issue, he also asked for more. "An Inquiry into the *Modus Operandi* of the Yellow Fever Poison" appeared in that journal's issue of July, 1875.

Other contributions, inspired by this initial success, followed rapidly. During the next forty years he was to be one of the most prolific medical authors in the history of journalism. Writing mainly about yellow fever, tuberculosis, cholera, and a few other diseases in which he was especially interested, he nevertheless ranged widely over the broad field of medicine and health. And as his by-line began appearing in practically every important medical publication, as well as a few well-known general magazines, his reputation extended to the most distant reaches of his profession and to a large segment of the nonmedical public. That initial publication in the *New Orleans Medical and Surgical Journal* set him on his way to national recognition. His reputation leaped international barriers when many of his papers, published originally in this country, were translated into French, German, Portuguese, and other foreign languages and published in leading European scientific and medical journals.

But Dr. Sternberg was to know yellow fever much more intimately before he became recognized as one of the world's outstanding authorities on that disease and others. Another battle with Yellow Jack, a desperately vicious one, was just ahead. It exploded in mid-July, 1875, just about the time his first by-line appeared over "An Inquiry into the *Modus Operandi* of the Yellow Fever Poison." About three weeks earlier—late in the afternoon of June 27—the S. S. *Von Moltke*, with five yellow fever cases aboard, dropped anchor in Pensacola harbor inbound from Havana. Having arrived too late to be inspected by the quarantine officers before the next morning, she remained overnight near the Fort Barrancas side of the bay, under strict orders that nobody was to board or leave her. Upon arrival of the quarantine officers the next day the captain signed an affidavit stating that these orders had been fully carried out. What he did not know, or did not mention, was that a small boat containing enlisted men from Fort Barrancas had pulled alongside during the night to get some of the Cuban whiskey she was carrying. On July 18 one of these men went down with yellow fever, and that first case was followed by others until every one on that liquor-seeking expedition got it.

The infection, of a particularly virulent type, soon spread to other parts of the encampment, with especially heavy concentrations of cases in the laundresses' quarters, the enlisted men's barracks, and the officers' quarters. Thirty-seven cases occurred in five days, and the total reached seventy-four before the epidemic came to an end. Twenty-nine of them ended fatally.

Almost the first thing Dr. Sternberg thought of, and he thought of it with a sinking, desolate feeling, was that the rapidly crescendoing outbreak would bring another hated, but necessary, separation for him and Martha. For, as heartily as he loathed the very thought of being away from her again, he was as firmly convinced as ever that she had no business at an army encampment, or anywhere else, during an epidemic. Aside from considerations of her own safety, he told her, her departure was essential to the morale of the post during the cascading epidemic. If she stayed, the men—even then in process of being moved once more to the comparative safety of Fort Pickens to be returned to the Fort Barrancas hospital whenever they developed the disease—would be wondering whether he was giving them all the time their condition demanded. Even if she should be lucky enough to stay well—which would be too much good luck for them to depend upon—those men knew his husbandly responsibilities would cut substantially into the time he would not require for sleeping and eating, time they thought he should devote to them. If she herself should become sick, the other sick people knew he would have to spend a great deal of time looking after her. Moreover, his anxiety over her would almost certainly affect his work. Such considerations did not make much difference in normal times, he told her. But these were not normal times, not by a long shot. He did not want questions like these bobbing up in his patients' minds while he was helping them fight a highly fatal illness made even more dangerous by the state of near panic that accompanies a serious yellow fever outbreak.

Of course she raised the same objections he had heard so many times in the past. She simply could not see why she should leave her own husband in a time of danger. While the matter was still in the discussion stage, a messenger arrived from the commanding officer of the post, General J. M. Brannon. Captain Sternberg was to report to his office at once.

The general was in trouble. He wanted some advice and some help as well. A young woman who had never had or been previously exposed to yellow fever was visiting his wife. Unless she got out at once, she would be kept there, in momentary danger of getting the disease and in a completely miserable state of mind, until the epidemic abated. Even now it would not be easy for her to get away, with quarantines springing up all around; it might be done if she left immediately. But she was young and quite inexperienced; the realization that she was gradually being trapped here in this epidemic center had brought her to the thin edge of hysteria. Something had to be done, and at once, or she would have to reconcile herself as best she could to virtual imprisonment until the quarantine should be lifted. And a young woman, spoiled and impatient, is not easily reconciled to anything like that.

Would Mrs. Sternberg take charge of her and get her away as quickly as possible? General Brannon looked to Captain Sternberg for an answer. The latter, remembering how stoutly his wife had resisted his urging her to leave, could not tell him. He said he would talk the matter over with her, would urge her even more strongly than before to get out while she could. If she should do so, he was sure she would look after this badly frightened, homesick young woman.

Martha Sternberg agreed to do as he wished in both matters. Then the two of them plunged into a round of chores even more arduous than those leading up to her flight from Governors Island a few years earlier. The harried C. O., happy to be rid of his pretty but distracting visitor, did everything he could to speed up the departure and reduce the danger of a last-minute change of mind. A government wagon was placed at Mrs. Sternberg's disposal to carry the two women and their supplies. An officer, a captain, who had won immunity to yellow fever by having had it in Mexico, was assigned to go along and help them in any way he could till they got settled. The Sternberg pony—not Robert E. Lee but a smaller animal—was hitched to the wagon, which had been loaded with enough food and supplies to last a month. There was another tearful leave-taking as husband and wife prepared once more to meet the uncertain and troubled future away from each other.

During the next few hours Martha Sternberg found out for the first time in her life what it means to be a yellow fever refugee—the discouragement, the heartlessness shown by others, the cruelty engendered by fear of the disease. As the slowly moving craft jogged along the dusty highway, a farm house would come in sight. The officer would dismount from his horse, knock on the front door and explain that two ladies fleeing from a yellow fever epidemic were in the wagon near the entrance. They were looking for a place to stay until they could safely return to Fort Barrancas or go somewhere else. They had money to pay for everything they would require. They also had an ample supply of food. Would the lady of the house let them stay there a while?

The lady of the house would not. She did not want anybody in her house, or anywhere nearby, who had had any contact with yellow fever. Then the door would slam shut in his face, and his ears would follow the rapidly diminishing sound of footsteps as the woman would hurry back to the rear of the house, fearful lest those few minutes of conversation had exposed her to a million yellow fever germs.

That sad little drama was re-enacted, with slight variations, time after time as the wagon would halt in front of one house after another, every kind of house. The officer was good-natured, persuasive, and persistent. Martha Sternberg, watching and listening, was worried and all but desperate. The pretty young lady from Georgia was badly frightened and crying. The pony was tired. At last, at nightfall, the dreary routine had a different ending. A woman, hostile at first and appearing on the point of doing what the others had done with terrifying monotony for hours, relented when she saw the frightened, desperate, and attractive women. She agreed to take them in.

"I have daughters of my own," she said simply. "I cannot turn you away."

She was poor, she said, confirming the testimony of the old, unpainted, neglected house. But she was kind. And kindness was what Martha Sternberg wanted just then more than anything else, except of course a place to stay. She was so grateful for it that she did not care a whit how poor the other woman was or how crude the living conditions. Here at long, weary last was a shelter, an end to the all but endless wandering along dusty, bumpy roads, avoided like villains.

Evidently the woman had not understood about the food and supplies they had brought along, for she worried about not having enough food in the house for herself, her family, and her visitors. That made Martha Sternberg even more grateful to her for taking them in. The woman's anxieties—those having to do with food at least—were soon allayed. Mrs. Sternberg told her to take charge of everything they had brought, using it as she thought best.

Unfortunately, that was not the end of their troubles. This woman with the rare hospitality was heavily penalized for it. A few hours after they arrived the word got around that she had given haven to a party of refugees from the Fort Barrancas epidemic. It got as far as Pensacola, twenty-five miles away, which, remembering its own recent experience with yellow fever, was determined to keep the disease away this time. Armed guards were posted around the building. When members of the family started to leave, they were stopped and turned back, prisoners in their own home.

Notwithstanding the rush and confusion of getting off, the Sternbergs had worked out a scheme by which they could, they hoped, hear from each other fairly regularly, in spite of the slow mail service or no mail service at all. As soon as she should get settled in her refugee home Martha was to find a suitable box and place it just above the lowest limb of a tree. They would write as often as possible, every day, if they could. One of the men at the fort would leave Dr. Sternberg's letters there and pick up hers. For some reason, typical of the peculiar workings of hastily set up local quarantines, these yellow fever refugees themselves and certain others were not kept inside the house, at least at first. The guards did not interfere when Mrs. Sternberg, with the assistance of the captain, located a box and a tree and firmly anchored the former in position. Then she wrote a message about it to be delivered by the officer, about to start back to the post.

Her first letter from her husband came two days later. The next day, however, the person she had sent to the mail box returned without one. The rules had been changed. The guards had been ordered not to allow anybody to go to the box from either direction. This damming of the flow of news was particularly unfortunate. For she had been troubled by that first—and thus far only—letter. It had spoken of the writer's extreme fatigue and of his working extremely hard. Knowing his tendency to minimize his own troubles to keep her from worrying, she feared he had left a great deal untold. Wifelike, she worried lest the untold news be bad news. Between the hastily and wearily written lines she read, or thought she read, actual or impending illness. It later turned out that she had read aright.

Consistent with the inconsistency which marked local quarantines of the time, the rules were again changed overnight. Or perhaps the guards decided to pay no more attention to them. At any rate they did nothing the next day to prevent ready access to the box from both directions. Martha Sternberg saw with delight that her mailbox emissary was carrying a letter in his hand. Her pleasure vanished, however, when she looked at the envelope. It was not addressed in her husband's familiar handwriting. This, to her tortured mind, could mean just one thing: he was ill.

He was. The unfamiliar handwriting was that of the commanding officer, at whose urging she had made this trip. Dr. Sternberg, he had written, had yellow fever. He made no effort to soften the blow: the sick man was dangerously ill. The Surgeon General had been notified by telegraph and had instructed that everything possible be done to help along his recovery. A surgeon had been transferred from another post to devote his entire time to this one case. Two others had been ordered to Fort Barrancas to take over Dr. Sternberg's duties.

General Brannon's letter also contained other news, almost as disturbing as the news of her husband's illness. Sentries along the highway and at other places had been ordered not to let her pass. She must not try to go to him. She had no choice but to stay right where she was, seize whatever scraps of news she could get, and hope and pray he would be more fortunate than many of yellow fever's victims.

She stood the waiting and anguish as best she could. News about Dr. Sternberg came far less frequently and was far less satisfactory than she had hoped. She had a worried feeling that much was being left unsaid. Those pages of generalities told very little; wifelike, she imagined that the untold was terrible. But there was comfort in one thought: she would certainly be notified quickly in one way or another if he should die. As long as that news did not come, every day was a day in his favor.

That day-to-day waiting and anxiety proved all but insufferable. Not getting any news of his death did not necessarily mean that death was not imminent or inevitable. As week followed weary week, she became almost unnerved waiting for letters that sometimes came, but often did not. At last, after about three weeks, she decided she had stood enough. "Please tell me the worst," she pleaded in a letter to General Brannon. "It cannot be worse than the agony I am suffering at present." Her letter ended with a threat that, unless he gave her some solid factual news, she was going to leave her farmhouse refuge and make a desperate effort to get back to Fort Barrancas, sentries or no sentries.

That plea proved effective. Dr. Sternberg had really been quite ill, desperately ill in fact, General Brannon wrote. In addition to yellow fever, he had suffered several complications. A septic infection was still causing him a great deal of pain. At times he had been virtually at death's frontier. He was still very ill and by no means out of danger. But the C. O. and the medical officers believed he would recover. At the same time, he considered it extremely inadvisable for her to try to return home. She must stay right where she was.

Meanwhile her troubles had been aggravated by the young woman still looking to her for mothering. The latter, getting more and more homesick for her family and friends in Georgia, was unhappy and rebellious under the strict restraints of her semi-imprisonment. She kept complaining that even her and her family's experiences during the war, when Sherman's army had taken away practically everything that could be moved and burned much of the rest, had been more endurable than this life as a yellow fever refugee in a cruel world of quarantines, suspicion, and fear.

At last the harrassed Mrs. Sternberg was relieved of this trouble at least. Some friends and relatives who knew the right people made it possible for the unhappy beauty to get back to the Georgia home she had left so light-heartedly several weeks earlier. It would be hard to say which of the two women was happier when they said good-bye.

Martha Sternberg's other source of worry was also causing

her less concern. Letters from the medical officer treating her husband started coming through much more regularly, and the news they brought was much more cheerful. Dr. Sternberg was still not able to write himself, but that would be only a matter of time, provided he suffered no relapse. The author of the letters that brought so much comfort to Martha Sternberg was Dr. Joseph S. Herron. Nobody could have done more for "the doctor," as he invariably called him, in those dangerous weeks than he, no one could have shown more consideration for the sick man's wife. He wrote her on August 1 that "the doctor" was "getting along very nicely now," but still weak. At that time there had been seventy-one yellow fever cases at Fort Barrancas in addition to Dr. Sternberg's. Twenty-five of them had been fatal. "The doctor" was "doing splendidly" two days later and "sends much love." His appetite was good, and he should regain his strength rapidly. He was "doing finely" the next day and again sent his love. On August 4 the faithful medical officer wrote: "I now consider him out of danger." The patient "will of course require care for some time yet, as he is still weak." Otherwise, he was "pretty clear of the effects of the fever." The next day "the doctor" was "progressing just as nicely as possible," so well in fact that, "if it were not for his being housed up, he would hardly know he was sick." "The doctor" was "doing splendidly" on August 6. His bed clothing had just been changed for the first time since he became sick. Dr. Herron told her her husband "would be able to sit up in bed tomorrow and out of it the next day." He "is now about out of all danger and gaining strength rapidly." He "sends much love and is glad to hear that you are so cheerful."

"The doctor" had had "quite a fine night's rest," the faithful friend wrote the next day. Moreover, as predicted, he had been sitting up in bed most of the day and was expected to be up in a chair the next day. He had been greatly cheered by news that she was getting along all right and by visits from "the General" and a number of other officer friends. He still could not write, however. He had developed a felon on the first finger of his right hand, an important finger as far as writing is concerned, and it had become quite tender and sore. So he was still having to depend upon Dr. Herron to serve as his letter-writer as well as his physician.

The next day's letter carried particularly bright and good news. "The doctor" was "doing nicely," although his finger continued too sore for him to use it. Moreover, "it will not be long till you will be able to see the doctor," for he "is recuperating rapidly."

He kept on making progress. He was overcoming the weakness into which the disease had plunged him. And he appreciated the articles—flowers and fruit mostly—she had sent.

General Brannon himself wrote on August 11. He had just left Dr. Sternberg, who was now completely free from yellow fever, although still far from complete recovery. As soon as the sick man felt able to travel, the general told her, he was going to apply for a three-month leave. At last the end of that agonizing separation was in sight. The patient was sure he would soon be able to travel. Still unwilling for her to return to Fort Barrancas, he asked General Brannon to use his good offices in obtaining permission from the Pensacola municipal and health authorities for her to go there to take the train for her old home in Indianapolis. The mayor, who was also president of the Pensacola Board of Health, sent the general the pass, which the latter handed over to Dr. Sternberg. It was sent immediately to Mrs. Sternberg by messenger.

Her painful imprisonment ended on August 17, but her troubles were not yet over. Starting out on that twenty-five-mile trip to Pensacola, she and her maid ran into a severe rain and electrical storm, which added greatly to the difficulty of travel over the rough roads. The carriage made only slow progress. They had not gone far when they were stopped by a man on horseback. He told them he was looking for Mrs. Sternberg.

What awful thing had happened now? she asked herself as she fumbled with the words that told him she was Mrs. Sternberg. Were more months to be added to the weary, heartbreaking period of separation? Was she to be prevented from going to Pensacola after all, in spite of the pass she was clutching in her hand? Was her husband—horrible thought!—worse or dead?

But this man had no bad news. Dr. Herron lived in Pensa-

cola, and Mrs. Herron was still there while he was on temporary
duty at Fort Barrancas. He had told her about Mrs. Sternberg's
plan to go there to take the train, and, probably at his suggestion, she had obtained permission from the mayor for her to stop
at the Herron home for a cup of tea, instead of going directly
and as quickly as possible to the railroad station, as she had been
told to do.

The two women followed the horseman to the Herron home
on a pleasant residential street, arriving after dark. They were
met at the door by a small woman with about the most pleasant,
charming, and hospitable manner Martha Sternberg had ever encountered. Mrs. Herron greeted her warmly and assured her that
she was eager to do everything possible to ease the discomfort
of her long, hard trip. The two women got along famously and
became great friends in a few minutes.

There were a number of things Mrs. Herron was able to do,
but her most welcome service was as a bringer of news: from her
husband she had just learned that Dr. Sternberg was much better. That short visit at the Herron home did wonders in lifting
Martha Sternberg's drooping spirits. Still uncertain of the wisdom of going so far from her still-sick husband, she nevertheless felt much better about him now. She was willing and glad
to accept Dr. and Mrs. Herron's assurance that it would be only
a short time before he could rejoin her in Indianapolis.

Several days after her arrival the telegram she had been waiting for came. Still too weak for the long, tiresome train ride all
the way, Dr. Sternberg was already enroute to St. Louis via New
Orleans and a Mississippi river boat. He asked her to meet him
there.

CHAPTER VI

Thunder in the West

THAT LONG-LOOKED-FORWARD-TO St. Louis meeting was not a happy one for Martha Sternberg. She was surprised and distressed, in spite of what she had been told, to find how severely her husband's illness had served him. Her exclamation of joy as their eyes met was quickly followed by an outcry of anxiety when she got a better look. He was so changed, she said later, that she would not have recognized him at all had she not known it was he.

His whole frame was shrunken and dwarfed. The bones stood out on his face and body like those of a shriveled corpse. His weight was down to less than a hundred pounds. His hair had thinned and whitened markedly. His skin had an unhealthy pallor. Getting about required a tremendous effort. Every part of him fairly shrieked of the long bout he had had with his old enemy, which appeared to have unleashed particular venom upon this man who had fought it so valiantly and so effectively in the hospital and in the laboratory.

With that first shocking sight of him fresh in her mind, she was not surprised at what he subsequently told her—things that would have been even harder to bear had she known about them at the time. He had been even worse than she had been told. Not once or twice, but time after time his friends had despaired of his recovery and had waited almost momentarily for death to come. Besides that felon on the first finger of his right hand, he had had several boils on the other hand. There had been boils on his face. His physical reserves had reached exhaustion. When it was all over and he began treading the long, slow pathway to recovery, the doctors had wondered many times by what miracle the candle that so often seemed to be out had managed to shine again.

He had, of course, had no difficulty in getting the extended leave he had requested. After his examination, Assistant Surgeon Harry E. Brown had certified that he was "suffering from the disability and exhaustion subsequent to a severe attack of yellow fever, complicated with acute peritonitis* of the index finger of the right hand." (For some reason, the medical certificate did not mention those boils.) The patient, the medical officer declared, was "not fit for duty in a less period than three months."

Her husband also told her about some other experiences growing out of his long illness and its aftermath. When he got ready to dispose of Bob—their nickname for the faithful Robert E. Lee—he had found a navy yard employee willing to pay a hundred and fifty dollars for the horse and buggy, but troublesome complications had arisen after the sale was agreed upon. The navy yard authorities, with still-fresh memories of the community's latest yellow fever epidemic, had raised objections. They had finally agreed that Bob might join the navy yard's animal colony, but only under certain conditions. First, Dr. Sternberg had to hire somebody to give the unhappy animal a vigorous scrubbing in a solution of carbolic acid to kill any germs he might have picked up from his association with the former yellow fever patient. Then somebody—not Bob's disease-dangerous master, of course—had to leave him tied to a tree at some distance from the nearest building. This done, the purchaser left the hundred and fifty dollars under an agreed-upon rock. Then he untied the horse, got into the buggy, and drove off.

It had been no easy or simple matter to take the river boat at New Orleans either. Before he was allowed to enter the city he had to wash all his clothing—suits, shirts, shoes, underwear, everything—in carbolic acid, apparently the best of all killers, those people thought, of yellow fever germs on both man and beast.

After that St. Louis rendezvous the Sternbergs took a long

* Dr. Brown appears to be in error here. He probably had synovitis in mind.

rest at the Pattison home in Indianapolis. She saw that he did not overexert himself or put too much strain on his enfeebled strength. She procured and cooked for him the food she thought he needed to put flesh on those gaunt, protruding bones and drive that haunting yellowness from his complexion. She arranged for him the kinds of amusement he needed to keep his spirits up. She set an early bedtime to insure his getting the sleep he needed. As week followed week, she was sure she was seeing improvement. He gained weight. That blundering feebleness diminished and all but disappeared. His complexion took on a more ruddy color. But he was not a well man yet—it would be many weeks and months before the damage done by Yellow Jack's harsh, vicious blows would cease to show.

After about a month and a half in Indianapolis, Dr. Sternberg went to Washington to report to Surgeon General Charles H. Crane, taking Martha with him. He had used only about half of his leave, but he wanted to find out where he was going to be sent at its expiration, it having been understood before he left Fort Barrancas that he would not return there. General Crane greeted him warmly and congratulated him upon the ground he had won in regaining his health. He insisted that Dr. Sternberg would not be well enough to go back on active duty for some time yet. To speed his recovery and make it more agreeable, he recommended a trip to Europe. The Surgeon General spoke enthusiastically of the pleasures, the beauties, and the sunshine of southern France and suggested that as an ideal place. The Sternbergs' reaction was not merely favorable but enthusiastic. General Crane promised a six-month extension of leave, and they went to New York a few days later to see about steamship reservations and attend to other details of the trip.

Dr. Sternberg both enjoyed and benefited from the ocean voyage. Traveling on the *City of Chester*, of the Inman Line, they had pleasant, congenial fellow-voyagers and a smooth, stormless crossing to Liverpool. After a brief stay in London— just long enough to get in some shopping, some sightseeing and a great deal of walking along historic streets that gave Dr. Sternberg a chance to try out his new-gained strength—they moved on to Paris. There they remained only long enough to recuperate from an unusually rough channel crossing which caused the doctor considerable discomfort and his wife considerable anxiety over its possible effects upon his health. Then they continued on to Nice, where they planned to stay a good long while.

The improvement that had begun at Fort Barrancas and continued in Indianapolis was almost completed in that peaceful segment of the Mediterranean paradise. They found a small hotel where there was a happy admixture of activity and opportunities to rest. From time to time they would run into friends they had first known at army posts here and there. Those were especially pleasant occasions for this man to whom personal friendships meant so much. The food, most of it grown in the pleasant rural comunities just outside the city, was fresh, tasteful, and nourishing. There was a wealth of opportunities to read. Chafing somewhat under his inability to devote any of his ample leisure to research, Dr. Sternberg, at the same time, eased his stern taskmaster's conscience somewhat by studying medical and scientific textbooks. From time to time they made brief excursions to other places, including Monte Carlo. They were not interested in the gambling but did get a tremendous thrill from a concert in the great music hall.

Dr. Sternberg's spirits received a great lift on, appropriately enough, Christmas Eve, from news from Washington. The promotion to which he had been entitled in 1869 and which had been snatched from his grasp at that time by Senate dilatoriness had come at last. Now he was no longer Assistant Surgeon with the military rank of Captain but Surgeon with the military rank of Major. This advancement in rank, carrying a substantial increase in compensation, was none the less welcome by reason of being considerably more than five and a half years overdue.

Early in the new year, 1876, the sick man's health had improved so much that they felt safe in extending their travels into Italy. Continuing the watchful care they had been maintaining all along to prevent his overdoing himself, they made the trip in short, easy stages, stopping along the way to combine rest pleasantly with sightseeing. Reaching the end of their journey at Naples, they rested and went sightseeing there for several days. Then they began, also in easy stages, the long trip back home, with extended stops in Paris and London. For the ocean voyage they chose the same ship on which they had made the eastward passage. They reached New York in late April. Dr. Sternberg was now ready and anxious to get back to work.

On reporting to General Crane, he was told he could have his choice between the Department of the Dakotas and the Department of Columbia. He chose the latter and was ordered on May 1 to report at Department of Columbia headquarters at Portland, Oregon.

The long trip to his new post was much more arduous than their pleasant excursion to Europe. It took eight days and nights to get from Washington to San Francisco. In the absence of dining cars, they ate at trainside dining rooms, some good, some very bad indeed, while their train took on water and fuel or just waited. The windows that had to be left open to provide ventilation in those pre-air-conditioning days admitted a great deal besides fresh air, including, as the travel-weary Sternbergs remembered for many a year, huge quantities of dry alkaline dust which got into their berths, their clothing, their mouths, their eyes. Beyond San Francisco they traveled by boat, far more pleasantly, although the ship was old and the sea rough. Dr. Sternberg stood the trip well.

Soon after their arrival at Portland they learned that this assignment was to be a brief one. The medical director left early in June, to be away about three months, and Major Sternberg took over his duties. Upon the former's return in early September, Dr. Sternberg was given his choice of stations at Fort Vancouver and Fort Walla Walla, both in the state of Washington. He chose the latter. One of the considerations that played a deciding part in this decision was the knowledge that, whereas the Fort Vancouver assignment would probably last only a short time, he apparently could depend upon being settled more or less permanently, as army people think of permanence, at Fort Walla Walla. The major was anxious to bring to an end the shifting assignments that had kept him either moving, or preparing to move, or trying to settle down after much longer a move than he liked. He thought, too, that the climate at Fort Walla Walla would be more healthful.

As at Fort Barrancas and other posts, Dr. Sternberg carried on at Fort Walla Walla a private medical practice among the civilian residents of the community, along with his official duties as a medical officer. As at his previous posts, he received no monetary compensation for much of that outside work but was handsomely paid in other ways. He never forgot, for example, the old packer who suffered a serious leg injury late one night. Unable to travel, he sent a friend to the Sternberg home for help. Dr. Sternberg, of course, got out of bed and started dressing at once, meanwhile telling the visitor to hurry back to the victim and apply a tourniquet to the injured leg, which was bleeding furiously. After examining the injury, Dr. Sternberg told the packer he must give up his leg or lose his life. The old man, probably thinking of the difficulty of earning a livelihood with only one good leg, decided not to submit to amputation, and stuck stubbornly to that resolution in spite of Dr. Sternberg's sternest warning that only amputation could save his life. While one man pleaded and the other resisted his pleas, the injured leg grew worse and the danger that the injury would prove fatal, amputation or no amputation, grew grimmer. At last the Sternberg eloquence and the Sternberg logic, aided by the ominous change in the color and general appearance of the shattered leg, wore down the old packer's resistance. As soon as possible after he consented to the amputation it was underway. Dr. Sternberg worked speedily and skillfully. The leg was severed at the knee, and prompt measures were applied to prevent infection of the stump. Fortunately, the delay had not been enough to prevent recovery. In time the old man was hobbling about the place on his one good leg and a peg leg that served its purpose fairly well. From then on, until Dr. Sternberg was ordered to another post, he never tired of singing his praises. And, whenever he would see him, he would ask to be allowed to "kiss the hand that saved my life." As far as is known, his gratitude was all he ever gave Dr. Sternberg for that life-saving service. But, as in the case of that poor colored woman in Florida whom he had saved from blindness, that was enough.

Another civilian patient at Fort Walla Walla—one able and willing to pay and also different from that old trapper in other

ways—was the son of a charming middle-aged woman, a native
of France, who had been unusually well educated in her native
country in anticipation of a teaching career. Romance had intervened. Instead of spending most of her adult life drilling important but unexciting knowledge into reluctant brains, she had
married and come to this country. She was now living in a frontier community as far from the cultured refinements of her native
land as could well be imagined. She had not entirely relinquished
her role of school teacher, however. At the time her son became ill and she called in Dr. Sternberg, she was teaching him
and the other junior members of the family not only her own
language, a strange one to these young Americans, but also Latin,
German, and Greek.

Major Sternberg recognized her as a clever and highly intelligent woman on his first visit. He was equally quick to note
her large collection of books, some of them rare volumes that
seemed strangely out of place in this wild frontier country. She
and the Sternbergs became great friends. The man of science,
who had inherited from his mother an alert interest in foreign
languages, saw here an excellent opportunity for cultural improvement, not for himself but for his wife. He was too busy
for anything of that sort, he thought, though it would be a great
thing for Mrs. Sternberg to take French lessons from their new
friend. Both ladies agreed, and the lessons began. Before long
Major Sternberg decided that, busy or not, he was missing something he ought not to miss, and became a French student too.
In time both Sternbergs felt entirely at home in the French language. Especially enjoyable were their wide explorations into
the vast treasures of French literature to which their growing
knowledge of the language became a wide, inviting gateway.
His ability to read the language of Pasteur and other famous
French men of science was to serve him well the rest of his life.

They made another valuable friendship about that same time.
A civil engineer employed in a civilian capacity near the fort
found that he and Dr. Sternberg had a common hobby—fossils.
The medical officer told him about those he had found in Indian
Territory while on that expedition some seven years earlier under
General Sheridan. Thereupon the other man not only told about,

but produced some striking specimens he had found on a sur-
veying expedition not so very far from where the two men were
then living. He had hardly scratched the surface of the fossil
fields he had visited, he told Dr. Sternberg. There were vast
beds still awaiting exploration. The latter resolved to visit them
and see what he could find.

It was not difficult to get away, and transportation was easily arranged. Recruits were being sent frequently to that part of
the country, and the commanding officer readily agreed to let
Major Sternberg go with the next party. His medical duties at
the fort were assumed temporarily by a local civilian physician.
The camp quartermaster provided tentage, horses, and a wagon,
and all other equipment likely to be needed. Mrs. Sternberg,
almost as ardent a fossil hunter as he, went along.

On the expedition's second day out they were encamped for
the night on the banks of the Snake River, not far from where
it empties into the Columbia. After a while they heard the mo-
notonous, repetitive beat of tom-toms, and on the opposite bank
they saw a band of Indians. While they watched, the red men
engaged in savage tribal dances in the late afternoon sunlight.
They seemed to be friendly, but there was no way of knowing for
sure, and Dr. Sternberg and the others could not help feeling
nervous. It was not a pleasant feeling to have so many red men
so close at hand, with night coming on. Their apprehension
was increased when some of the Indians began leaping into the
water and swimming toward the opposite bank. But they did not
go all the way across, circling and turning back several feet from
land.

After dark those nervous watchers saw several boatloads
of Indians leave their side of the river and row swiftly in the general direction of the campsite. Unlike those late afternoon swim-
mers, they did not turn around soon after passing midstream but
went all the way across and landed. However, only two, the chief
and an interpreter, left the boats. Going boldly to the camp,
they asked for the "medicine man." (Dr. Sternberg subsequently learned that some soldiers had told them that a medical officer
was in charge of the expedition.) They wanted to know how
many recruits were in the party and where they were going.

That, Dr. Sternberg decided, was none of their business. Nevertheless, not wishing to anger them unnecessarily, he gave them an evasive answer that was polite enough but told them nothing. They did not press the point, nor did they seem offended.

The chief had a favor to ask. (Perhaps, Dr. Sternberg decided, that was why he did not show any resentment he might have felt.) He told Dr. Sternberg, through the interpreter, about his sick daughter. She had been coughing for "two snows." Would the "medicine man" give him something that would cure her? The "medicine man" doubted his or anybody else's ability to do that. From his studies in medical college, his experience as a medical officer, and his research, he knew, as doctors generally knew, that the Indians were tragically susceptible to tuberculosis. They contracted it upon the slightest exposure and put up little resistance to it whenever it developed, dying from this white man's plague in far greater numbers than they were dying from any other form of illness or from all that their human enemies put together could do to them. Any Indian who had been coughing for "two snows" almost certainly had tuberculosis. Nothing in Major Sternberg's medicine kit and no knowledge in his head was likely to slow up materially the disease's rapid progress toward death.

But he could help a little, and this he was glad to do. Among his medical supplies were some drugs with which he prepared a cough medicine. This might give the sick girl some temporary relief and help her sleep. The chief accepted the medicine with gruff thanks. That did not end the interview: he wanted more. He had no coffee. Major Sternberg ordered one of the men to let him have some. Then he mentioned sugar: he didn't have any of that either. Sugar was supplied. There were some other things he needed, or said he needed. Major Sternberg saw that he got them. Even then he was in no hurry to leave.

The expedition split up the next morning. The main body of troops—the recruits and those accompanying them—headed north to their new post. The others—the Sternbergs and four or five soldiers—moved on toward Washtuckna Lake, where their civil engineer friend had told them about finding the fossil specimens. It was too far away for them to get there in one day;

they had to camp out another night. With their numbers so greatly reduced, they took particular precautions against the Indians and other possible troublemakers. But they passed the night peaceably, except for the howling of the coyotes just a stone's throw from the tents, huddled close for protection.

They did have a visitor, however. A man on horseback, attracted by the campfires, asked if he might camp nearby. He was driving cattle to new grazing lands and had seen a great many Indians, most of them traveling in small bands. Some, he said, were in an angry mood toward the whites. The members of the party felt safer with one more strong man within calling distance.

The campsite was only some eleven miles from the fossil field, and the party arrived about noon. Disturbed by that enveloping wall of Indian hostility, Dr. Sternberg decided to keep them in this exposed position for as short a time as possible, consistent with his wish to do a thorough exploratory job. After getting into the fascinating labor of fossil-finding, he was entirely willing to accept his friend's statement that nobody but himself had been there ahead of the present party. Both Dr. and Mrs. Sternberg were overwhelmed by their great wealth of discoveries, including the skeletons of whole animals, such as horses, elk, deer, etc. She, as happy as he as one magnificent find followed another, theorized that these animals, thousands of years earlier perhaps, had gone to the nearby lake, now dried up, to drink. Sinking helplessly into the morass of sand along the shore, they had perished from suffocation and starvation. The excited couple marveled at their great good fortune in accidentally finding out about this field and being practically the first to have an opportunity to explore it.

They subsequently shared their treasure with Professor Edward D. Cope, of Philadelphia, and several other authorities in this field. Specimens they especially prized were kept in their home the rest of their lives to be shown pridefully to their guests.

They had planned to return by way of the famously beautiful Shoshone Falls, whose majestic roar they could hear from their camp, but Dr. Sternberg could not rid his mind of the danger of remaining longer than necessary with so very little protection in the heart of the Indian country. That herdsman's story was only one of many he had heard regarding the Indians' mounting hostility toward the whites. The slightest incident might erupt into a bloody massacre. The party might be wiped out in a few minutes by one of those roving bands. He therefore decided that he and the others for whom he felt responsible ought to be satisfied for the present with hearing Shoshone's mighty thunder and pass up until a more favorable time the chance to see it. Carefully packing their fossil treasures, they headed back to Fort Walla Walla by the most direct and quickest practicable route.

CHAPTER VII

Conflict on the Clearwater

A WISE DECISION INDEED: they found when they arrived that their friends, hearing about those wandering bands of angry red men, had been greatly worried about them. There was general agreement that serious trouble was coming, and soon.

The primary cause of the Indians' hostility was, of course, the gradual taking over of their land by the white man. They had seen what was left to them shrink rapidly as settlers, government officials, and others, singly and in groups, arrived to set up towns and trading areas. They had been backed into a small corner of the Northwest, with every reason to think they would soon be forced out of much of the area they were holding so tenuously.

Particularly disturbing to those at Fort Walla Walla was the changed attitude of the Nez Percés. Unusually friendly and helpful to the first settlers to arrive, these brave, fine-looking, and intelligent Indians had turned bitterly and militantly hostile. Their leader was a strikingly handsome chief whom the white men knew as Joseph but whose Indian name was Halla Kalla Keen, meaning Eagle's Wing. Even those who were expecting to meet him and his men in battle readily conceded that he was a remarkable person. Fiercely eager to right what he considered the wrongs of his people, he was, nevertheless, a strong believer in settlement by negotiation and was opposed to precipitate action or bloodshed as long as it could be avoided or postponed. He thus acted as a restraining influence over his aggressively militant warriors. All in all, Joseph was one of the finest examples of the red man at his Indian best, energetic, forceful, and deliberate.

with a persuasive power that made him almost irresistible as a pleader of causes.

The particular cause of friction at the time was what the Nez Percés regarded as a clear violation of the terms of a treaty. This tribe, which had originally occupied a wide expanse extending over what is now much of western Idaho, southeast Washington, and northeast Oregon, had ceded much of this vast territory to the United States in 1855—largely because they had little choice in the matter. However, they had retained a considerable area which included the Wallowa Valley in Idaho. Later, with the influx of thousands of miners and settlers attracted by the finding of gold on the west coast, pressure was applied to them to cede other extensive areas that would limit them to the Indian reservation at Lapwai, Idaho. Certain of the Nez Percés had agreed to this further shrinking of their territory, but the group led by Joseph's father, who was also known as Joseph, had refused to recognize the treaty. Before the trouble boiled to a climax the elder Joseph was succeeded by his son, who had been born in the Wallowa Valley and had grown up there, developing for it a sentimental attachment surprising in a supposedly stolid, unsentimental Indian. The idea of being pushed out was a bitter one to him, yet he still hoped his beloved valley could be saved for the red man without fighting those with whom he had traditionally been on friendly terms.

This hope was cruelly dashed when General Oliver O. Howard was ordered to occupy the Wallowa Valley, ostensibly to protect the government's Indian agent in enforcement of the treaty. Learning of this action, Joseph sent a message requesting that a meeting between them be arranged at Walla Walla. General Howard agreed to the request, and the meeting was set for April 20, 1877. Illness prevented Joseph from attending, but he was represented by his younger brother, Ollicutt.

Mrs. Sternberg, who attended the meeting as a spectator, was favorably impressed by Ollicutt, whom she described as tall, strong-looking, and handsome. The Indians sat an benches on one side of a long table. Most of the white men occupied benches on the other side. A few officers, Mrs. Sternberg, and a handful of other ladies sat on the few chairs available.

Ollicutt was as conciliatory as his elder brother could have been, but he was outspoken and vigorous in objecting to what he called the injustices of the treaty. Producing a colored map which he had drawn himself on a piece of cow skin, he spoke at some length, though with marked restraint, of the plight in which his tribesmen would find themselves if they should be forced to leave the broad, beautiful, productive Wallowa Valley and to crowd themselves inside the narrow confines of the Lapwai reservation. Compared to what they were expected to give up, he said, the latter was a virtual wasteland, barren and unproductive. His tribe had long depended for a livelihood upon the raising of horses. This would be all but impossible in the Lapwai reservation. Indeed, he went on plaintively, it would be extremely difficult for the Lapwai reservation to support the new immigrants, in addition to those already there, under any conditions or mode of living.

Nothing was decided and no agreements were reached at that meeting. Others were held, also without results. Finally, on June 14, Joseph and the other members of his delegation signed a treaty in which they promised, in behalf of their tribesmen, to leave their traditional homeland in the Wallowa Valley within a month and get along as best they could on the Lapwai reservation. Their decision was influenced greatly, if not actually dictated, by the arrival after the negotiations had begun of heavy reinforcements of troops sent to back up the white man's demands.

Unfortunately, this abject surrender did not bring its promised peace. Ever since the white man had been arriving in sizable numbers in the Northwest, the Indians had been complaining about his hogs. Many were not fenced in at all. Others were kept in flimsily fenced fields from which they escaped whenever the notion struck them to break out and go wandering and rooting about the neighborhood. The Indians' chief complaint was that they destroyed the small bulb known as the camas root which the red men and their families had been using for generations in baking bread. At times these animals had been so destructive that the Indians were faced with actual hunger. Complaints and requests that the white men prevent their hogs from running wild were often treated with contempt. Usually there was nothing the Indians could do but get along as best they could with the bread they were able to bake.

One incident of that kind did not turn out that way, however. When an Indian complained to a white man named Larry Ott, living in a small white settlement known as Slate Creek, about his marauding hog, the complaint grew into a bitter argument, and the argument into a fight in which the Indian was killed. Regarding the killing as murder, three or four of the dead man's Indian friends went to the Ott farm. When Ott appeared, he was killed.

When news of the double killing reached the encampments at Lapwai and Walla Walla, practically everyone regarded it as a prelude to war. Preparations were made for battle. Supplies at both places were checked. Arms and ammunition were packed for transport to the general area where, it was assumed, Joseph and his men were readying for war as assiduously as were these men. Meanwhile, couriers brought disturbing news of Indian movements.

Because of his health, which was not yet quite back to normal after his bout with yellow fever, Major Sternberg's official superiors had given him to understand that he would not be sent on active duty with the troops. Reconciled to the less arduous and less dramatic work of caring for the sick and wounded in the comparative safety of a regular encampment, he and Mrs. Sternberg got busy doing whatever they could for those under orders to march out to meet the enemy. These simple but useful services were gladly accepted by the departing troops and their families. And when the last battlefield-bound unit of the Walla Walla garrison marched away on June 9, 1877, the major and his wife rode a short distance with it to receive last-minute messages to families left behind and perform other chores they were still able to attend to.

Upon their return to the fort in the late forenoon, a surprise awaited them. Evidently his official superiors had changed their minds regarding Major Sternberg's fitness for battlefield duty, for almost the first thing they saw upon entering the house was an order to report as soon as possible at Fort Lapwai, joining other troops en route. Three hours after first reading his orders he was on a train for Wallula, where he was to rendezvous with those other troops. His horse and equipment left on the same train.

At Wallula he boarded a river boat already crowded with troops, including two companies from Fort Walla Walla. En route to Lewiston, he attended several shipboard conferences at which plans were worked out for dealing with the rampaging Nez Percés, who had already inflicted terrible defeat upon a body of troops under Captain David Perry at White Bird Canyon.

"We are on our way up the river," he wrote his anxious wife soon after his departure, "and of course have heard no news since we left Walla Walla. I will mail this as soon as we reach Lewiston and will write you again as soon as I learn what the actual state of affairs is." He told her about the two companies of troops from Fort Walla Walla and two others traveling with him. He also told her that three other companies, just returned from Alaska, and an outfit from San Francisco had been ordered to continue up the river to Lewiston immediately after reaching Wallula and were expected to join the others in a short time. With such heavy reinforcements on the way, he assured her, "we will be able to move out, if necessary, with quite a strong force." The letter closed with an expression of love, a promise to return "just as soon as I can," and an admonition to "be brave and don't allow yourself to be alarmed by sensational rumors."

Reaching Lewiston about 1 A. M., Major Sternberg and the others started out immediately on the overland journey to Fort Lapwai. There they received additional supplies and pack mules, were brought up to date regarding the situation at the front, and received their orders. The trail soon became pretty rugged. The weather was cold, and a disagreeable rain was falling most of the time. The terrain was so rough that even the horses of Major Sternberg and the others fortunate enough to be on horseback and pack mules found it difficult to keep a footing. They slipped and almost fell several times, threatening injury to their riders.

Passing through White Bird Canyon, the men saw the bodies of their dead comrades, lying where they had fallen in the battle. A few days later, after they had halted a short distance away for

a rest and a rendezvous with the expected reinforcements, Dr.
Sternberg returned to the battlefield on an extremely unpleasant
errand:

> We visited Major Perry's* battleground yesterday and buried the
> dead. The greater part of the command went and marched very cau-
> tiously, fully prepared for a fight, but we saw no Indians. The dead were
> very much scattered, and you can imagine that the troops had a very dis-
> agreeable duty to perform in burying them. It rained nearly all day and
> we returned at dark tired, wet and hungry.

That letter also brought welcome news about himself. He was
feeling "quite well and stronger than when I started." He had
"a splendid appetite" and was "sleeping well." Kitty, his horse,
"carries me bravely and seems to enjoy campaigning."

Another letter told her some things he had learned about
the battle. The men "did not behave well and were badly
whipped." Twenty-four, including an officer, had been killed.
However, "the balance of the command is entrenched and can
protect itself until reinforcements arrive." He was to leave the
next day with six companies of infantry and two of cavalry for
"the scene of operations." He again admonished her not to worry
about him:

> We will have a pretty strong column and you need not apprehend
> any disaster. Matters are not as bad as we feared. Keep up your courage
> and write to me very often. Do not be uneasy if you do not hear from
> me very often. Our command will be off the mail route and couriers
> will probably only be sent when we have important news to send....
> Kitty has come through all right and will carry me handsomely.

He wrote her on June 23 that he was in camp, along with
the survivors of the White Bird Canyon disaster and another
company of troops, on "good camping ground." They were to
rest there over the weekend. He was "feeling quite well," in
spite of having marched in the cold and snow since half past
three in the morning. The Indians were reported to be about
thirty miles away. The long march "has not fatigued me much
and my cough is better." Kitty was still serving him well "and
seems to enjoy the expedition."

That thirty-mile gap between the troops and the enemy was

---

* Dr. Sternberg was in error here. Perry, although breveted a colonel in
1868, still held the regular rank of captain.

sharply reduced the next few days. He wrote her on June 24 that he was to march eighteen miles the next day and "will then be getting pretty close to the hostile Indians." More troops, including medical officers, were expected soon.

That gap had been almost completely closed four days later. Only the Salmon River separated the hostile armies. The Indians appeared to be numerically strong "and may dispute our crossing tomorrow." However, reinforcements had just arrived, and "I think it probable that the Indians will retreat after a little skirmishing." Even if they didn't, he was not worried, for "we are strong enough to whip them without any trouble." The troops were "advancing very cautiously and I do not fear any further disaster." Again he urged her not to worry.

We have plenty of fresh beef and hard tack, and I eat my camp fare with a good appetite. At night I roll myself up in my blankets and sleep comfortably or rather soundly. I can hardly say comfortably. It is unnessary to tell you that my comfortable bed at home, my regular, delicious meals, strawberries and cream, etc. and, above all, the society of my darling wife would be a thousand times preferable to this rough life. But I try to make the best of it.

The river crossing the next day was not as easy as he had expected. Not only did the Indians harass them constantly, but the current was strong and treacherous, and the men had to row with all they had to keep from being swept downstream with their valuable supplies and equipment. But they made it. By the time they got across the Indians were not disposed to do much fighting. Instead, they started marching, with the troops close behind.

He reported "the hardest march we ever had" on July 2. Camp was broken at three o'clock in the morning, but the columns could not get going until eight because of delays in getting the baggage and equipment loaded on pack mules. The route was "up the steepest and roughest kind of mountain trail," so rough that "several mules fell over and rolled down the mountain." It rained most of the day and night. When he wrote about the trip the next day he was in camp "on a plateau on top of the mountain, where grass is good for the animals and we have good water in abundance." He had arrived hours ahead of his equipment and supplies, lashed to the backs of those plodding pack mules. Some officers who had arrived ahead of him had treated him to a cup of coffee, ham, and crackers. One of them also shared his blankets with him. Even at that, "we all got thoroughly wet during the night and did not sleep much." They had lost contact with the Indians and had no idea where they had gone, but scouts were out looking for them.

There was more hard marching the next few days, and it was impossible for him to write, but there was no fighting. From his camp on the banks of the Salmon River, he managed to send her a letter on July 9. It told about difficult travel over mountain trails (which he underscored for emphasis). It also mentioned "hot days and sometimes cold, wet nights."

> Our marching for the past week has been of no use. We have not seen an Indian, and we learn that we left them behind us and that the cavalry has been doing all the fighting. . . . I do not know which way we will move next. Today the command is engaged in crossing the Salmon River at the same place where we crossed with such difficulty a week ago. This crossing of rapid rivers is a difficult undertaking. We tried to cross lower down stream by means of a raft but failed and our raft was carried down stream. We have here two small boats and by working as rapidly as possible it takes 24 hours to cross the command.

After all that hard marching, he welcomed the chance to stay in one place and take it easy:

> I have improved my time here by fishing. I caught a nice string of white fish yesterday and another lot today. They make an agreeable change in our bill of fare. I read occasionally in my French Testament, but there are two officers in the tent with me (Lieutenant Leary and Col. Miller) and they are generally talking. Then too, when we come into camp in the evening, I am too tired to read.

He asked her to order him a new pair of cavalry boots: those he had been wearing were "too light for this mountain climbing."

There was certainly no reason to think "this mountain climbing" would end soon, although actually it was already practically over, as far as he was concerned. Two days later—on July 11—Joseph decided to stop running and make a stand. The site he chose for that decisive struggle was along the rocky banks of the Clearwater River.

The battle came perilously close to ending in disaster for the whites before it had fairly started. In a movement so quickly accomplished that it overwhelmed the white troops involved, the enemy fell upon a pack train at the rear of the cautiously advancing column and almost captured the main ammunition supply. In another swift thrust, he placed the expedition's main food supply in extreme jeopardy. Had either move not been thwarted by heroic stands by small bodies of men, the helpless white men would hardly have been able to go into battle at all. Surrender or massacre would have been their only choice.

After missing disaster so narrowly, the troops advanced with extreme caution against the main body of the enemy, who were firing furiously from behind stone barricades set up during the night. From time to time the Indians would leave the comparative safety of those barricades to make sudden, furious, reckless attacks of their own, some on horseback, others on foot. Even those in the thickest of the fighting paid grudging, reluctant tribute to Joseph's generalship. He was making every man, every gun, and every piece of ammunition weigh as heavily as possible in the delicately balanced scales. But every Indian attack was thrown back.

The white men were doing somewhat better. Led by the cavalry and using every man not desperately needed for non-combat duties—orderlies, those charged with the handling and feeding of the animals, etc.—an attack was launched in the early afternoon. The distance between the white troops' lines and the staunch enemy barricade had been substantially shortened, but the enemy had not been driven out. He was still in a position to inflict frightful casualties.

Besides caring for the wounded already back of the lines, it was Major Sternberg's responsibility, with the help of two other medical officers, to remove other wounded from the battlefield. The Indians had a reputation for mistreating those who fell into their hands, and the medical officers were anxious to get them to a place of safety before the enemy could get to them. In that they were completely successful. Not a single Indian got his hands on a single wounded white soldier during the whole afternoon.

The troops' position when the battle was brought to an overnight halt was not a favorable one. They were continuously exposed to enemy fire, especially from sharpshooters posted behind breastworks to watch for any sign of movement. The snipers' particular concern was to isolate a nearby spring, the white men's only safe water supply, and they were able to do so. The men went thirsty rather than risk almost certain death by attempting to run that blockade. As the night advanced, their thirst became all but unbearable, their suffering pathetic. Some were so desperate that they drank, or tried to drink, water from the only other source within reach—a shallow, muddy stream through which the dirty, sweaty mules had been driven before and during the battle.

Meanwhile, Major Sternberg, still stalking the wounded, had been moving cautiously over the stretch of wasteland separating the troops and the enemy about a hundred yards away. At times he was so close to those nests of deadly rifle power that he could hear the Indians talking, but "the night was dark, and they could not see me." He found two wounded men and took them to a place of comparative safety. As he moved about among the unwounded, he heard pitiful cries from water-starved throats. "For God's sake," they implored, "bring us water to drink."

As soon as he had discharged his immediate duty to those two wounded men, he determined to do something for the others. Going to the officers' tent, he made an urgent plea for volunteers to help him run that deadly blockade. Several responded, and he gave them detailed instructions about avoiding any movement that might attract attention. Then each member of the party made his way as silently and inconspicuously as possible to the spring, returning with as much water as he could carry. Luck was with them, and the intense darkness was a great help. The task had called for great physical courage and cold-steel nerve. The records do not show how many, if any, failed to complete that round trip, but few men have risked their lives more courageously, more deliberately, and with such great devotion to their comrades. Dr. Sternberg himself escaped without a scratch.

He had an even closer brush with death that same night. Called to the firing line to care for a wounded man, he found him in a serious condition and losing a great deal of blood. Fearing it would be fatal to move him, Major Sternberg decided to operate on the spot. He would need light for the operation of course, but any gleam in such an exposed position would al-most certainly be instantly seen by alert sharpshooters, who would let loose a concentrated burst of rifle fire. The best arrangement he could think of was to operate by candle light behind a blanket held in place by two men, but the blanket did not hide the light and from the Indian lines came a noisy barrage aimed at that tiny target. The candle was quickly snuffed, and Major Sternberg went ahead with the operation as best he could in the dark. The wounded man survived and recovered. Again Dr. Sternberg escaped injury.

He said nothing about the incident, and, as no other officers were present, it was not reported to his commanding officer. Not until some thirteen years later was this act of rare medical skill combined with rare physical courage made a part of his official service record. The person responsible for that belated recognition was Major Chat R. Greenleaf, who wrote the Surgeon General about it. Major Greenleaf had heard about the incident from a packer whom he had met while on duty in Montana. His informant had either seen the operation himself or talked to someone who had done so. When Dr. Sternberg was asked about it, he said it had occurred substantially as Major Greenleaf had described it.

In spite of having become a conspicuous target, Major Green-leaf wrote to the Surgeon General, "Major Sternberg proceeded with the operation with the utmost coolness and terminated it successfully."

While Dr. Sternberg was getting water to those thirst-crazed troops and carrying on his darkness-shrouded battle to stem that flow of blood, most of the others were taking advantage of the darkness to build stone barricades in preparation for the next day's battle. The next morning it could be seen that the Indians had been similarly engaged during the night. Every man physi-cally able to handle a gun was in position when the first feeble light of the new day started to filter through the bushes and trees. All the food each man would require all day was ordered cooked at once, to be kept close at hand and eaten whenever, or if, the fighting should become relatively light on his part of the battle-field.

The battle did not come aflame with the dawn, however. The morning's activities were slight in comparison with those of the day before. As Dr. Sternberg wrote a few days later, "it consisted only of the exchange of an occasional shot." That slow, desultory pace ended suddenly in the early afternoon, when "a charge was made along the whole line and the enemy was driven in confusion from their [sic] chosen position and from their camp." The rout was complete. Those brave red men, who had contested their ground foot by foot, almost inch by inch, the day before and had undertaken some strong offensive action of their own, disintegrated into a wild, disorganized, demoralized mob. With the troops close to their heels, they tried to lose themselves in the primeval forest, clambering up and sliding down mountainsides and leaping recklessly from high river banks to the swirling waters below. Many drowned when they found themselves unable, in their weakened state, to swim across the swift current. Others were killed when they struck rocks just below the surface of shallow streams. Still others died of their wounds. Seldom has the American Indian been so decisively defeated in battle.

Obviously, Joseph and his braves had not anticipated anything like this. Back of their lines the advancing troops found their camp intact, so hastily had they abandoned it. Indian blankets were there in profusion. So were buffalo robes, food of all kinds, and any number of articles of personal use. Buried deep in the ground but easily located by the souvenir-hungry victors were artistically beaded ceremonial costumes, belts, robes, and trinkets of many kinds. That was indeed a souvenir hunter's heyday. Major Sternberg carried off two of those battlefield souvenirs, a beaded Indian robe and a bag which allowed the Indians to load additional equipment on the backs of their ponies. After his death Mrs. Sternberg gave them to Representative Edward Keating of Colorado in appreciation of a particular favor he had done her.

Those Indian articles were not all that Major Sternberg netted from that battle. General Howard breveted him a lieutenant colonel "for his heroic conduct in the performance of duty at the

Battle of the Clearwater, Idaho, July 11th and 12th, 1877, against the hostile Nez Percés Indians."

While General Howard took personal command of the pursuit of the defeated and scattered enemy, Major Sternberg was ordered to carry the wounded—twenty-seven in all—to Grangeville, some twenty-five miles away, and set up a hospital for them. A single company was assigned to go along for protection. The best horses and mules, in fact all that were at all good, had been kept with the main forces, where they would be needed in case Joseph should rally his men and make another stand. For the same reason, only the wagons that were considered unsuitable for service with the pursuit troops were left behind for Major Sternberg's use.

It would be no simple or easy task to transport twenty-seven wounded men twenty-five miles through wild territory in ramshackle wagons pulled by weary, worn-out animals. But that was not Dr. Sternberg's main worry as he watched General Howard and his troops march away and lose themselves in the descending darkness. He was thinking, rather, about a disaster that might befall his wounded, their handful of escorting troops and himself even before they started out. He and the others "passed an anxious night," he wrote in his next letter to Mrs. Sternberg, realizing "it was not improbable that the Indians might come to our side of the river again and, finding how weak an escort was left behind with the wounded, might murder us all."

That, fortunately, was not to be: "But they were too badly whipped to try anything like this, and we could see them on the bluffs, on the other side of the river in great numbers making their way downstream." Those three old wagons were not enough to carry all the wounded, but Dr. Sternberg took care of the others. Emulating the Cheyennes he had seen and fought against in Indian territory, he built "travois" out of the long lodge poles left behind by the fleeing Nez Percés, lashing one end of each pole to each side of a pack saddle. The other end dragged on the ground. Between the two poles was suspended a wooden bridge on which blankets were placed for comfort. The overflow wounded rode there. Those fifteen wheelless vehicles were much more comfortable than they would appear to be, either from their appearance or from this description. Indeed, some of the wounded said they were having easier rides than those in the wagons.

As they approached the end of their first daylight hours of slow travel, Dr. Sternberg again became anxious. Suppose the crafty Joseph and some of his men should pounce upon them out of the darkness. The danger was as great now as it had been the night before, and indeed greater. Joseph had had more time to rally his followers, and the white men were in a less easily defended position. Had he known then what he knew later, Major Sternberg would have realized how utterly demoralized and scattered the enemy had been, how incapable of putting up a fight. As it was, he awaited the dawn with eagerness and anxiety. Of course, nothing happened.

Fatigue proved a real danger, however. He had slept very little for several nights before the battle. The steady traveling had proved exhausting. The battle itself had been extremely taxing upon his physical reserves. The result was that, in spite of his worrying and his heavy responsibility, it was all he could do to keep awake as he rode along. To fall asleep in the saddle might be disastrous. The captain in charge of the escorting troops saw what an effort he was making not to do so, and he told his orderly to ride beside Dr. Sternberg and guide his horse. The orderly also kept him talking and so helped him stay awake.

In the early morning, several hours before they were due in Grangeville, Major Sternberg sent a soldier ahead on horseback to make arrangements for the wounded men's comfort after their arrival. This proved a considerable task, as the town had no hospital and indeed was poorly equipped in every way to care for them. However, the women of the community were quickly mobilized: some made coffee; some prepared sandwiches; some collected the makings for hot soup. A large building which had been doubling as a community meeting place and carpenter shop was turned into a makeshift hospital. Everything that could be done for those wounded—only twenty-five now, two having died en route—was done. When the weary expedition finally showed up, the survivors were found to have stood the trip much better than expected, and the hot food proved a great boost to spirits and bodies alike.

With all their hospitality, the Grangeville people did not want them to stay there any longer than necessary, however, for they knew how much Joseph loved this country and how glad he would be to take revenge upon this small segment of his conquerors. As long as troops remained in the village, they feared that the Indians would attack. Dr. Sternberg was also anxious to get going again. In addition to the danger and the terrible responsibility it placed upon him, some of his wounded needed attention he could not give them there. At Lapwai there was a small, but excellent, hospital. He wanted to get them there as soon as he could.

Nevertheless, he had to wait several days at Grangeville. The wounded, now resting in their comfortable beds at the Grangehall, kept him fairly busy. Most of his leisure time he spent trying to catch up with his correspondence, which had suffered during the battle and the march that followed. From here he wrote to Mrs. Sternberg on July 16:

I have my hospital in good running order, and the wounded are doing as well as could be expected and are as comfortable as possible. The ladies of the village brought them a nice dinner today consisting of chicken, green peas, custard, soup, pies, cakes, &c., &c. There are about a dozen houses in this place and as many more families who have come in for protection. . . . I am reveling in luxury. Have a straw bed on the floor of my office and get three regular meals at a neighboring house with plenty of fresh bread and butter and beef. I am quite well and nearly rested from the excessive fatigue of the past few days.

Three days later, on July 19, he was ordered to move the wounded to Fort Lapwai, and the expedition got under way at four o'clock that same afternoon. They had made about eighteen miles at nine o'clock, when they struck camp for the night. Starting out again at five the next morning, they kept going until noon, when they stopped at a deserted ranch to eat, rest, and dress the wounds. Four hours later they started moving again and spent that night at another deserted ranch. During the night one of the men with a leg wound began bleeding profusely. Dr. Sternberg was afraid he would not live long enough to reach the Fort Lapwai hospital without an operation, so preparations were made for an immediate amputation at the knee. The wounded man lay on the ground while Major Sternberg operated by candle light. The patient stood the operation all right, was tenderly lifted back into his wagon after resting there a while to regain some of his strength, and was in fairly good condition when he arrived at the hospital.

Dr. Sternberg's troubles were not at an end, for the Fort Lapwai hospital was not large enough for so many new patients. Some were placed in tents and others on the front porch of the small building. He wanted to take the wounded to Fort Walla Walla, where the hospital was large enough to take care of them. The suggestion was turned down by his official superiors.

The welfare of the wounded was not the sole inspiration for his desire to take them all the way to Walla Walla. His wife was there, and he was hungering to get back to her after those weary and trying weeks of exposure, physical strain, and hardship. Since he was unable to go to her, the next best thing was to have her come to him. He had been staying with an officer friend and the latter's wife but would soon have to make other arrangements, as the other man was about to go on field duty, his wife's health was bad, and their servant was threatening to leave. It would be an excellent arrangement, Dr. Sternberg suggested to Mrs. Sternberg, for her and the Sternberg's Chinese cook to move in and take over the running of the house. The doctor's wife was all for it, of course. The past several weeks had not been easy for her either, and she was as eager to see him as he was to see her. But she was not sure about June (a strange name for a Chinaman). Would he go along? He would. He liked the major and wanted to see him, too. The Chinese servant and the American housewife started packing.

Major Sternberg met them at Lewiston, where they left the boat. As they started to the hotel to await the arrival of the carriage that would take them to Fort Lapwai, twelve miles away, he, in mock seriousness, threatened to send her back to Walla Walla by the next boat. The air was tense at Lapwai, he told her. A large number of Indians captured at the battle of the Clearwater and other places were being held prisoners there, and trouble was expected from other Indians. There were even rumors that an attempt would be made to affect a wholesale liberation. It was no place for a lady.

But the lady insisted upon going on with him, danger or no danger.

She sensed the air of tenseness as soon as their driver made a sharp turn and they found themselves virtually inside the encampment. And about the first thing she saw was the heavily guarded stockade, crowded with miserably unhappy Indian captives. Guns and ammunition had been distributed to the troops, with orders to keep them close at hand for instant use, day and night. Twenty soldiers, trained not for combat but for making music in the regimental band, represented the camp's full protective force in addition to the doctors and the wounded. Soon after arriving, Mrs. Sternberg was told about the block house and the part it would play in case of trouble. In the cellar of this sturdy building, converted from an officer's residence, large stores of water, food, and other supplies had been cached. To give it added protection against rifle fire, cord wood had been stacked against its sides. Should trouble break out, the women and children were to go there as quickly as possible.

The uneasiness was increased by the arrival of many supposedly friendly Indians from the reservation. The women, the doctors, and that pitiably small military force could not be sure they were really friendly and not intent upon rushing the stockade and tearing down the barricades, an easy task in view of their overwhelming numerical superiority. Then there were rumors, spread by white men arriving from the wilderness, that Joseph had managed to escape General Howard's pursuing troops and was on his way back with heavy reinforcements. Meanwhile, the stockaded prisoners became more and more restless, more and more resentful of their confinement. The tenseness of the situation and its grave potentialities were reported to military and Indian affairs officials in Washington, who decided to do something about it. The prisoners were ordered removed to distant places, where other Indians could not see them and where they would be beyond any possible help from the crafty Joseph.

The Indian's stoicism, his lack of emotion, are traditional, as much a part of him as his copper skin, his war paint, and his deepset eyes. But the people at Fort Lapwai learned the day the Nez Percés left how emotional and even sentimental they could be. These braves, who had scorned fear in battle and disdained pain and fatigue on long marches, broke down and cried like overwrought women. Their moans were enough to melt the hearts of even those who had fought against them at the Clearwater and on other fields of strife. Those outside the stockade were as demonstrative as those inside, for many of the men who were leaving were close blood kin of those who had won comparative freedom by agreeing to live on the narrow, barren reservation set aside for them by the powerful white man. Other prisoners had friends and sweethearts on the outside. There was a veritable surge of copper-colored bodies toward the stockade barricades as the two groups got as close to each other as they could. Farewell gifts, as sentimental as those given by any white girl to her departing sweetheart, were tossed across the barriers. Beaded ornaments were torn from the free Indians' necks to adorn the necks of the men about to begin that last long, sad march. Beaded cloth ripped from dresses and coats was hurled into the air in the hope that it would land near those for whom it was intended.

At last the wide, lumbering gates were thrown open, and the men were told to get going. Major and Mrs. Sternberg were there to watch them, and, like others who witnessed this spectacle, found what they saw extremely depressing. They could not get away from the idea that is was unjust. They were not prepared to say that this beautiful valley ought to remain forever, as it had been for centuries, a hunting and camping ground for the red man. Perhaps it was time for another race of men to take over. Where these men had built campfires, the white man would create factories. The wood in this beautiful valley would not be left to stand in majestic uselessness additional hundreds of years but, instead, would be made into furniture and any number of other articles that would make people more comfortable all over the world. Farms would soon dot the hillsides. Towns and cities would spring up. But all this did not prevent the studious, serious-minded doctor and his wife, with their deep sympathy for unhappy people, from wishing from the bottoms of their hearts that the white man could possess all this vast and beautiful land without having to drive those who formerly possessed it away like cattle. Those whimperings and those shouts of anguish kept ringing in their ears as they stood there and in their memories for a long time afterward. These two who had contributed much to the victory which those copper columns symbolized—he on the field of battle, she by sending him off to battle and spending tortured days waiting for news—watched that march into a new part of the country, a new life, and a new era as long as they could. When at last it had dwindled to a tiny dot on the dusty horizon, they turned sadly away, got into their carriage, and drove home.

CHAPTER VIII

Laboratory Warrior

MAJOR STERNBERG'S main incentive for getting back to Fort Walla Walla as soon as he could ended with his wife's joining him at Fort Lapwai. Nevertheless, he still wanted to do so. Having helped his wounded to get a good start on the rugged road to recovery and having provided them with satisfactory care at the small but efficient Fort Lapwai hospital, he did not see why their treatment should not now be turned over to some other medical officer. His official superiors agreed and honored his request for a transfer back to Walla Walla. He looked forward to an extended period of relatively light duties which would give him a chance to recoup his strength after the strenuous life he had been living since leaving there on such short notice several weeks earlier.

Neither his stay in Walla Walla nor his rest was to last long, however. Early in November, 1878, he was ordered to represent the Medical Department of the Army at the impending meeting of the American Public Health Association in Richmond, Virginia. Again he had to get away on short notice. The meeting was to begin in less than three weeks, and he had a continent to cross to get there. Checking the schedules, he found that he did not have time enough to take the more comfortable route, largely by water, by way of Portland and San Francisco, but would have to travel some four hundred and fifty miles by stage coach to Winnemucca, Nevada, where he would transfer to a train. The wisdom of undertaking such a trip so soon after undergoing several weeks of hard campaigning and battle became questionable soon after he set out. His stomach, which had taken without protest such food as he had been able to get during the war, rebelled militantly against the jostling of the stage coach, the dust of those crude roads, and the unsavory and ill-cooked meals he and the other passengers had to snatch during brief stops along the way. Bacon, fried potatoes, and bread were all a traveler could get in most places, and the first two were particularly hard on his mistreated digestive and nervous systems. Once, some time before reaching Winnemucca, the strain and the indigestion proved altogether too much: he "passed out" completely. So did a fellow passenger, a lady. Both were soon revived, however, and managed to endure the rest of the journey to the railroad terminal. The train trip was, of course, much more pleasant and comfortable.

Whatever earlier doubt Major Sternberg may have had about the wisdom of attending the meeting was quickly dissipated after his arrival. There he found a number of old friends he had not seen in years. New friendships were formed among the distinguished speakers and discussion leaders. The addresses he listened to stimulated his enthusiasm, and he entered heartily into the informal discussions that followed the presentation of the formal papers. Hard campaigning and routine army post duty had nothing like this to offer a medical man with a burning zeal for research and for wide exploration beyond the normal frontiers of medicine. He began the long, tiresome return journey with a new enthusiasm, a new zest for discovery, a new pride in his profession.

But he took even more back to Walla Walla with him. A great deal of the discussion at the meeting had been concerned with disinfection, a new field of medical concern at that time. In Europe men like Pasteur, Lister, and Koch were beginning to arouse the medical world to the part played by tiny organisms in life and health. Here, he was convinced, was the explanation of many of mankind's great disease enemies and their ability to slay humans like an advancing army. What could be done to curb and kill them? If enough could be done, then many of mankind's most troublesome disease problems would be solved; a new era in medicine would be born. The subject's vast possibilities challenged him. He determined to become a pioneer in the new science of bacteriology. The spare-time work he had been doing had been an excellent beginning—but no more than a beginning. That Richmond meeting had thrown open a door to a dazzling new world of exploration and adventure.

As soon as possible after getting back he began finding out everything he could about disinfectants, devoting himself particularly to what the scientists called "the thermal death point of pathogenic organisms." Tests were made in his crude laboratory. Every product he could get his hands on that might throw new light on the power of chemicals to destroy disease organisms or render them impotent was put under scrutiny. There were many problems that needed to be mastered. As before, he received very little encouragement and no help from his official superiors in the Medical Department of the Army. Not that he needed any encouragement or help—he was perfectly willing to spend his own money, as he had been doing for several years, for the materials and supplies he needed. No time or worry was wasted upon those who thought he was off on a wild goose chase. Nor was he entirely without financial and moral supporters. The American Public Health Association made him chairman of a committee devoted to a study of disinfectants and made a small fund available to meet a few of the committee's expenses.

He realized at the outset that he had set himself a lengthy task, a job much more likely to fail than to succeed and with countless temptations to give up in discouragement and disgust. Here was no self-imposed duty that could be discharged in a matter of weeks or months. The study he had undertaken would move at such a slow pace that it could not be completed in less than several years. Actually, he did not begin to see worthwhile results for about five years.

In mid-April, 1879, some five months after his return from that Richmond meeting, he was ordered to cross the continent again, this time for assignment to the office of the Surgeon General. He had no idea what was ahead of him, but the transfer orders pleased him greatly, in spite of his and Mrs. Sternberg's attachment to Fort Walla Walla. Regardless of the nature of his future work, he would be working directly under the Surgeon General, and that would, or should, make it easier for him to carry on the independent research upon which he had embarked. Too, even if his new work should prove no more conducive to concentration upon disinfectants than his work at Walla Walla, he would have, in and around Washington—assuming that he was to be stationed there more or less permanently—what he had missed so much at Walla Walla, excellent college and university laboratories. There, in whatever spare time he might have, he would find the physical equipment he needed. Of equal importance, he would find scientific-minded men like himself with whom he could exchange views.

When he reached Washington Surgeon General J. K. Barnes told him he was to work with the Havana Yellow Fever Commission of the National Board of Health. His successful handling of those yellow fever epidemics in New York harbor, Pensacola, Fort Barrancas, and New Orleans, and the personal immunity he had won so dearly, were regarded as excellent preparation for this new assignment. He welcomed it, even though it would not permit him to spend much time in Washington, for a while at least, because it promised an opportunity to do a great deal of research in a field in which he was greatly interested. Others on the Commission were Dr. Stanford Chaillé, of New Orleans, T. S. Hardee, a civil engineer, also of New Orleans, and Dr. Juan Guiteras, of Havana. Dr. Guiteras was then a relatively unknown physician but destined to win fame as an associate of Major Walter Reed in one of the most brilliant series of experiments in medical history. Dr. Chaillé was named chairman of the group, Dr. Sternberg secretary.

The Commission's primary task was to find out as much as it could about the cause and spread of yellow fever, which for centuries had been wreaking terrible devastation in the West Indies and along the Atlantic and Gulf coasts. Concentration upon that task was implicit in the official instructions issued by the sponsoring National Board of Health. But these men were also instructed to find out as much as they could about general sanitary conditions in the Cuban capital which might affect health on the mainland.

Major Sternberg took with him to Cuba a firmly formed opinion regarding yellow fever transmission: the many hours he had spent studying the disease in his makeshift laboratories and in the fever-wracked bodies of its victims, including himself, had convinced him almost to the point of certainty that, somewhere in the patient's body, there was an organism which set the disease aflame in its current victim and served as the spark for new fires in other bodies. He leaned heavily to the belief that that harboring place was the blood stream. The fact that all efforts to find it there had failed did not strike him as conclusive. Sooner or later, he hoped, the mechanics of examining the blood for such organisms would be so greatly improved that this deadly germ, or bacillus, or whatever it was could be exposed to human sight and examined as readily as a piece of flesh being studied for skin texture. Naturally, he dreamed fond, exuberant dreams of being able to make that great discovery himself with equipment born in the Sternberg brain.

For the coming true of that fond dream and his ability to prove its reality, he placed a great deal of reliance upon the relatively new technique of photomicrography, in which he had been a pioneer and in which he was still a leader. Thanks to his skill and delicate touch—even so slight a jar as that caused by a vehicle passing on a nearby street was enough to ruin a carefully planned photomicrograph—he was able to obtain clear and permanent pictorial records of what he saw momentarily through his microscope lens.

After enjoying "charming weather" and a pleasant trip generally, he arrived in Havana early in July, 1879. Almost the first thing he did was to write to Mrs. Sternberg, telling her, among other things, that he should not lack for material upon which to work: "There is plenty of yellow fever, chiefly among the soldiers and sailors." In another letter about a week later, he told her he was "working away in the laboratory" and had "commenced some experiments." That day he had been making microscopic studies of bacteria which he had been culturing in coconut milk, or liquor, as the Cubans called it. He had not been out of his hotel for several days except to pay a short visit to a Cuban doctor who had invited him to inspect his laboratory. In spite of the hard work, however, he was not faring at all badly:

I have not as yet suffered from the heat. The thermometer does not go much above 85 degrees and indeed has been exactly 85 degrees every time I have looked at it. I sleep well under a light blanket, have a good appetite and do justice to the fruits and dishes of the country. . . .I assure you that I am doing very nicely and trust that I will remain quite well until the happy day when we meet again.

Still working on the theory that somewhere, probably in the blood, a sufficiently industrious, sufficiently observant, sufficiently persevering, and sufficiently fortunate researcher would eventually find the yellow fever organism, he kept "much interested in my work" during the weeks of toil that followed. And at last that toil appeared about ready to pay off handsomely: "I have already made some observations of value on the blood." Moreover, "I am not sure but [that] I have discovered the yellow fever germ." However, "we shall see." Meanwhile, he was going to the hospital the next morning " to get some more blood." Later letters expressed continuing hope that he was making steady progress in the right direction, although he did not want his wife to expect too much. "I am much interested in my work," he told her, "and hope to arrive at some results of value." The animals he needed for some of his experiments were slow in arriving, and that delayed him somewhat. Finally they did show up, and "we will commence experiments at once."

Mrs. Sternberg had sent him newspaper clippings telling about the Memphis yellow fever epidemic of that year, one of the worst in the disease's long and tragic history. The news disturbed him: knowing the misery caused by yellow fever on a rampage, he felt sorry for its victims; and, from a more personal standpoint, he feared that, should the disease become too bad in the United States, he very likely would be ordered back to the mainland to help fight it. "I hope," he wrote, "the Board of Health will not send for us until our three months have expired. I consider our opportunities here so good for accomplishing something of value that I would be sorry to lose such a chance." He need not have worried. As far as is known, his official superiors never had any plans to recall him and the others from Havana.

His letter of August 8 brought disappointing news to the wife who was as eager for success as he was. After about a month, "I have not made any wonderful discovery yet." Nevertheless, he had made "a fine lot of photographs of yellow fever blood and of preparations of air from infected places." He had just submitted to the National Board of Health a preliminary report covering his early findings, particularly those concerned with the study of the blood of yellow fever patients—nothing startling or revolutionary, however.

He had better news, he thought, a few days later. He wrote that he was sending her, along with a few pictures of Havana's famed beauty, some examples of his work in photomicrography. Concerning the photomicrographs he said:

> I have made one valuable discovery. In the views of yellow fever blood you will see in the white blood corpuscles certain granules that are peculiar to yellow fever and that have never been described before.... [And] as I find them also in the blood of a dog just imported from the north* I hope that they may prove to be a test of the exposure of dogs to infected localities and that this may prove of great value in future investigations and experiments on animals.

His expected return home, still more than a month off, was much on his mind when he wrote her on August 22. The date of his departure had been set as October 2; the ship on which he would sail was to be the *City of Washington*, on which he had come south. The remaining weeks, he assured her, "will soon slip away" and they would again be together "well and happy by or before the 10th of Oct." He asked her to meet him in Washington, where he would have to spend some time working on his report and attending to other official business.

On September 22, he reminded her that:

> Three weeks from tomorrow we are to sail. It will be a happy day for me when I reach Washington and take my dear wife in my loving arms again. I feel that I need rest and the comforts of home and the company of my dear wife. This living in a hotel and working from 7 in the morning to 10 at night gets to be an old story after a while.

He had to confess finally that his hope of discovering the exact cause of yellow fever had been disappointed. But his trip had been fruitful and successful nevertheless:

> I have not discovered the yellow fever germ, but I have done good work here and think I will get credit for it with the Board of Health. ...My work here is about the same thing every day. Going to the hos-

* From the United States.

pital for specimens and looking through the microscope at blood and bilge water and black vomit and urine and all those nice things.

The happy reunion in Washington did eventuate as scheduled. With his wife, Major Sternberg settled down in the pleasant suburban community of Georgetown, and there he completed his report. He also continued some investigations that had been cut short by his return home.

The National Board of Health certainly showed no dissatisfaction or disappointment over the results accomplished. His report won commendation not only from Board members but also from other scientists and researchers. His inability to expose yellow fever's most important secret during that brief period did not dim in the least his belief that that eventual exposure of the secret was possible. He had accomplished much in a negative way. He had demonstrated that a number of avenues which had formerly been considered promising actually led nowhere. Thus he had considerably narrowed the field of research, making much easier the work of those who were to follow him. And of course he still hoped it would be his own great good fortune to make that vital discovery. The National Board of Health showed how pleased it was with the Sternberg accomplishments at Havana by selecting him a few months later for another important, albeit troublesome, task. This assignment took him back to New Orleans, where he had been stationed three times already.

The disease upon which he began concentrating his investigative fire in those early months of 1880 had baffled the scientists and hamstrung human progress for many centuries. Malaria, believed to have been introduced into Italy during the Second Punic War and into Greece two or three centuries earlier, almost certainly played an important part, if not the dominating part, in the decline and fall of those two great powers. It has plagued military leaders in practically every major war. The National Emergency Council in 1938 estimated its current victims in the southern United States alone at some two million and said it was probably reducing that region's industrial output by a third. Malaria, probably more than any other disease, caused President Franklin D. Roosevelt to label the South "the nation's

Economic Problem No. One." In his *Preventive Medicine and Hygiene*, the late Dr. Milton J. Rosenau calls it "the scourge of the tropics. . . . the tyrant of tropical diseases, sovereign over a vast domain, retarding progress, influencing history, destroying millions." Alabama's late State Health Officer, Dr. J. N. Baker, said malaria had "probably had a greater effect upon the South's well-being than Sherman's March to the Sea."

The choice of New Orleans as the center of operations for the Sternberg malaria experiments was solidly based. Not only was it situated in the South, the area of the greatest malaria endemicity in the Western World, it was also situated in a particularly marshy area, an ideal breeding place for mosquitoes, which some advanced-thinking scientists were associating with the disease, under storms of sarcastic witticisms from their fellows.

Dr. Sternberg's task at New Orleans was a negative one. His job was not to try to find the organism causing malaria or the method by which it is spread. Rather, he was sent there to test the soundness of other persons' claims to having discovered that tiny organism.

Several months earlier two well-known and highly respected scientists, Edwin Klebs of Germany, and Corrado Tomassi-Crudeli of Italy, had announced that they had isolated the malaria bacillus. Because of these men's renown, there was a general willingness, not to say eagerness, to accept their claims without dispute. But some officials of the National Board of Health had their doubts. So did Dr. Sternberg. He was far from satisfied with the reasoning Klebs and Tomassi-Crudeli had advanced in support of their claims.

In his New Orleans laboratory Dr. Sternberg diligently duplicated their experiments. The results he obtained differed radically from those they had reported: not one of his discoveries gave him any reason to think the *Bacillus malariae*, the Klebs-Tomassi-Crudeli organism, had anything whatsoever to do with malaria. Long before he wound up his studies he was certain that the malaria-like illnesses his experimental rabbits were developing (and, presumably, also the cases resulting from the Klebs-Tomassi-Crudeli experiments as well) were not malaria cases at all.

It called for a great deal of confidence in his own findings and the risk of considerable loss of face to make those findings public. The *Bacillus malariae* had been widely accepted by physicians in this country and England as the cause of malaria. The Klebs-Tomassi-Crudeli "contribution" to world scientific knowledge had been described, with full approval, in medical journals all over the country and in other countries. Standard medical textbooks had given the bacillus a place among the properly authenticated disease organisms. But Major Sternberg was sure of his ground. He had risked embarrassment of this kind before. Boldly he announced that the European scientists had failed to prove their claim; then he prepared to defend himself and his position against the expected deluge of protest. Fortunately, that was not difficult, for others soon began sharing his assurance that his position was sound. Some years later he was able to write: "Today no one speaks of the *Bacillus malariae* of Klebs and Tomassi-Crudeli except to refer to it as one of the pseudo-discoveries which for a time passed current, like a counterfeit coin, which was detected and thrown aside when subjected to approved scientific tests."

Dr. Sternberg's labors in New Orleans in the early 1880's were not all of a negative nature. Before returning to his Washington headquarters for reassignment he had made a substantial positive contribution to the science of bacteriology. In September, 1880, he injected a small quantity of his own saliva beneath the skin of a laboratory rabbit. As this was done as part of a control experiment, by which to judge the results of another experiment, a negative reaction was taken for granted: the rabbit was not expected to show any reaction at all to the injection. But Dr. Sternberg had a surprise. The rabbit died. Puzzled by this unusual outcome, he dissected its body and found a great many oval organisms of a kind quite foreign to normal rabbits. Pursuing his search for an answer to this puzzle, he injected some of this rabbit's blood into another rabbit. It died too. He isolated some of those oval micrococci in pure cultures and injected them into still other rabbits. They succumbed like those used earlier. Each of these experiments was repeated over and over. And each repetition brought repetition of the results. Those oval micro-organisms, formed from his own saliva, which he had never had the slightest reason to consider as otherwise than completely harmless, were a deadly poison.

He prepared a preliminary report on these experiments and their results. Before his paper was published (in the *National Board of Health Bulletin*) Louis Pasteur announced to the French Academy of Sciences that he had discovered what he called a "new disease." He had produced it, he said, by injecting under the skin of laboratory rabbits saliva obtained from the mouth of a child who had just died of rabies in a Paris hospital. He knew nothing at the time of the Sternberg experiments, and Dr. Sternberg knew nothing about his.

As soon as he learned about the Pasteur announcement, Dr. Sternberg recognized the Frenchman's "new disease" as identical with the disease he had produced with injections of his own saliva. However, he disagreed with the Pasteur opinion that the rabbits in the Paris laboratory had died from anything related to rabies. The fact that the child had that disease at the time of her death had nothing at all to do with the case, he contended: those rabbits would also have died if that youngster had succumbed to heart disease or injuries received in a traffic accident. For that matter, she need not have died at all: she might have been alive and perfectly well, as he himself had been. Later experiments established the soundness of the Sternberg contention, and Pasteur did not press his claim to having discovered a "new disease."

Dr. Sternberg's wide explorations in this fascinating field led to a number of important and interesting discoveries having to do with the harmless-appearing deadliness of human saliva. Not all people have that organism in their mouths. Those who do may have it at one time and not at another. He found in his own case, over a three-year period, that from time to time his saliva had no effect on laboratory rabbits. Whenever it did, there would be wide variations in the time required for it to prove fatal—the range was from forty-eight to seventy-two hours. Similar variations were noted by other scientists.

Positive as he was that this accidental discovery of his constituted an important advance in scientific knowledge, Dr. Sternberg, nevertheless, did not realize at the time how important it really was. It apparently did not occur to him that there was any connection between his *Micrococcus pasteuri* and the organism responsible for any other disease. As it happened, others were toiling energetically about that same time in allied fields. In 1882 Carl Friedlander, a German, reported that the previous September he had observed unusual organisms in the sputum of eight pneumonia patients. Those cocci, as they were called, had also been found, he said, in the fluid drawn from the chests of pneumonia victims. Scientists were strongly inclined, on the strength of this presentation, to credit him with the discovery of the pneumococcus, the pneumonia-causing organism. In April, 1884, however, Albert Fraenkel, another German, appeared before a medical group in Berlin to dispute Friedlander's right to that honor. He himself, he declared, had carried on a number of experiments that antedated Friedlander's, and his results had largely duplicated those achieved by his fellow countryman.

After carrying on additional experiments, Fraenkel stated positively in 1886 that his organism—which he had named the microbe of sputum septicemia—and the Friedlander organism were different, but that Fraenkel, Pasteur and Sternberg organisms—each discovered independently of the others—were identical. Moreover, he declared, this thrice-discovered organism—and not the one discovered by Friedlander—was the actual causative agent of true fibrinous, or lobar, pneumonia.

He gradually began winning support for his claim. Present-day medical volumes list both Friedlander's bacillus (*Klebsiella pneumoniae*) and Fraenkel's pneumococcus. The former, according to the *American Illustrated Medical Dictionary*,* is "associated with various pathologic conditions of the nose and accessory sinuses." It "is found in certain cases of pneumonia but is not considered pathogenic for that disease." Fraenkel's pneumococcus, on the other hand, "is the organism. . . which causes lobar pneumonia." The latter, clearly, is the winner in the struggle for recognition, as between these two.

But, Dr. Sternberg and his friends contended, if the Fraenkel organism is recognized as the true cause of lobar pneumonia,

* W. A. Newman Dorland, *The American Illustrated Medical Dictionary*, 22nd ed. (Philadelphia and London: W. B. Saunders Company, 1951), p. 784.

should credit for its discovery not be accorded to the person who was the first to discover it? Should it not be called the Sternberg pneumococcus?

In his *Manual of Bacteriology*,* published in 1892, Dr. Sternberg states that the pneumococcus was "discovered by the present writer in the blood of rabbits inoculated subcutaneously with his own saliva in September, 1880; by Pasteur in the blood of rabbits inoculated with the blood of a child which had died of hydrophobia in one of the hospitals of Paris in December, 1880; identified with the micrococcus in the rusty sputum of pneumonia, by comparative inoculation and culture experiments, by the writer in 1885." Moreover, this organism was "proved to be the cause of croupous [lobar] pneumonia in many of the researches of Talamon, Salvioli, Sternberg, Fraenkel, Weichsel-baun, Netter, Gamaleia"—scientists studying pneumonia's cause and mode of transmission—"and others."

He repeated his claim to recognition as that organism's dis-coverer nine years later. In the second edition of his *A Textbook of Bacteriology*,† published in 1901, he reviewed his own and others' experiments and added: "Under these circumstances the writer feels justified in again calling attention to his priority in the discovery of this important pathogenic micrococcus, and in objecting to its being described as 'Fraenkel's pneumococcus,' the 'diplococcus of Fraenkel,' etc."

Mrs. Sternberg contended to her death that her husband was in reality and beyond dispute the discoverer of pneumonia's caus-ative agent. From time to time between his death and hers she took issue with occasional writers and speakers who awarded to Fraenkel the credit for this discovery. The earnestness and de-votion with which she entered the fray and carried on the fight for recognition after he was no longer able to do so were of course commendable. Nevertheless, there are, as has been point-ed out, those who differ with her and with him, although generous in their praise of the Sternberg contribution to the over-all vic-tory.

* New York: William Wood & Co., 1892, p. 298.
† Second revised ed. (New York: William Wood & Co., 1901), p. 339.

The dispute will never be completely resolved to everybody's satisfaction, of course. Like the controversy over the discovery of anesthesia, it will divide the medical and bacteriological worlds for a long, long time. However, Dr. Sternberg's great admirer, Colonel (later General) Edgar Erskine Hume seems to have been eminently fair to him and to others when he wrote:

> While Fraenkel is entitled to credit for this important discovery, it was Sternberg who first recognized and described the organism, though he did not associate it in his first publication with pneumonia, since it was found in his own and the buccal secretions of other healthy subjects.*

Dr. Crawford Long of Georgia was unquestionably the first to use ether or any other anesthesia to make endurable the pain of surgery. But he was in no hurry to announce what he had done and in fact very probably did not realize its true significance and importance. He thus made it possible for others, who used it after him, to beat him to the printing presses and speaker's platforms with their announcements. Likewise, Dr. Sternberg was undoubtedly the first, as Colonel Hume points out, to see the pneumococcus and recognize it as a separate organism. But he too waited several years to realize and proclaim the real significance of his discovery. And, as Dr. Long also found out belatedly, waiting a few years can make a vast difference, especially if others are hard at work in the same field. While Sternberg adherents and their rivals wrangle over the honor, one great fact stands out: Dr. Sternberg at the very least made a valuable contribution to the mastery of one of mankind's greatest enemies. Uncounted millions who have escaped death from that master killer certainly owe much of their good fortune to him.

* Edgar Erskine Hume, "Sternberg's Centenary, 1838-1938," *Military Surgeon*, LXXIV (May, 1939), 420-428.

CHAPTER IX

Berthside Doctor

EARLY IN August, 1881, Dr. Sternberg was ordered back to the Pacific coast and assigned to duty at Fort Mason, California. Mrs. Sternberg called it "a beautiful post." Their house was quite small, but it had an excellent view, with a broad sweep of the bay. The post hospital, in which he was most interested, was "clean and bright." As the post was a small one, consisting only of a company of artillery and a handful of officers, the hospital, too, was small.

However, it was big enough to provide room for a tiny laboratory, which Dr. Sternberg set up and maintained at his own expense. It is here that he demonstrated and photographed the tubercle bacillus, which had recently been discovered by the German bacteriologist Robert Koch. "I am informed on good authority," Mrs. Sternberg wrote later, "that this was the first demonstration of the organism in America." On another occasion she was more positive in crediting this achievement to him, calling him "the first in America to demonstrate the tubercle bacillus discovered by Koch in 1881." *

These statements, other admirable examples of this woman's devotion to her husband and of her determination to assure for him the credit she considered his due, have been challenged by a number of authorities. She was certainly in error in giving the year of the Koch discovery as 1881: he did not make his epochal announcement until March 24, 1882.

Mrs. Sternberg was not alone in giving Dr. Sternberg credit

* Martha L. Sternberg, *George Miller Sternberg: A Biography* (Chicago: American Medical Association, 1920), pp. 87, 255.

for being the first to demonstrate the tubercle bacillus in this country and in stating that he did so prior to the date of the Koch announcement. One other who made substantially the same statement was Colonel Hume, who wrote in the May, 1939, *Military Surgeon*: "In 1881, while on duty at Fort Mason, California, Sternberg demonstrated and photographed for the first time in America the tubercle bacillus, which had been discovered in that year by Koch." Another Sternberg admirer, Dr. G. M. Kober, said at the banquet celebrating his friend's seventieth birthday: "In 1881, while stationed at Fort Mason, California, he demonstrated and photographed, probably for the first time in America, the tubercle bacillus, which had been discovered by Koch the same year."

There is no reason to doubt that Dr. Sternberg both photographed and demonstrated the causative organism of tuberculosis while he was stationed at Fort Mason. Unfortunately, the evidence at hand does not prove that he was the first to do the latter in this country. As in the case of priority in the discovery of the pneumococcus, there have been other contenders for top honors, each with his supporters. In an article in the *Yale Journal of Biology and Medicine,* Dr. E. R. Baldwin calls Dr. Edward L. Trudeau "one of the earliest in America to appreciate the discovery made by Koch in 1882."[*] The founder of the famous tuberculosis sanatorium at Saranac Lake, New York, he says, "quickly acquired the technique of staining the bacillus from Prudden and Hodenpyl of the old laboratory of the College of Physicians and Surgeons in New York, as he has so graphically told in his *Autobiography.*"

Now let us see what the *Autobiography* says about Dr. Trudeau's part in this bit of health pioneering:

In 1882 Koch published in Germany his epoch-making paper on "The Etiology of Tuberculosis," and I read in my medical journals one or two extracts of the long and painstaking experimental work which had led him to the startling conclusion that a specific germ, the "tubercle bacillus," was the cause of this widespread disease. There was every reason why this announcement of Koch's should make a deep impression on me.

* Edward R. Baldwin, "History of Tuberculosis Research in America," *Yale Journal of Biology and Medicine*, XV (Jan., 1943), 301-309.

But, eager as he was to get full information about the Koch experiments and their results as quickly as possible, he was thwarted. Koch's paper had not yet been translated, and Dr. Trudeau did not read German. So "there would be no use of my trying to obtain Koch's paper." Some time later—he does not say how much later—Dr. Trudeau had "one of the pleasantest surprises of my life." A good friend of his had the entire Koch paper translated into English and gave it to him. "Surely," the happy recipient wrote, "I never had a Christmas present that meant more to me than that big hand-written copy-book. I read every word of it over and over again."

It did not take much persuasion on Koch's part, if any, to make Dr. Trudeau a Koch disciple, although medical opinion generally was extremely skeptical. After reading the paper he "became strongly convinced of the soundness of his deductions and the far-reaching importance of his discovery." Moreover, he was "intensely anxious to test his experimental results." A formidable obstacle stood in his way: he "knew nothing about bacteriology; had never heard the name before." However, he had his microscope and determined to spend as much time as he could on his next trip to New York "learning how to stain and recognize the tubercle bacillus under the microscope." He realized that "the first thing to do was to learn to find and recognize the germ."

When he got back to the city Dr. Trudeau did spend several days at the laboratory of his alma mater, the College of Physicians and Surgeons, working under the guidance of Dr. T. Mitchell Prudden and his assistant, Dr. Eugene Hodenpyl. Before he returned to Saranac Lake he was easily finding the deadly bacilli under the powerful magnification of his microscope.

When was this? He does not tell us. One would assume from his interest in the Koch discovery that he made that trip to New York as soon as possible. But, unless there was an unusual and extremely unlikely time lag between that trip and the putting into use of the knowledge gained there, it did not occur until two or three years after the Koch announcement, for the *Autobiography* gives "the fall of 1885" as the time when he got his "little laboratory-room" equipped and started to work examining his patients' sputum for tubercle bacilli.

There is another reason to think Dr. Trudeau did not begin looking for tubercle bacilli until sometime in 1885. Neither Dr. Prudden nor Dr. Hodenpyl, presumably, could teach him before then for the simple reason that neither of them knew how. In the article cited above, Dr. Baldwin tells us that Dr. Prudden "visited Koch's laboratory in 1885 and brought back a thorough knowledge of the methods of the master." Presumably, he subsequently passed on his knowledge to Dr. Hodenpyl, as well as to Dr. Trudeau—some three years after Koch's announcement.

Another American, Dr. William T. Belfield, happened to be in Europe, though not in Berlin, when the Koch paper was presented. He obtained as much information about it as he could and passed it on to the readers of the *Chicago Medical Journal & Examiner*, which published the Belfield correspondence in its issues of June and July, 1882. It is not known when Dr. Belfield first put his newly acquired knowledge to use, but it was not later than October of that year. In that month he is known to have demonstrated the tubercle bacillus at a meeting of the Chicago Pathological Society. An anonymous writer in the *Journal of the American Medical Association*, presumably a member of the editorial staff, says this "appears to be the first public demonstration of the bacillus in this country."

Others insist that Dr. W. H. Welch, then professor of pathological anatomy and general pathology at Bellevue Medical College, deserves to have this honor added to the many others he accumulated during his long and productive career. In *The Life of Herman M. Biggs*,* Dr. C.-E. A. Winslow says another member of the Bellevue faculty, after reading about the Koch discovery in his morning newspaper, "jumped into a cab, drove down to Welch's lodgings on East Twenty-first Street and rushed to the bedside of his more indolent young colleague waving the paper in the air in his enthusiasm." Some weeks later, Dr. Welch, still under the spell of the great German teachers and researchers with whom he had studied and worked for three years, "had succeeded in staining the tubercle bacillus by the Koch methods and

* (Philadelphia: Lea & Febiger, 1929), p. 56.

had demonstrated it to his colleagues and to his most eager student, Biggs."

Sternberg's definite statements make it clear that, unless the Welch demonstrations occurred prior to August 8, 1882, they did not antedate but followed the Sternberg demonstration. And the same is true of the demonstrations conducted by others, for he tells us in a medical journal that on that date he saw the bacilli in the sputum of a tuberculosis patient. Their presence "was clearly demonstrated." The technique he employed was not exactly that used by Koch but was an adaptation of the Koch method devised by Dr. Paul Ehrlich soon after the Koch discovery was announced. The Ehrlich method, he wrote, "is very definite, and distinguishes clearly these [tubercle] bacilli from other micro-organisms—bacilli and micrococci—also present in the same preparation [sputum specimen]." Tests on August 10, 12, and 14 also showed the bacilli.*

There are also references to the Sternberg tests and their success in a paper prepared by Drs. Henry Grable and H. Woltman and read by the former in January, 1883, to the Chicago Medical Society. Near the beginning they mention "Korab in France, and Sternberg in this country" as having "made short communications corroborative of Koch's experiments." Somewhat later they refer to a point raised by some of Koch's critics and insist that such an objection "can not weigh in opposition to the positive statement by the discoverer that such *is* the case, a statement fully confirmed by Ehrlich, Gibbes, Sternberg, Balmer and ourselves." Again, in a footnote to a lecture he delivered some time later at the Chicago Medical College, Dr. Grable named seven research workers in various parts of the world who, he said, had confirmed "the invariable presence of these [tubercle] bacilli in the tubercular products." The seven included Dr. Sternberg.

And so the question whether he was the first to demonstrate the tubercle bacillus in the United States remains without a very definite answer. If he was not the very first, he certainly was one of the first. Most of those who question his right to that dis-

---

* "Is Tuberculosis a Parasitic Disease?" *Medical News,* XLI (Sept. 16, 1882), 311-314.

tinction freely accord him another having to do with the tubercle bacillus: they concede that he was the first in this country to photograph it. Colonel Hume wrote in his *Victories of Army Medicine:** "It was General Sternberg who first photographed the tubercle bacillus. His negative is still in the Army Medical Museum, and the photograph is an excellent example of his skill as a photomicrographer."

Dr. Sternberg's professional interest was by no means confined to yellow fever, pneumonia, malaria, and tuberculosis in the early 1880's. He was also asking himself some searching questions having to do with the human body's defenses against disease. At the 1881 meeting of the American Association for the Advancement of Science he read a paper to which he, or those arranging the program, gave the unwieldy title "A Contribution to the Study of the Bacterial Organisms Commonly Found on Exposed Mucous Surfaces and in the Alimentary Canal of Healthy Individuals." In it he threw out the suggestion —two years before the Russian biologist Elie Metchnikoff announced the theory now known by his name—that the white corpuscles in the blood might attack and destroy invading disease germs:

> It has occurred to me that possibly the white corpuscles may have the office of picking up and digesting bacterial organisms which by any means find their way into the blood. The propensity exhibited by the leukocytes for picking up inorganic granules is well known, and that they may be able not only to pick up but to assimilate, and so dispose of, bacteria which come in their way does not seem to me very improbable. . . .

During much of 1883, the year Metchnikoff announced his theory and received credit as its originator, Dr. Sternberg was hard at work on his book *Bacteria*, finishing it in mid-August. There is nothing to indicate that he knew anything about Metchnikoff's experiments at any time the manuscript was in preparation. Nevertheless, he was now much more certain than he had been two years earlier that the blood contained powerful organisms which protected the body against invading disease germs. He called attention to what he and other scientists had clearly demonstrated: if harmful bacteria are added to blood which has

* Edgar Erskine Hume, *Victories of Army Medicine* (Philadelphia and New York: J. B. Lippincott Co., 1923), p. 169.

been withdrawn from the body and kept at body heat, a rapid multiplication of those invading bacteria takes place. But, if a similar number of harmful bacteria are injected into the blood stream of a living animal, they not only do not multiply, they quickly disappear. "It requires no great stretch of credulity," he wrote, "to believe that they [the white blood corpuscles] may, like an amoeba, digest and assimilate the protoplasm of the captured bacterium, thus putting an end to the possibility of its doing any harm."

These two Sternberg pronouncements contain the essence of the present-day conception of the Metchnikoff theory. According to that theory, announced at the 1883 Naturalists' Congress in Odessa and published some time later in medical and scientific journals, the small organisms known as ameboid cells, which are present in the blood and in certain tissues of the body, "engulf" solid particles and bacteria, destroying the latter by the process known as phagocytosis. The Russian scientist gave those ameboid cells the name "phagocytes," explained that they served as scavengers, and pointed out that whether the victim of an infectious illness died or recovered depended upon the outcome of the battle between the invading and defending organisms.

Dr. Sternberg had a great admiration for Metchnikoff. He freely conceded that the Russian had been the first to use the term "phagocyte," which soon became closely associated in the scientific world's collective mind with the Metchnikoff theory. But he insisted that it was he, and not Metchnikoff, who first clearly stated what he called "the theory of phagocytosis." This claim he vigorously defended in a letter to the editor of the *Journal of the American Medical Association*:

> The theory, so ably supported by Metchnikoff, which ascribes to the leukocytes the function of picking up, and destroying bacteria which find their way into the blood or tissues (phagocytosis) is now generally accepted as having been demonstrated by observation and experimental evidence.
>
> I have no desire to detract from the credit due to Metchnikoff in connection with this theory, but in justice to myself desire to call attention to the fact that this theory was suggested by me several years before the publication of Metchnikoff's first paper on the subject.*

* "The Metchnikoff Theory," *Journal of the American Medical Association*, LXIII (Nov. 14, 1914), 1779-1780.

The Sternberg letter contended that his failure to use the term "phagocyte" in any of his writings prior to the Metchnikoff pronouncement did not make any difference, since "the theory of phagocytosis" had been very clearly stated in his pre-Metchnikoff publications.

Actually, neither Dr. Sternberg nor Metchnikoff was the first to see and comment upon phagocytosis. Two or three other experimenters, notably the German surgeon Wilhelm Roser and the Swedish physiologist Peter Ludwig Panum, did so before either of them. But these men's explanations of its significance were, at best, vague. Moreover, they offered no experimental evidence. Dr. Sternberg, on the other hand, gave an explanation of the procedure which is substantially that taught to medical students today. Metchnikoff's claim to fatherhood of the theory and to the right to give it its name is based upon the fact that, as the *American Journal of Public Health* pointed out editorially, he was the first "to formulate the theory and prove it by experimental work."

Notwithstanding the trouble he was having in getting the credit he considered justly his, Dr. Sternberg had little reason to complain of his standing in medical and scientific circles. Even those who sided with his rivals in the disputes over priority were eager to honor him as a great bacteriologist. Some, even then, with much of his best work still ahead, were calling him the greatest this country had produced. And they were publicly predicting much greater things from and for him.

This recognition could not fail to please him greatly. It also made him impatient to get back East, in spite of his and Martha Sternberg's pleasant life at Fort Mason and their "charming little house on the side of a high bluff, overlooking the bay." He was working under a great handicap. The "clean and bright" little post hospital gave him little to work with. Laboratory facilities, ready access to some of the world's largest and best medical and scientific libraries, the daily association with scientific-minded fellow workers which he had found so stimulating on his previous assignment, all were lacking here. For an army officer who was primarily an army officer, Fort Mason was almost ideal. For an army officer who was primarily a researcher, bacteriologist and experimentalist, it was about the worst place he could have been. His tiny laboratory and study, with their scanty and out-of-date equipment, left him feeling like a long-distance runner with a bad leg. He longed yearningly for the freedom to do research exclusively which he had enjoyed in Havana and during those few busy months in Washington just before being ordered West again.

His friend, General Barnes, had been succeeded as Surgeon General by General Robert Murray. He did not know what kind of reaction his new superior would have to a request for a transfer, but he decided to try for one anyhow. On November 27, 1883, he put his dissatisfaction into words and sent his letter to Washington with a mental mixture of hope and pessimism. He told General Murray:

> It is my earnest desire to devote my time to scientific and literary work and especially to microscopical and experimental studies relating to the etiology of infectious diseases. Since leaving the National Board of Health, August 2, 1881, I have been obliged to prosecute my experimental work at my own expense, and to purchase expensive microscopical apparatus, in order not to drop out of sight as an investigator in a field in which I have gained some distinction. And this notwithstanding the fact that apparatus of this kind, purchased with government money, has been for two years lying idle at the Army Medical Museum and also in the hands of the National Board of Health.

He called General Murray's attention to "the experience and special training I now have" and expressed confidence that, with suitable backing, he could make substantial contributions to the science of bacteriology and the curbing of infectious diseases. Given the tools he needed and a congenial environment in which to work, he was sure he would be able to "accomplish more for humanity, for the credit of the Medical Corps of the Army, and for my own reputation" than by spending additional months or years performing the routine tasks of an army surgeon. So discouraging had been his efforts to carry on his investigative work under the prevailing handicaps, he complained, that "I am satisfied that it is useless to continue my attempts in this direction, at a post remote from the centers of learning and without encouragement and material assistance from some source." Dr. Sternberg complained as vigorously about the difficulties encompassing the writing and publication of his articles as about his

lack of scientific facilities. He was much too far away from
libraries and other sources of material and from publishers. He
mentioned having had to spend a considerable sum—his own
money, of course—and a great deal of time in order to do some
necessary research in the library of the Surgeon General's office.

He had his eye on two positions in Washington, either of
which would have been ideal for carrying on the kind of work
in which he was so greatly interested. One was the curatorship
of the Army Medical Museum, which in time was to display
mementos of Sternberg achievements as some of its most prized
exhibits. The other was membership on the National Board of
Health.

Army machinery usually moves slowly in peacetime, and it
did in this case—but it moved. In April of the following year
the orders he had been hoping for finally came. They were not
very informative. He was merely ordered to report to the Surgeon General's office in Washington for reassignment.

On this transcontinental trip the Sternbergs found no alkaline dust in their car to get on and into everything they had, or
at least they said nothing about any. Travel generally was much
more pleasant than they had found it in 1869, when they had
traveled extensively through the West for the first time. One
improvement they especially liked was the introduction of dining
cars on the better trains. They were glad to say good-bye forever
to those trackside meal stations where they had wolfed indigest-
ible food while they kept their eyes on their train lest it pull out
without them. There was luxury, contentment, and leisure in taking their time in the diner while they swept over mountains and
plains and through the multitude of small cities and large towns
which had sprung up along the railroad since they first came this
way, headed in the opposite direction.

Being between assignments, Dr. Sternberg might be supposed
to have shed temporarily his responsibilities as a man of medicine.
On that trip, however he found that, like the sloppily dressed
British officer who drew a sharp rebuke from the Duke of Wel-
lington, a doctor is never really "off duty." Late one night, as
they were crossing the mountains, he was shaken lightly but excitedly by the porter. A woman in the car ahead was sick. Would

he see what he could do for her? He was glad to do all he could, of course, and his ready and sympathetic response brightened somewhat the anxious look on the face of the woman's husband, who had accompanied the Negro to the Sternberg berth. There was nothing very comforting in what Dr. Sternberg found in the course of his examination: the woman was suffering from advanced tuberculosis and a serious heart condition. The high altitudes through which they were then passing had aggravated the latter. The porter had not exaggerated a bit when he told him his passenger was "bad off."

The woman was not especially afraid of dying. She seemed reconciled to it. But she was on her way back home and wanted supremely to get there and see her children before she died. That was a modest desire, certainly, and Dr. Sternberg did all he could to make its coming true possible. After administering the medicine he hoped would partly counteract the effects of the high altitude on her heart, he stayed there with her to see how effective it would be. He was sympathy and understanding incarnate. No country doctor fighting for the life of an intimate friend could have fought harder with what he had to fight with—the medicines he had happened to bring with him. As the darkened train finally reached the highest point of its route and began the descent to more normal atmospheric pressures, this distinguished medical scientist turned general practitioner thought he saw a chance that this mother with the sharp pains in her chest and the labored breathing and those homeside youngsters would see each other again before she left them for good. As lower altitudes began to have a beneficial effect upon her heart, that hope and that belief became stronger. But she still had far to go. All he dared tell her was to keep up her spirits and hope for the best. That she was willing to do.

There would be a change of trains a few hours later, for the Sternbergs as well as for the sick woman and her husband. She was in no condition to walk from this train to her berth in the other one. The conductor wired ahead for a wheel chair to be ready upon her arrival, but the message was inexcusably delayed or the person who was supposed to attend to the matter at the junction point was inexcusably negligent. There was no wheel chair at the station when the porter leaped off the train to get it. The woman's revived hopes of seeing her children froze in despair. It would take a long time to obtain another one, and her train would be pulling out soon.

"I'll surely miss my train," she kept gasping over and over. "I'll never see my darling children again."

But she had not taken this army doctor, long experienced in handling difficult situations, into sufficient account.

"Don't worry," he assured her. "You'll make your train. Just wait and see."

There had not been any wheel chairs on the battlefields of the Civil War and the war against the Nez Percés either—often there had not been enough litters to go around—but the wounded, or most of them at any rate, had been carried off to first aid stations without too much suffering and without aggravating their wounds. This situation called for the same kind of treatment.

He asked for a blanket and called upon the woman's husband and two other men to help him. Firmly seizing one corner and asking the others to do the same, he told them to lower it to berth level. Then he asked her to move over onto it as gently as she could while they braced themselves to support her weight. Walking slowly down the aisle to the vestibule and handling their heavy bundle with great care, they carried her out of the car and across the tracks to the waiting train. She showed no ill effects from her unconventional ride, and was most appreciative

The Sternbergs went one way and the sick woman and her husband another, not to see each other again. Dr. Sternberg gave the man his address and asked him to let him know how she got along. The man kept his promise. A week or ten days later Dr. Sternberg tore open a letter addressed in an unfamiliar handwriting. The woman's wish had been granted. She had lived long enough to get home, though not much longer. The reunion with her children had been something the husband and father would never forget. The letter was no literary gem: its author obviously was not an educated man. But, both in what had been written in that semiliterate scrawl and in what had been left unwritten, Dr. Sternberg read an eloquent and heartfelt "Thank you" for his part in bringing that final exciting reunion to pass.

CHAPTER X

Doctor on the Go

DR. STERNBERG did not get either of the posts he coveted, although he did get one which might be considered almost as good, and perhaps in some respects better. He was detailed as attending surgeon and examiner of recruits at Baltimore. There he was just an hour's train ride from Washington and its vast research facilities. He was also within a few blocks of young and vigorous Johns Hopkins University, which was rapidly developing into the sort of institution a medical researcher dreams of. Delighted with the new arrangement, he settled down for what promised to be his best chance to carry on extensive research since he entered the army.

As so often happened to him, events about which he knew nothing were shaping up other things for him. On April 24, 1885, when he had been in that comfortable situation less than a year, he found a telegram on his desk. "The Surgeon General," it said, "wishes to see you at once." Hurrying to Washington to find out what it was all about, he was told that he had been chosen as the American delegate to the International Sanitary Conference to be held the next month in Rome. The main purpose of the conference was to launch an international campaign against cholera, which had appeared in epidemic form in several European countries. The Italian government had requested Secretary of State F. F. Bayard to send two delegates to represent the United States, a technical expert and a diplomatic envoy, but he had decided to send only Dr. Sternberg. The selection had been made in the usual way. The Secretary of State had asked the Secretary of War to recommend someone: the latter had dis-

cussed the request with the Surgeon General, who, in addition
to recommending Dr. Sternberg, had praised his "eminent qualifications" for the assignment. In his letter of instructions Secretary Bayard himself expressed confidence in the appointee's "scientific knowledge and good discretion."

Through Dr. Emile Roux,* to whom he had a letter of introduction, Dr. Sternberg met Pasteur in Paris en route to Rome.
The American visitor later referred to that meeting as one of the
great moments of his life. Pasteur took him on a tour of his laboratory and the nearby buildings where he was also carrying on experimental work. At that time the Frenchman was deeply en-
grossed in his search for an effective preventive for rabies, or hydrophobia. His experiments with animals had been satisfactory,
almost convincing him and his assistants that the vaccine he had
developed would prevent a person bitten by a mad dog or other
rabid animal from developing the fearful disease. He had not,
at the time of Dr. Sternberg's visit, submitted the vaccine to the
supreme test. His reluctance to expose a human being to rabies in
order to demonstrate the preventive power of his vaccine at the
risk of a horrible death in case of failure is altogether understandable. Several weeks later—after Dr. Sternberg had returned
to the United States—the army surgeon learned about nine-year-
old Joseph Meister—how he had been bitten fourteen times by a
mad dog; how his mother had taken him to Pasteur with a plea
to do something—anything—to prevent him from getting hydrophobia; how, after deep soul-searching, Pasteur had given him
the treatment he had formerly been afraid to use on humans;
how the scientist had walked the floor night after night hoping the
treatment would prove successful and prepared to condemn himself if it did not; how, in the slow hours of darkness, he had
dropped off to sleep and dreamed fitfully that the Alsatian lad
had died; how day after day had passed without hydrophobia
developing; and how at last, after those agonizing days and
nights, Pasteur had had the glowing realization that he had really
given humanity an effective defense against one of its most terrifying illnesses. However, there was nothing to make either man

* Dr. Roux some years later developed the diptheria antitoxin.

think such epochal events were just ahead as they discussed Pasteur's work in Paris that day.

Pasteur had suffered a stroke about eighteen months before, and Dr. Sternberg had been concerned about him. He found Pasteur "a vigorous and well preserved man," although not entirely free from evidences of the attack. "There is still some paralysis of some muscles of the left leg," the American wrote in a letter to a medical journal, "and he is obliged to go up and down stairs with caution, but he did not show any indications of fatigue from the extended trip which we made together through the laboratory and the yards in which the animals were kept, which are two or three squares distant from it." The visitor commented more informally on that afternoon's experiences in a letter to Mrs. Sternberg. He told her he had been "well received" and that Pasteur had spent two hours showing him around. Thanks to his knowledge of French, "I understood him perfectly and was able to make myself understood by him." It had indeed been "a very profitable day for me."

In Rome a few days later he met Dr. Koch, his fellow worker from Germany, presumably for the first time. The two men spent a great deal of time together, discussing not only cholera and the other matters that had brought them to the conference but also a great many others in the broad field in which they were both clearing new ground.

Dr. Sternberg delivered a brief address at the opening of the conference on May 20. It was devoted principally to the accomplishments of the last gathering of this kind, held four years earlier in Washington.

On June 8, his forty-seventh birthday, he and the other delegates began a four-day excursion to Naples as guests of the Italian government. Another social diversion that greatly lightened the burden of technical discussions was a state dinner in honor of the delegates, given at the royal palace by King Humbert. His Majesty was "extremely civil." Each delegate was presented to him individually; each had an opportunity to discuss with him the work of the conference or anything else he wanted to. The whole affair, Dr. Sternberg wrote his chief correspondent, "will be remembered with special pleasure."

The American delegate took a prominent part in the conference deliberations. Because of his knowledge of French, he was asked to translate the proceedings into English. The technical subcommittee, of which he was a member, recommended and the conference approved a number of measures to prevent and control outbreaks of cholera. They included the establishment in each country of a "central bureau of sanitary information and notification" to keep in touch with those in other countries and warn of actual or threatened epidemics anywhere in the world. Another measure which received approval provided for the publication and distribution of bulletins describing health conditions in every important city, with particular emphasis upon epidemic diseases. Another called for the immediate reporting by telegraph or cable to all participating governments of the first case of yellow fever or cholera to appear in a community, especially in port cities. Still another had to do with sanitation and the isolation of suspected cholera and yellow fever cases.

On the eve of adjournment Dr. Sternberg received one of the most highly prized distinctions of his career—honorary membership in the Royal Italian Academy of Medicine.

After his return home, he found a number of diseases challenging his searching mind. Malaria did so especially, and with good reason: on November 6, 1880, Alphonse Laveran, a French surgeon on duty in Algeria, had discovered the malaria parasite, but his claim to this distinction had been clouded by those of Klebs and Tomassi-Crudeli. Having shown those latter claims to be baseless, Dr. Sternberg was naturally much interested in Laveran's work. This interest had been increased considerably while in Rome, where he had witnessed, at the San Spirito Hospital, a memorable demonstration conducted by Ettore Marchiafava and Angelo Celli. There, in the blood of malaria patients, he had clearly seen the *Plasmodium malariae* found and demonstrated by Laveran some five years earlier. After that demonstration, he wrote later, "no doubt was left in my mind that I saw living parasitic micro-organisms in the interior of red blood corpuscles obtained from the circulation of malaria fever patients." He was anxious to conduct a similar demonstration of his own as soon as he could.

That opportunity came on March 24, 1886. On that day he received from a physician friend a blood specimen drawn from the finger of a malaria patient. Using Dr. Welch's laboratory at the Johns Hopkins University and in the presence of Dr. Welch and a few others, he saw there in Baltimore the same type of organism he had seen several months earlier in Rome. He subsequently stated on several occasions that this was the first demonstration of the Laveran organism in the United States. The claim has never been seriously challenged.

Meanwhile, Dr. Sternberg had been continuing his work with disinfection and disinfectants. What he had learned he described in an essay entitled "Disinfection and Individual Prophylaxis against Infectious Diseases," which he entered in the 1885 competition for the Lomb Prize, awarded by Henry Lomb, of Rochester, N. Y., through the American Public Health Association. It was declared the winner and brought its author a prize of five hundred dollars. The work, concerned largely with a technical discussion of disinfection, was widely hailed as a notable contribution to medical knowledge. Colonel Hume called it and the studies that packed it with valuable scientific facts "a glorious gain in the battle against communicable diseases." It still ranks high among medical and scientific publications and has been published in many languages practically around the world.

As his work in tuberculosis, disinfectants, malaria, and other fields of investigation caused him to be compared more and more to Koch, Dr. Sternberg wanted more and more to know the German bacteriologist better. He began laying his plans to go to Berlin as soon as a trip could be arranged. In 1886, about a year after his trip to Rome, he was at last able to go.

Dr. Koch showed much interest in all of Dr. Sternberg's work and was especially interested in his chance discovery of the pneumococcus. He asked for a demonstration of its presence in the Sternberg saliva. The request caused the visitor considerable anxiety. For he had learned that pneumococci were not constantly present in his saliva. He could not tell when it would be found and when it would not. It would be extremely embarrassing to fail to produce it for such a distinguished witness. As it turned out, however, his anxiety was groundless. After worrying about it all night, he returned to the Koch laboratories, produced some saliva, and found numerous pneumococci.

Back in Baltimore, Dr. Sternberg began exploring still another field. Several years earlier—in 1880—Karl Joseph Eberth of Halle, Germany, had discovered the *Bacillus typhosus* in the tissues of typhoid fever patients, definitely linking the organism with the disease. But in a decade crowded with revolutionary discoveries in the fields of medicine and bacteriology, this one had not attracted a great deal of interest, even among physicians. However, Dr. Sternberg was much interested in it. And at the 1886 meeting of the Association of American Physicians he read a paper telling in considerable detail about Eberth's work and the part it was likely to play in the future effort to curb typhoid. The interest stimulated by that paper did much to make American medicine typhoid-conscious and, to a considerable extent, advanced the eventual curbing of this once highly fatal, now relatively unimportant, disease.

At its 1885 meeting in Washington, at which Dr. Sternberg won the Lomb award, the American Public Health Association had adopted resolutions requesting Congress to send a commission of yellow fever experts to Brazil and Mexico to investigate the claims of men in those countries that they had discovered the yellow fever germ and had provided protective immunity to the disease. Members of Congress introduced the requested legislation, but it failed to stimulate much enthusiasm. The effort was renewed two years later, however, and this time fared better. The legislation that resulted provided, not for the suggested commission, but for a single yellow fever expert, to be appointed by the President.

Grover Cleveland turned to Surgeon General John Moore for a recommendation. The latter promptly recommended Dr. Sternberg, calling him "a physician thoroughly equipped by many years of special study in the line of special investigation." The Surgeon General wrote that he "would be the choice of nine-tenths of the most eminent medical men in civil life in this country." The President officially informed Dr. Sternberg of his appointment on April 28, 1887. He was directed to go first to Brazil to evaluate the claims of Dr. Domingos Freire and then to make a similar evaluation of the claims of Dr. Carmona y Valle in Mexico. An October 1 deadline was set for the completion of both missions—not much time to travel so far and accomplish so much.

Less than a week after his appointment he sailed, with Mrs. Sternberg, on the S. S. *Alliance* for Rio de Janeiro. Taking no chances on finding himself handicapped by inadequate facilities, he carried along a complete set of laboratory equipment.

There was a brief stop-over at St. Thomas. There they had a tragic reminder of the grim fury of the enemy he was then tracking. In a small cemetery not far from the pier they saw the graves of several Moravian missionaries. A single disease had killed all of them—yellow fever.

Already fretting over the necessity of having to do so much before that October 1 deadline, Dr. Sternberg found himself threatened with the loss of a great deal of time because of other people's heedlessness. Coolly disregarding warnings that Para was ablaze with yellow fever, two women passengers went ashore during a stop-over there. A few days later both developed the disease. Knowing that their condition upon arrival would determine whether and for how long the ship would be quarantined, he watched their day-to-day progress with considerable anxiety. Here again, however, his worry was unjustified. The two ladies made an excellent recovery and were among the first to leave the ship at Rio.

Dr. Sternberg had discussed the Freire claims with Pasteur during his Paris visit two years earlier, and the Frenchman had left no doubt as to his complete lack of faith in them. His extreme skepticism, Pasteur had told Dr. Sternberg, had caused him to turn down an invitation from the Emperor of Brazil to do what Dr. Sternberg was now doing—to go to that country and make a thorough-going test of the Freire claims. The invitation had been due, the Frenchman had told the American, to the Emperor's own lack of faith in Freire's claims.

Even without Pasteur's skepticism, Dr. Sternberg would have been strongly inclined to consider the claims baseless. He had been studying them and trying to evaluate them, as best he could at such a great distance, for some time. His conclusions had made him as great a skeptic as his French friend. Nevertheless, he had started out on this mission with an open mind and a determination to get at the truth, regardless of whether it agreed or failed to agree with his own preconceived ideas. As he wrote in his report, "the writer was glad to undertake the investigation," although "the published work of Dr. Freire... did not impress him with confidence as regards the scientific value of the alleged discoveries." He realized that, in spite of the evidence which had already accumulated in his mind, "the possibility remained that there was a germ of truth in the background."

Nevertheless, to both of Dr. Freire's claims—that he had discovered the causative organism of yellow fever and that he had protected nonimmunes against it by inoculation with a vaccine made from that organism—Dr. Sternberg, after completing his experiments, replied with a firm and positive "no." Each claim, he reported, was "without scientific foundation."

In spite of his early belief that he probably would have to make this kind of report, the making of it was an extremely distasteful duty to this friendly man of science, who not only hoped for great things from the infant science of bacteriology but also was reluctant to hurt a fellow scientist. He never made a more truthful statement than when he said after his return: "It is always an ungrateful task to criticize the work of those who have earnestly and conscientiously sought to elucidate unsettled questions in science, and especially so when the object in view is the amelioration of human suffering." Although his opinion of Dr. Freire as a man changed later, he appears at that time to have considered him a serious, honest, and truthful, though badly mistaken, scientific investigator.

His job at Rio finished, Dr. and Mrs. Sternberg took ship on August 11, less than two months before that tantalizing October 1 deadline, for the long trip northward. He intended to travel on this ship only as far as Barbados or St. Thomas. At one of those places he expected to transfer to another ship bound for Vera Cruz.

One night, several days out of Rio, Mrs. Sternberg awoke with chills that made her shake and shiver violently in her berth. These were not a sure-fire symptom of yellow fever, but they were enough to frighten her husband, who had seen similar chills followed by bad cases of that disease. The ship's surgeon and the stewardess became worried too. They and Dr. Sternberg began worrying a great deal more when Mrs. Sternberg began having sharp pains and dull aches here and there over her body. News, especially that kind of news, travels swiftly on shipboard. By breakfast time the word had spread around that the army medical officer's wife had yellow fever. Suddenly the general area of the Sternberg stateroom became the most unpopular part of the ship, and their neighbors requested the purser to move them.

Fortunately both Dr. Sternberg's fears and that mercurial evacuation of that part of the ship turned out to be unjustified. About the time Mrs. Sternberg made a yellow fever diagnosis seem practically inevitable by developing a voracious thirst and running an extremely high temperature she also experienced itching and pain in her left arm. Both were traced to a small-pox vaccination which Rio authorities had insisted upon her taking soon after their arrival, weeks earlier. Her husband, vast-ly relieved, nevertheless found it hard to believe any smallpox vaccination had waited so long to "take." A young woman who had been vaccinated at the same time had a severe reaction a few days afterward. Dr. Sternberg had an explanation: "That English virus must have been contaminated." Contaminated or not, slow-acting it undoubtedly was, though it nevertheless ran true to form. After the usual day or two of itching and pain, the angry area on her arm cleared up nicely, leaving an orthodox vaccination scar that stood between her and smallpox infection for many years.

At Barbados the Sternbergs found there was no ship sched-uled to sail for a Mexican port anytime soon. Even if there had been, they would not have been able to take it, for the smallpox epidemic at Rio which had caused Mrs. Sternberg to submit to that delayed-action vaccination caused the local health authori-ties to slap a quarantine on the ship and its passengers. They ran into the same difficulty at St. Thomas, and had no choice but to stay with the ship all the way to New York. An exasperat-ing delay, but there was nothing they could do about it.

Dr. Sternberg moved as rapidly as possible after the ship docked. Dismissing any idea of proceeding to Vera Cruz by boat, he went, without Mrs. Sternberg this time, by train. The Surgeon General acceded to his request to move back that deadline twenty days.

Both Dr. Carmona y Valle and his principal assistant, Dr. Angel Gavino Yglesias, received him cordially and assisted him in every way possible. But their courtesy and co-operation did not prevent him from making the kind of report they hoped he would not make. The Carmona y Valle organism, he concluded after completing his experiments, was present in the blood and urine of yellow fever patients only by accident. It did not have anything at all to do with causing the disease. That being true, inoculation with a culture made from that organism could provide no immunity whatsoever to those who had not had yellow fever.

"The claims of Dr. Carmona y Valle of Mexico to have discovered the specific cause of yellow fever have no scientific basis," Dr. Sternberg reported, "and he has failed to demonstrate the protective value of his proposed methods of prophylaxis." However, he was not willing to let that cold statement stand alone. He told of his personal regret that he could not bring news more favorable to his fellow scientists in both Brazil and Mexico and more promising of good things for the people of the world:

No one regrets more than I do that the question of the etiology of yellow fever is not yet solved in a definite manner, but I at least have not to reproach myself with want of diligence or failure to embrace every opportunity for pursuing the research. . . . It would have been extremely gratifying to the writer if he had been able to announce as a result of his investigations that the specific germ of yellow fever had been discovered in Brazil, or in Mexico, and that a reliable method of prophylaxis by inoculation is now successfully practiced in one or the other of these countries. Such a report would be easily written and gladly received by the medical profession in this country and in Europe, but unfortunately I am unable to make a favorable report, and to sustain a negative [report] and show wherein these gentlemen above named have in my opinion been mistaken calls for an elaborate and extended statement of facts, which I am aware will have but little interest for the majority of the profession; but those who do take the pains to read it will find, I trust, that I have fully sustained the position taken. . . .

Subsequent events showed that he had indeed "fully sustained the position taken." Although Drs. Freire and Carmona y Valle continued to peddle their wares for some time, they had no standing among American men of medicine. And of course others eventually found out for themselves what Dr. Sternberg had made plain—that their claims were entirely unjustified.

CHAPTER XI

Bodies and Bacilli

DR. STERNBERG received a short leave after his return from Mexico, then went back to Baltimore as attending surgeon and examiner of recruits once more. This proved an extremely pleasant, though, again, a brief interlude. The infant but lusty Johns Hopkins University, which had previously made him an honorary fellow, gave him the full run of its laboratories. He worked alongside the stimulating Dr. Welch and the others who were making the Johns Hopkins Medical School an institution of distinction. President Daniel Coit Gilman went to special pains to make him feel welcome. Mrs. Gilman added her gracious bit to the feeling that he and Mrs. Sternberg were among warm friends. And beyond the university campus there was a rapidly growing city where Dr. Sternberg found other men of science who made extraordinarily congenial company.

As pleasant as all this was, however, he did not find it altogether satisfying. In Havana, in Brazil, and in Mexico he had been greatly handicapped by his inability to obtain all the research material—more specifically, human bodies—he needed. Many hospital administrators, he had found, were frankly or covertly opposed to post-mortem examinations for any purpose. They had rushed the bodies of yellow fever victims off to the cemeteries as soon as possible after death. Even when hospital officials themselves had been willing to co-operate, others had not been. Usually the latter had been motivated by the prevailing fear that to handle or even be around such a body was deadly dangerous. Such people were little interested in scientific advancement and greatly interested in getting the cadavers out of the hospitals and underground quickly and with a minimum of handling. Often they were afraid to be around a body even long enough to prepare it decently for burial. Many were committed to the earth without benefit of caskets and with only such protection as might be provided by bed sheets saturated with bichloride of mercury or carbolic acid solution. Dr. Sternberg had learned from frustrating experience that human bodies were practically useless for experimental purposes unless obtained within two hours after death.

Having been unfortunate enough to be in Havana when there were relatively few yellow fever cases, he decided to go back there during an epidemic. His request for permission to do so was readily granted, and he sailed on April 23, 1888. He had another good reason for making the trip at that time. Still another scientist had announced the discovery of the yellow fever organism. Dr. Paul Gibier, of France, had become interested in the Freire claims some time earlier and had been in Havana since the previous fall trying to find the bacillus the Brazilian claimed to have identified. Having failed to do so (understandably enough, in the light of the Sternberg revelations) and therefore having lost faith in the Freire claims even before the Sternberg report was made public, he had embarked upon studies of his own in an effort to do what Dr. Freire had obviously failed to do. After several months of experimentation and tests, he had tentatively announced the discovery of the yellow fever organism. He had found it, he said, not in the blood but in the alimentary tract of yellow fever patients. Dr. Gibier had been by no means positive in his claims, however. In fact he had gone to considerable pains to present them with marked reservations. But he had indicated that he thought the organism he had been studying probably was the long-sought agent of yellow fever.

Dr. Gibier co-operated wholeheartedly with Dr. Sternberg, turning over to him a culture of his bacillus immediately after the latter's arrival. But once again the American found himself under the extremely unpleasant necessity of refuting a fellow scientist's claim. The Gibier organism killed laboratory animals all right. But Dr. Sternberg's researches "give no support to the supposition that it is concerned in the etiology of yellow fever."

Having exposed several other people's claims as unfounded, Dr. Sternberg again set out to find that baffling organism himself. He wrote Mrs. Sternberg on May 14 that he was "having some interesting results" from his experiments. However, he had found "nothing definite yet," although "it is possible that I am on the right track." Three days later he told her:

I have some good news for you. I believe that at last I have discovered the yellow fever germ in the stomach and intestines. I have also obtained it in cultures from the kidney and urine. I will not attempt to give you particulars but there are several good reasons for believing that the bacillus which I get in my cultures is the long sought yellow fever germ. Last night I went to the Military Hospital at half past one for an autopsy and this morning at 5 o'clock I was at work in my laboratory. I have only had two autopsies as yet, but they were typical cases and both give me the bacillus in question. . . . It is not found in the blood. As I am the first one to cultivate it and to describe its characters [sic] I must be considered the real discoverer. . . . I am feeling very well and very cheerful at what I believe to be a successful search.

A few days later he was in even higher spirits:

I am getting on famously and as I wrote you believe I have at last discovered the yellow fever germ. I have now had three autopsies and find it in every case, not in the blood but in the stomach and intestines. It kills rabbits and guinea pigs and in a guinea pig which died on the 4th day the characteristic black liquid was in the intestines in large quantity. . . . I am feeling very well and very happy at having accomplished that which I so long have been trying for.

His next letter, written on May 23, was still more optimistic:

I am getting on all right with my work. The announcement I made to you is fully confirmed and I shall publish the discovery very soon. Dr. Gibier who has been here four or five months has published the discovery of a different germ and he is wrong. I have not encountered his bacillus in any of my cases. . . I keep very well and enjoy my laboratory work on account of the very definite and satisfactory results I have attained.

During the next week, however, he began to be assailed by doubts. As more autopsies were performed he thought he found his germ in the stomachs and intestines of those who had died from other diseases. But his optimism returned early in June. On the fifth he wrote:

I am regaining confidence in my germ. Indeed there was no good reason for losing it. I thought I had found the same thing in other cases, not yellow fever, but it turns out that though similar in appearance they are not the same thing.

His hopes fell once again soon afterward. On June 8, his fiftieth birthday, he confided his increasing doubts to his chief correspondent and most sympathetic confidante:

> I can see now that I will not be able to make a definite announcement of a discovery. The best I can say is that there is some probability that my *Bacillus A* is the yellow fever germ. I shall have a lot of work to do again after my return home.

His crescendoing doubts were fully justified. Although he wrote to Mrs. Sternberg on June 16, five days before sailing, that "I still have hopes," there was a marked absence of the enthusiasm and almost complete confidence he had expressed earlier. In the end, he had to give himself the same sad news he had been obliged to give those others searching for the yellow fever organism. The Sternberg *Bacillus A*, after offering bright promise at first, faded into disappointment and failure under the stern tests of laboratory experimentation.

One of Dr. Sternberg's fellow workers during that brief stay in Havana was Dr. Carlos Finlay, a Cuban with a passion for finding hard-to-find truths. The two men, different in so many ways, became warm friends. Dr. Finlay had been doing considerable exploration in the fascinating world of yellow fever transmission, and his diligent labor and brilliant, searching mind had come up with the conviction that a certain micrococcus, which he named *Micrococcus tetragenus febris flavae*, was the object of his and other scientists' search. He had isolated it, not in the blood or alimentary tract of yellow fever patients, but in mosquitoes which had fed on the blood of those who had this disease. This discovery led Dr. Finlay's methodical mind to the conclusion not only that his microorganism caused yellow fever but also that the mosquito played a part in yellow fever transmission. In this latter and revolutionary conclusion he had the support of a few other medical scientists, notably Dr. Josiah Nott of Mobile, Alabama. As early as 1848 Dr. Nott had strongly suggested that the mosquito was an important link in the chain of yellow fever transmission. Dr. Sternberg himself had given the mosquito-transmission theory a measure of indirect support: he had gone counter to the almost universally held medical opinion that yellow fever was contracted by physical association. He had written as early as 1881:

> There are doubtless many facts upon record which seem to point strongly to personal contagion, and one recent writer [Berenger-Feraud] considers the question settled in the affirmative. . . . [However] the writer may be permitted to say that in his personal experience. . . no facts have come under his observation which give the least support to a belief in personal contagion.*

After his return to Baltimore Dr. Sternberg received and test-ed in his Johns Hopkins laboratory a number of cultures which the energetic Dr. Finlay had made of the organism which had stirred his enthusiasm. The latter asked Dr. Sternberg to study them and report upon their place in the yellow fever picture. In spite of his great admiration for Dr. Finlay, however, his re-port was negative: while the Finlay organism was undoubtedly present in the blood of yellow fever patients, its presence was only accidental, due probably to contamination of the blood while it was being collected. The American had found it in the blood of victims of other diseases too. "There is," he reported, this time with particular reluctance, "no reason to believe that this organism has anything to do with the etiology of yellow fever. . . ."

In late September, 1888, Dr. Sternberg was in Decatur, Ala-bama, then being swept by one of the most explosive yellow fever epidemics ever to appear in the South. There he was closely as-sociated with Dr. Jerome Cochran, Alabama State Health Officer. Both men had good reason to remember that Decatur epidemic as long as they lived. Dr. Cochran won the militant hostility of the local physicians and the citizenry generally, was roundly de-nounced as an ignoramus and a fraud, and was all but run out of town because he had publicly (and, of course, correctly) diag-nosed those mysterious cases as yellow fever. Local civic pride was hurt, and it was feared the statement that there was yellow fever in Decatur would have a bad effect on business. As for Dr. Sternberg, it was at Decatur that he got his first chance in this country to try out a new treatment he had devised for the

---

* "Yellow Fever," in *The Cyclopedia of Practical Medicine,* Supplement (Philadelphia: Blanchard and Lea, 1881), pp. 45-73.

disease. Now inclined to believe the yellow fever organism was to be found in the alimentary canal, in spite of his failure to link his *Bacillus A* with this form of illness, he had been giving much study to a form of therapy aimed at attacking that organism in that part of the body. Acting on the well-established fact that the urine, vomited matter, and other discharges from the intestines are strongly acid, he had assembled a highly alkaline treatment to curb the development of microorganisms in the alimentary canal. It consisted of the administration of an extremely weak solution of bicarbonate of soda and bichloride of mercury.

The new mode of treatment had an auspicious beginning in Decatur. (It had previously been tried out on a limited scale in Havana.) He wrote Mrs. Sternberg as early as October 10 that "two of the physicians are now using my treatment and report excellent results thus far." Ten days later he told her the results to date had been "excellent." The only death that had occurred among the dozen Decatur yellow fever victims who had received the Sternberg therapy had resulted from "a bad case in a plethoric man addicted to drink." During the entire epidemic 40 per cent of the white and 20 per cent of the Negro patients treated by the conventional methods had succumbed. Not one of the 32 Negroes and only an eighth of the white people receiving the Sternberg alkaline treatment had done so.

Successful results were also reported from other epidemic centers. During an Havana outbreak 10 cases at Garcini Hospital, including 6 that were particularly serious, received the Sternberg treatment, and all recovered. At another Havana hospital all 3 patients under this mode of treatment recovered. A Jacksonville, Florida, physician who used it along with other procedures on 216 patients reported that the bichloride and soda treatment "gave the best results by all odds." More specifically, the mortality rate among his white patients treated by the Sternberg method was only 6.3 per cent, against a rate of more than 22 per cent among white people treated by other methods. There were no deaths at all among 27 Negroes receiving the Sternberg alkaline treatment. No mention was made of the number of deaths or death rate among Negroes treated by other methods.

"Magnificent results" were reported from its use in a Brazilian epidemic: of 34 patients treated in that way, only one had died.

Still unwilling, in spite of the evidence of his own tests, to concede that his *Bacillus A* was not the yellow fever organism, Dr. Sternberg was eager to be in Havana during the 1889 epidemic season and continue his studies, which had been cut short the previous summer by the arbitrary deadline set by his official superiors. His request for permission to make the trip was readily granted. Remembering that earlier experience, he asked for and was given enough time to do a satisfactory job—from mid-March to early September.

A few days before sailing he again expressed confidence in the existence, somewhere in the human body, of a specific organism responsible for yellow fever. On March 5, 1889, he told a quarantine conference in Montgomery, Alabama:

> I may say, before going any further, that my faith in a living infectious agent as the specific cause of this disease is by no means diminished by my failure thus far to demonstrate the exact form and nature of this hypothetical "germ." The present state of knowledge with reference to the etiology of infectious diseases in general, and well known facts relating to the origin and spread of yellow fever epidemics, fully justify such a belief. The *a priori* ground for such faith I stated as long ago as 1873, in a paper published in the *Journal of the Medical Sciences;** and the progress of knowledge since that date has all been in the direction of supporting this *a priori* reasoning. But yellow fever is by no means the only infectious disease in which satisfactory evidence of the existence of a living infectious agent is still wanting.

Back in Havana, Dr. Sternberg got in touch with Dr. Finlay, who of course bore no resentment over the outcome of the Sternberg investigation of his *Micrococcus tetragenus febris flavae.* On the contrary, he had accepted the report in good grace and freely conceded that he had been mistaken. Soon after Dr. Sternberg's arrival both men attended a meeting of the Academy of Sciences, at which Dr. Finlay told about the Sternberg studies and publicly acknowledged the correctness of his American friend's conclusions.

Dr. Sternberg was pleased to find that the Cuban officials

---

* "An Inquiry into the Nature of the Yellow Fever Poison, with an Account of the Disease as it occurred at Governor's Island, New York Harbor," *American Journal of the Medical Sciences* (new series), CXXIX (January, 1873), 398-406.

were much interested in his work—a great deal more so than the previous summer—and were apparently eager to help him. That was encouraging in view of his inability on his earlier visits to obtain the bodies he needed. Soon after his arrival he had interesting news from Brazil. From a clipping from the Rio de Janeiro *Journal do Commerce* which someone had sent him, he learned that Dr. Freire had continued large-scale inoculations against yellow fever in spite of the Sternberg findings, which the Brazilian was apparently determined to ignore. The results of these inoculations, the paper said, had been altogether unsatisfactory, causing Dr. Freire to be criticized "without mercy." The article included a long list of people who had died of yellow fever in spite of the immunity supposed to have been conferred by the Freire inoculations. Somewhat later Dr. Sternberg learned that all nine members of a certain family which had been "protected" in this way had developed the disease. Two of them had died. Convinced as he long had been of the baselessness of the Freire claims, he did not find this news particularly surprising, but he did find considerable satisfaction in having this additional evidence of the soundness of his own findings.

In spite of those promises of full co-operation he had received from the Havana authorities, he again faced the same problem that had given him such great concern the previous summer, a shortage of bodies of recently deceased yellow fever victims. The blame did not lie with those officials: there just were not many bodies. The expected epidemic had not materialized. That was a great blessing to the people of Havana, of course, but it was disastrous to yellow fever research. He wrote Mrs. Sternberg after he had been there about three weeks that he had not had a single autopsy. Moreover, the outlook for the future was far from bright: "There are only three or four cases at present in the Military Hospital and none in the civil hospital."

He complained again about the lack of experimental material two days later. He was "not getting on at all' with his investigations, because "I have not yet been able to get an autopsy." However, "it can't be long before some of the unfortunate Spanish soldiers will fall victims to yellow fever."

He was able to make some headway nevertheless. And the

results seemed promising. His hopes of doing for yellow fever what Koch had done for tuberculosis received a substantial boost when—having succeeded in obtaining a few bodies—his studies led him to conclude that a certain type of organism, different from any he had yet thought of in connection with this disease, was uniformly present in yellow fever cases. He hoped to be able to identify it positively with yellow fever as soon as he could obtain enough bodies to make a satisfactory study. Sobered by his earlier disappointment, he curbed his enthusiasm this time. He reminded Mrs. Sternberg on May 6 that "the discovery [of the yellow fever organism] is not an easy one to make." Even if this search should prove as fruitless as his earlier one however, he was sure it would advance the eventual conquest of yellow fever: "Whether I demonstrate the germ or not, my work will stand as scientific work of value in this department of research."

Later tests were disappointing. He wrote Mrs. Sternberg on May 13 that, while he had found some other organisms that seemed to have possibilities, "so far as I can see, I am no nearer a solution of the main question." However, he had no thought of quitting:

I am doing my work thoroughly and, if I don't demonstrate the specific germ, it won't be for want of working faithfully by the most approved methods, and no one else is likely to make an easy discovery in the field if I have to give up in the end.

He was more encouraged after making a few more tests:

My big anaerobic bacillus* is coming to the front as the possible yellow fever germ. I have obtained it more frequently than any other organism in material kept in the lab. for forty-eight hours. It is the most difficult organism to cultivate I have ever encountered.

He was not any too optimistic, even then: "However, I have not as yet any satisfactory evidence that it is the thing I am after."

He found in mid-May that one of his anaerobic bacilli produced yellow fever in guinea pigs. An animal which had been inoculated with the bacillus had died on the second day thereafter. A few days later he was "beginning to entertain pretty strong hopes" of that bacillus, but still had nothing definite in the way of results. Eventually he realized that that bacillus,

* An organism which grows best in the absence of air.

which he had named *Bacillus N*, was not the cause of yellow fever. He had found the very same organism in the liver and kidney of a person who had died of tuberculosis. A little later he found it also in the body of someone who had succumbed to heart disease. Still, he was not defeated: there were some other anaerobic bacilli which had also given yellow fever to laboratory animals, and he was going to put them to the test.

His best hope after that disappointment appeared to be an organism he had named *Bacillus X*. He had found it to be "very pathogenic for guinea pigs." It was "now principally engaging my attention." At any rate, he was not yet ready to throw in the sponge:

> If I remain in good health and keep on with my work for a couple of months yet, I shall feel that I have done all in my power to settle the question and, if it is not settled, will have to give up to [the?] job, for I am quite sincere in saying that I want to make this last effort.

His enthusiasm for his *Bacillus X* soon equaled and even exceeded that which he had formerly had for the other one. In a letter to Mrs. Sternberg written on May 23, he called it "the most promising yet" and "very pathogenic." A few days later he referred to it as "my main hope" and wrote of his grim determination to "follow this trail until I have evidence that is satisfactory one way or the other." At the fatiguing end of a busy day in which he had performed two autopsies, he wrote her that he was "encouraged with reference to my *Bacillus X*." His tests had shown it to be "very pathogenic for rabbits and guinea pigs." He hoped he would continue to find it in the bodies of yellow fever victims and, of course, nowhere else. In that happy event, "it may turn out to be the specific microbe I have so long been in search of."

His letter of June 9 told her he was "getting along very well with my work." He still had "considerable confidence" in his *Bacillus X*. However, the outlook turned dark early in July. He kept on finding new bacilli in the intestines of yellow fever victims, but none of them was found with sufficient regularity or constancy to make him think it was a causative factor in the disease. Even his *Bacillus X* had failed him. He felt "quite discouraged at times," he confessed on July 9 to the only person who was following the irregular course of his hopes and disappointments. Nevertheless, he was sure he had not been wasting his time, for "at least I have gone over the ground faithfully, and, if I fail in the end, it won't be for lack of patient and careful work."

His pessimism regarding his *Bacillus X* did not last long. Later studies, as more bodies came under his efficient scalpel, revived his faith in it. "I am feeling more encouraged with reference to my *Bacillus X*," he told Mrs. Sternberg on July 26, "and I think now I will probably be able to announce it as a probable specific agent, even if I can't claim to have made a complete demonstration of it." His optimism rose even higher a little later. He wrote her on August 7:

> I am again quite hopeful with reference to my *Bacillus X* and have proved by experiment that it produces a deadly volatile ptomaine. I have collected this in distilled water from culture of *Bacillus X* and injected it into rabbits, which die from such injections in a few hours. ... You can say to my friends who ask you that I have strong hopes that I have discovered the right germ but am not yet prepared to announce positively that this is the case.

He still was not prepared "to announce positively that this is the case" when he started packing in late August for the return trip. But he could say, as he did in one of his letters, that "I have done all I can in this way" and that "I have in my collection all of the germs to be found in yellow fever cadavers, unless it be by accident or exception, in which case they have no importance so far as etiology is concerned." He was looking forward to continuing his studies after getting back home, using the material he had assembled.

Unfortunately, both the Sternberg alkaline treatment procedure and the *Bacillus X* in which he had placed so much hope eventually went the way of the Freire and Carmona y Valle organisms, Dr. Sternberg's own earlier organisms, and the others that had been subjected to the severe test of extended laboratory experimentation. As more and more yellow fever patients were treated with the sodium bicarbonate-bichloride of mercury formula, the ratio of recoveries to cases treated dropped sharply. During the next decade and longer, or until the nature of the disease, its exact method of propagation, and the measures by which it can be prevented were definitely revealed—under the Sternberg guidance—yellow fever continued its unchecked sweep whenever conditions favorable to its appearance arose. Those who developed it continued to die from it. As for the Sternberg effort to isolate and identify yellow fever's causative organism, later studies were to show that he was then completely on the wrong track. It was not in the patient's intestines or liver, but in his blood, that that yellow fever organism was finally to be found, identified, and rendered impotent.

These twin failures, however, were apparent, not real. Dr. Sternberg, now unchallengeably the country's leading authority on yellow fever, did not waste his time in Havana. Negative though his results were at the time, they made vastly easier the work of others who were to follow him in the search for the answers to yellow fever's vast mysteries. Having, as he said, collected and studied practically all the organisms present in the intestinal tract and having found all of them unrelated to the cause or propagation of this disease, he had greatly limited the field of research. Those who took up the quest after he went on to other tasks were able to concentrate their efforts upon those relatively small areas of exploration that still remained, after the Sternberg eliminations, as potential hiding places of that organism. Indeed it is not too much to say that, without these preliminary studies, the eventual mastery of this ancient and destructive enemy would have been delayed indefinitely.

CHAPTER XII

Microscopes and Men

DISAPPOINTED though he was over his failure to isolate and identify the yellow fever organism, Dr. Sternberg nevertheless had found a serene contentment in that work. In the last few years he had learned, if he had not fully realized it before, that at heart he was not an army officer, not even a doctor in the usual sense of the word, but a bacteriologist, a miner for the priceless treasure of medical knowledge. Frustrations and disappointments had not prevented him from being extremely happy. He was never to be so congenially employed again as long as he lived.

The first intimation he had that this was soon to end came about a year after his return from that 1889 trip to Havana. A vacancy occurred in the grade of lieutenant colonel in October, 1890, and, as the ranking major in the Medical Corps, he was therefore directly in line for promotion. Advancement is almost always pleasant, but in his case it would demand a price he was reluctant to pay. It would mean the end of his work as a bacteriologist, at least on the scale on which he had been doing it, and a return to the conventional duties of an army medical officer.

It looked for a while as though Major Sternberg might step even higher than a lieutenant colonelcy. Surgeon General John Moore retired in August, 1890, and was succeeded by Colonel Jedediah H. Baxter, who died before the year's end. Immediately a number of Dr. Sternberg's friends began boosting him for the post. Dr. James K. Barnes, Surgeon General at the time of the Fort Barrancas yellow fever epidemics, wrote the President about his "valuable and efficient services" in controlling them. Another booster, Enoch Pratt, president of the National Farmers and Planters Bank of Baltimore and founder of that city's Enoch Pratt Free Public Library, called him, in a letter to the White House, "the most capable and most creditable" of all those available. "Surgeon Sternberg is one of the most eminent medical scientists of the age and has contributed very greatly to the advancement of that science," Major General John McAlaster Schofield, commanding general of the Army, wrote to the Secretary of War. "He has also performed ably and bravely every variety of duty devolving upon a medical officer of the Army, with an Army in the field in time of war, in campaigns against hostile Indians and in the midst of epidemic diseases."

A particularly hearty and enthusiastic endorsement came from one of the cities where Dr. Sternberg had served during the Civil War. Dr. George T. Leick, Cleveland health officer, praised his "rare executive ability" and his "zeal and devotion to those under his charge," which, Dr. Leick affirmed, "won him the respect and admiration of all those who were fortunate enough to come in contact with him." Moreover, he continued, "I will further add that no American surgeon stands higher in the eyes of his foreign confreres than Dr. Sternberg. The older surgeons and physicians of this city who are familiar with his work while here are unanimous in their praises of his management and rare executive ability during those trying days." Others promoting the Sternberg-for-Surgeon General movement included Andrew Carnegie, Marshall Field, ten United States senators, numerous public health officials, and a large number of business executives.

In spite of all this praise, however, Dr. Sternberg did not win the appointment. The presidential favor fell upon Colonel Charles Sutherland. The orders that accompanied the official notice of Sternberg's own military promotion sent the new lieutenant colonel far from his beloved Baltimore, almost as far indeed as they possibly could without taking him out of the country entirely. When his Baltimore and Washington friends came to tell him goodbye and wish him success and contentment in his new assignment as medical purveyor at San Francisco, he experienced a sadness of farewell that was particularly deep. These friendly expressions were all poignant reminders that he was indeed bidding a long farewell to a work he loved as much as he loved those friends he was leaving behind.

Mrs. Sternberg called that San Francisco tour of duty "a sudden and complete change of mental occupation" for her husband. The change was even greater than he had anticipated and feared. It was like plunging into a cold bath, this giving up, or at least greatly curtailing, his quest for tiny organisms and trying to transfer to the tedious details of his new work some of the enthusiasm that had made him so happy in the old. It would be hard to imagine a nearer approach to a pole-to-pole change. Inevitably, the uprooted bacteriologist had a struggle to adjust himself and his thinking to his new duties and his new environment. He did manage to find odd hours he could do with as he pleased—the time a less devoted researcher would have spent in social activities or in other forms of relaxation and amusement. Many of those jealously hoarded hours he devoted to work in his crude laboratory. Others he spent reading the medical and scientific journals he had brought with him and those to which he had subscribed since his transfer. But the most ambitious task he gamely set for himself was the completion of his *Manual of Bacteriology*, on which he had been working, as conditions permitted, for some time.

Ironically enough, his troubles were increased by his reputation as America's top bacteriologist. There were insistent invitations to address learned societies, business groups, and the general public. Many of them he was able to turn down; others, for one reason and another, he was constrained to accept. Besides the time he had to spend at the meeting places and en route, it was necessary for him to devote many hours, sacrificed from his time for independent research, to the writing of his papers or the taking of extensive notes and the making of the photomicrographs which he found so useful and informative. One reason Dr. Sternberg found it hard to turn down speaking engagements of this kind was that he liked them. He enjoyed being with people, found it stimulating to be facing a mentally alert, questioning audience, and was pleased with the responses these public appearances brought. No orator in the spell-binding sense, he was nevertheless a forceful speaker. His manner was impressive. His voice was strong and pleasant. Whether he read a formal paper or spoke from notes, he gave an impression of being completely at home with his subject and of knowing what he was talking about.

Between the work he was obliged to do and that which he undertook on his own, he was obviously an extremely busy man. The heavy double burden he was carrying caused Mrs. Sternberg a great deal of anxiety lest he overdo himself. He "scarcely ever gave himself an hour's leisure," she complained of those San Francisco months, and she was constantly oppressed by fears of a physical breakdown. To protect him from his own excessive industry as much as she could, she would drag him as often as possible away from his laboratory and writing desk to engage in lighter pursuits. She managed to revive to a certain extent his early enthusiasm for botany after years of neglect, and from time to time persuaded him to go with her on brief trips to Monterey and other places where there was a chance of their finding rare plants. Occasionally they would drive to Golden Gate Park, a thousand-acre blanket of exotic plants and rare growths that ended only at the very edge of the blue Pacific. Once away from the happy slavery of his work, he enjoyed these outings. Mrs. Sternberg was sure they were doing him lots of good.

In spite of these reluctant but pleasant diversions, he managed to make steady headway on his *Manual of Bacteriology*. Week by week it crept onward toward completion. At last it was finished, a monumental work of some nine hundred pages, covering in magnificent detail every phase of its subject. Nearly half a thousand different specimens of microorganisms were listed, classified, and described. The work was extensively illustrated with a wealth of original photomicrographs, the choicest items in his vast collection. The book easily stood at the top in its field for many years as the standard textbook and reference work for students and research workers. In both its original form, as published in 1892, and its revised edition, which appeared in 1896, it caused many of Dr. Sternberg's friends and also others who did not know him personally to write him enthusiastic letters. One that he especially prized came from Walter Reed, then on duty with the Department of Dakota and later to be closely associated with him in an epochal adventure in health protection.

"How an Army medical officer, in the midst of daily routine work, could have written so excellent and exhaustive a work, I can't understand," he wrote. "Besides reflecting the greatest credit on our Corps, it must always stand as a monument to your energy and ability." Reed complained of being plagued by the same trouble that was making Dr. Sternberg so unhappy—the difficulty of carrying on what research he could in the face of working and living conditions extremely unconducive to original work on either his own or the army's time. He thanked his friend for some cultures the latter had sent him—what kind, he did not say. Then he went on to say that "I should be very glad to give more time to bacteriology, but, alas, my dear doctor, when most interested I must stop for practical things, so that I can only do the merest 'dabbling'."

A Philadelphian, Dr. H. C. Wood, wrote him soon after his *Manual of Bacteriology* appeared: "What a worker you are! To see a man like yourself really doing scientific work fills me with great disgust and envy; disgust at my own laziness and good-for-nothingness; envy of the restless spirit that gets you up early in the morning and keeps you up late at night."

Dr. Sternberg was not in San Francisco when the *Manual of Bacteriology* was published. The first copies reached him in New York, after another transcontinental change of stations. His new duties, as attending surgeon and examiner of recruits, were considerably more pleasant than those he had recently relinquished, and, being so close to research centers and the leading publishers, he found himself much more congenially situated in every way.

One of the most pleasant byproducts of this change was the opportunity it gave him to use the excellent facilities of the Hoagland Laboratory, which had been established for the promotion of bacteriologic research, in Brooklyn. He had been an absentee director for some time. It provided a profitable and pleasant interest for Mrs. Sternberg too. As an unpaid and unofficial assistant to her husband all those years, she had gained a great deal of experience in that type of work. When Dr. E. H. Wilson, who was then in charge of the laboratory, asked her if she would like to work there, both she and Dr. Sternberg welcomed the opportunity.

One of her tasks was the periodical examination of samples of the city's public water supply. On one of those tests she found an organism that startled and disturbed her. It looked to her exactly like the tubercle bacillus. Calling in her husband, she asked him to study it. To him too, it looked like the tuberculosis organism. If the Brooklyn water supply contained organisms of that kind, something drastic needed to be done at once. On the other hand, it would be a tragic mistake to terrify a whole city by a public announcement that was later found to be untrue. He decided to wait a while; as it turned out, this was a wise decision. Subsequent tests showed that it was not the tubercle bacillus at all, in spite of that striking similarity, but a theretofore unidentified organism which, fortunately, was entirely harmless. As its discoverer, Mrs. Sternberg had the proud privilege of giving it a name. She named it in honor of the laboratory's founder, Dr. C. N. Hoagland, a wealthy Brooklyn citizen. This naturally pleased him immensely. A culture of the find was kept in the laboratory for many years.

Dr. Sternberg returned to his old role of cholera fighter in September, 1892, when a ship arrived in New York harbor from Hamburg, then in the grip of a vicious cholera epidemic. Point-of-entry epidemiology was not normally within his official orbit, but his success in fighting this disease at Fort Harker and other places caused a member of the Special Cholera Committee of the New York Chamber of Commerce to request his help in preventing a transatlantic cholera invasion. Although nominally working under the regular quarantine officials, he was actually in command of the defensive forces, the others readily bowing to his leadership. When the crisis passed without the appearance of a single cholera case that could conceivably have been brought by that ship, to him was freely accorded full credit for the achievement.

The magnitude of that Sternberg feat was enhanced by the fact that the victory had been cheaply won. Having for some time had serious doubts regarding the necessity for the usual wholesale destruction of articles from infected localities, he tested the validity of those doubts in hurried but thorough experiments at the Hoagland Laboratory. The tests left him fully convinced that his doubts were completely justified. The proper use of disinfection and desiccation made other and more expensive measures entirely unnecessary, he was sure. He therefore did not require the destruction or even the disinfection of cargo or mails, if they had been clean and dry at the time of loading and had not been subjected to dampness en route. With a few exceptions, he approved the admission of all freight that could be exposed to extended periods of sunning, high temperatures, or currents of hot air. Relatively simple and inexpensive disinfection of the staterooms occupied by cholera patients was also pronounced sufficient. Dr. Sternberg realized that these were revolutionary measures and that a fearful responsibility rested upon him in using them in lieu of the standard procedures, but he felt sure of his ground. He was willing to act on his conviction in the confident assurance that this demonstration of the effectiveness of vastly cheaper procedures would prove a boon to shipping companies and health officials all over the world.

Naturally, public health officials and the general public in New York and across the country waited in anxiety for the feared epidemic to burst in full fury or die aborning. When it became evident that not a single spark from that Hamburg conflagration had reached this country, all were quick and enthusiastic in their praise of the man who had prevented a blaze at the nation's doorstep. Among them was Dr. William Jenkins, health officer of the port of New York, who was in a particularly good position to appraise Dr. Sternberg's generalship. Dr. Jenkins attributed "very much" of the success of that defensive effort to Dr. Sternberg's "calm, practical, deliberate judgment." "At no time," he said, "was he panic-stricken." He had been instrumental in rejecting the "extremely impractical suggestions" made by medical men and others. Largely because of him, "the very extreme measures which were proposed by scientific men" were disregarded.

That crisis having been met successfully, Dr. Sternberg turned to other and less stirring tasks. He took part in an investigation of sanitary conditions at Madison Barracks, where there had been a typhoid epidemic. He also served on two or three physical fitness boards examining officers up for transfer and promotion. He was then thinking about promotion for himself too: not merely stepping up a grade as another vacancy might occur, but something much more important. Just a few months ahead was the impending retirement for age of Surgeon General Sutherland, who had been appointed over him some three years earlier. There were a number of medical officers who exceeded him in seniority. Other things being equal, they would be given the preference. But practically all of them, if not all, were almost as old as General Sutherland himself. If one of them should be appointed, he would have only a short time to serve before retirement, which might not be good for the service. In view of this fact, it was believed that President Cleveland would not pay too much attention to seniority. If this should be true, Dr. Sternberg and his friends felt that his record, with service in the Civil War, against the Nez Percés, and in several cholera and yellow fever epidemics, along with his high standing as a bacteriologist and his extensive medical writing, would give him an edge over his rivals. So, after learning that several officers junior to himself had applied for the impending vacancy, he did so too. On May 16, about a fortnight before General Sutherland's retirement, he sent the President a detailed transcript of his service record, including the already mentioned citations by General Sykes (referring to his Civil War service) and General Howard (concerning his service against the Nez Percés) and letters of commendation from numerous others.

"I do not wish to be considered an applicant for the position to the prejudice of my seniors in the Medical Corps of the Army," he wrote the President. "But if in your judgment the interests of the service call for appointment of a medical officer who has several years to serve before retirement, I most respectfully ask that my claim receive due consideration."

His application was strongly supported by a number of other persons who wrote directly to the President after it became known that he was a candidate. Among them was Dr. S. B. Ward, an Albany physician and presumably a close friend of President Cleveland. Dr. Ward reminded the President of Dr. Sternberg's work as a yellow fever investigator under the President's appointment and of "your gratification at his turning back in the Treasury about half of his appropriation" for expenses in carrying on his studies—apparently then, as now, an almost unheard of thing among government workers. Moreover, the Ward letter reminded Cleveland, "His report, you may recollect, was so interesting that you sat up nearly all night reading it."

The President made up his mind on May 30, 1893, presumably upon the advice of Secretary of War Daniel S. Lamont. The latter immediately informed Dr. Sternberg that he had been selected for the post. The appointment carried an unusual promotion in military rank; from lieutenant colonel he jumped to brigadier general, over the heads of ten other officers—six colonels and four lieutenant colonels.

Martha Sternberg was at work at her table at the Hoagland Laboratory when a messenger brought her a telegram containing the good news, sent by a friend. A few minutes later her husband arrived, excited and hoping he would be the first to tell her. Momentarily disappointed when he found he had been deprived of that pleasure, he ordered her to "put up your microscope" and get ready for some kind of celebration. But that initial jubilation gave way a few minutes later to soberness as the full realization of the responsibilities he was assuming began to weigh down upon him. What had just come, he realized with a sense of second-thinking disillusionment, was not just a conspicuous honor. It was also a tough job, with the certainty of many frustrations, much criticism—a great deal of it unjust and unfair —, long hours of work of a kind for which he had no enthusiasm, and practically a farewell to research. As those sobering second thoughts swept over him, he began to wonder if he really wanted this position after all.

He confessed those sober second thoughts to Mrs. Sternberg as soon as they were alone. He could not say "whether I am happy or not." He spoke of the tremendous responsibilities he would have to assume and his realization that "it is not an easy matter to satisfy everybody." Whenever he would recognize and reward one person's capabilities, he would disappoint and antagonize many others. Considering all these things, he told her solemnly, "I scarcely know whether I am to be congratulated or not."

Martha Sternberg remembered these fears and doubts when she wrote about this phase of their life together.* She also remembered his pride in the Army Medical Corps, the satisfaction it gave him to be its head, and his eagerness to make it even greater. Except for her, he had no close relatives. As Surgeon General, he would regard the Army's medical officers as "my family" and, like a good parent, try to "give every man a chance." He was also determined, he said, to promote "a truly scientific spirit" in the Corps, and, in spite of the likelihood of disappointment and disgruntlement, would keep on the watchout for opportunities to reward unusual merit.

There was the inevitable disappointment of those others who had aspired to the post and of their friends and supporters; this was especially true of officers senior to him. But accepting such personal disappointments in good grace is part of the indoctrination of Medical Corpsmen, and the disappointed ones were among the first to send their congratulations and pledges of full cooperation and support. One whose telegram, and letter that followed, were completely free from disappointed ambition was Walter Reed. From his Department of Dakota headquarters at St. Paul, Minnesota, he wrote of his gratification over "the President's handsome tribute to honest merit." The letter, which brought so much satisfaction to its recipient, went on:

> When I think that it [the appointment] places at the head of the Corps the one man who preeminently stands forth as the representative of progressive scientific medicine, and that it means the fossil age has passed, I have an irresistible desire to toss my very hat into the air!
>
> I know what pleasure it will give to Professor Welch, Dr. Abbott and Dr. Councilman, all of whom have so many times spoken of your untiring energy and ability. I shall always remember Dr. Abbott's remark made to me on one occasion, when he said: "All that I am and know concerning bacteriology, I owe to a member of your Corps—Dr. Sternberg."
>
> Having no favors to ask, my dear doctor, I can all the more sincerely congratulate you.

Dr. A. Walter Suiter, assistant secretary-general of the Pan

* Martha L. Sternberg, *George Miller Sternberg, A Biography,* p. 131.

American Medical Congress, told Sternberg that "no appointment has ever been more enthusiastically received by the profession at large than your very meritorious promotion." Warm congratulations came from Assistant Surgeon William C. Gorgas, who was to occupy the Sternberg seat and suffer the Sternberg frustrations in the First World War. Equally warm were those sent eastward from his Chicago headquarters by Major General Nelson A. Miles of the Department of the Missouri, who was to be closely associated with the new Surgeon General in the Spanish-American War. Dr. Hermann M. Biggs congratulated him "not so much on the promotion, as that was deserved, but on the fact that your ability and scientific work have received the recognition they merit." Dr. John B. Hamilton of Washington recalled having nominated Dr. Sternberg for the presidency of the Pan American Congress's Section on Military Surgery and, more recently, having named a quarantine boat for him. "I had no idea," he added, "that I was speaking for the future Surgeon General."

The nonmedical public was also well pleased with the choice and, with a few exceptions, was strongly inclined to commend President Cleveland for going down the list to get the right person. The Washington correspondent of the New York *Tribune* pointed out that the appointment "prevented the ultimate advancement of no less than thirty-four officers of various grades in the Corps, owing to the fact that they are senior and retire from active service before himself." However, "aside from the military features," he called the appointment "a happy one," adding: "Professionally, he stands among the ablest officers in his Corps." The New York *Times* devoted a long editorial to the appointment, in which it averred that "there is no question of the eminent qualifications" of the appointee.

Dr. Sternberg's selection over the heads of more "conventional" candidates was properly interpreted as recognition by President Cleveland of the dawn of a new day in medicine, one which the army dared not disregard. The tried-and-true procedures which had protected soldiers' health in war and peace for well over a century still had their place. But the President and his advisers saw the need for greater emphasis upon preventive medicine. The new-born science of bacteriology was crowding many old concepts of health protection out of the picture, and the needs of the times demanded a military medical leader who was in the best possible position to make full use of the powerful weapons which that brand-new science had forged. Such a leader pre-eminently was Dr. Sternberg. As Colonel P. M. Ashburn observed in *A History of the Medical Department of the U. S. Army:**

> President Cleveland's appointment of George M. Sternberg to be Surgeon General was symptomatic of the times. The world was changing, and few things in it were changing more rapidly than medicine. Bacteriology and hygiene were existing facts which promised vast good to mankind. The old, dogmatic systems, the scholastic era, of medicine were passing. It was becoming recognized that disease was not a punishment sent for violation of the precepts of religions, but that it was the result of definite, physical, earthly causes, and the hope was growing that the laws governing its causes, progress, prevention and cure could be worked out as could the laws of physics and chemistry and that, once known, they could be utilized for man's advantage. The new ideas were as new to most medical men as to well-informed laymen, and they were as readily grasped by the latter as by the former. This gave rise to a great popular interest in medicine, and in its newest branch, bacteriology. Sternberg stood as the greatest and the most productive man of bacteriology in America. He was representative of the new thought and progress in medicine. His selection to be Surgeon General was natural, symbolic, almost inevitable. It is probably true that Greenleaf† would have been a greater administrator, but the Medical Department was not then looked upon as one calling for great administration. It was concerned with medicine, it needed to be led into the ways of medical advancement, and Sternberg was in the position to so lead it.

One man to whom the appointment brought particular satisfaction was Major (later Lieutenant Colonel) William Cline Borden. Major Borden was like Dr. Sternberg in one respect: he much preferred toiling in the laboratory to the usual off-duty activities of other medical officers. And, also like Dr. Sternberg, he got precious little encouragement or help from his superiors in the Medical Corps. On a visit to Washington one day, he called at the office of Surgeon General Baxter to pay his respects. This was a duty he dreaded, for the Surgeon General, while Chief Medical Purveyor of the Army several years earlier, had done

---

* Boston and New York: Houghton Mifflin Company, 1929, p. 148.
† Lieutenant Colonel Charles R. Greenleaf, another candidate for the post.

his best to prevent Major Borden from getting a new microscope and some other equipment he very much wanted. Finding General Baxter out, to his vast relief, he was received by Major Greenleaf, who fully shared his superior's low opinion of research, in the army or anywhere else, and welcomed this opportunity to get his views across to the other man. The burden of his admonition was that Major Borden ought to "quit fooling with the microscope" and devote his time to more practical things. His visitor pointed out, with some heat, that he was not sacrificing his regular work to research—he was doing that on his own time. He could not see, he told Major Greenleaf, how in the world the Medical Corps could object to his spending his spare time working in a laboratory if he chose to do that instead of drinking, hunting, playing cards, and engaging in other purely social and recreational activities. Major Greenleaf conceded that the Medical Corps could not dictate how an officer spent his leisure time or object if he spent it the way Major Borden was spending his. But that was not the point he was trying to get across. He was thinking of personal advancement in the Corps. He made it clear that, in his opinion, the worst possible way to get ahead was to do what Major Borden and a certain other misguided laboratory enthusiast insisted upon doing. "Look at Sternberg, over there in New York," he declaimed, "spending all his time with a microscope. Can you tell me one earthly bit of good Sternberg is to the Medical Corps?"

Major Borden had to wait some time for a satisfactory answer to that question. When it came, the man who considered off-duty research a sorry way to get ahead in the Medical Corps was immensely surprised and chagrined to find that that misguided officer who had been "spending all his time with a microscope" all those years had been chosen over him for the Corps's top job.

CHAPTER XIII

Doctor Out Front

DR. STERNBERG'S fears regarding his inability to do any research to speak of were fully confirmed. To all practical purposes, he had put his microscope and test tubes aside for good. But, except for that, he found his new work very much to his liking.

He soon found himself a frequent caller at the White House. President Cleveland's close friend and personal physician, Dr. Joseph D. Bryant, lived in New York. The President's health was not at all good, and getting to his bedside from such a distance in case of emergency would have taken a great deal more time then than now. Dr. Bryant, with Cleveland's approval, asked the new Surgeon General to be ready for a call at the White House whenever needed. Well pleased with this arrangement, the President and his physician turned over to Dr. Sternberg more and more of the responsibility for keeping the President in good health. These two men—both upstate New Yorkers and both sons of ministers—found a great deal in common. They soon became warm personal friends.

This pleasant relationship led naturally to Dr. Sternberg's being named unofficial medical guardian of other members of the White House family. This resulted, in turn, in Mrs. Sternberg's becoming a member of Mrs. Cleveland's small circle of personal friends and a frequent guest at White House social affairs. She called them "brilliant and enjoyable." Mrs. Cleveland, she stated, "always said and did the correct thing" and had a reputation for "never having made a mistake while presiding in the White House." This the other woman considered a particularly notable feat for one who had to face the slippery pitfalls of Washington society at an extremely early age.

As for the bacteriologist turned administrator, he won praise for the conscientious way in which he carried on his heavy duties, as well as for his kindly nature and personal magnetism. A magazine writer, referring some years later to the Dr. Sternberg of the Surgeon General era, called him "a genial gentleman beloved by all with whom he came in contact." To Lieutenant Colonel Edward L. Munson he was a man "of clean and lofty purpose, kindly nature and almost womanly sympathy." In his recommendations for promotion and his other official acts that inevitably brought pleasure to some and disappointment to others, he stuck faithfully to the promise he made to Martha Sternberg in the sobering afterglow of his appointment—that he would constantly be on the lookout for exceptional merit and eager to encourage and reward it. In such acts, Colonel Munson said, he "played no favorites." He "leaned backward in his effort not to be influenced by personal preference." When it came to official decisions, he "had neither friends to reward nor enemies to punish." Of Sternberg's personality, Colonel Hume wrote: "He had the power of drawing men about him and bringing out their best."

One of his ways of "bringing out their best" was to make medical officers feel that he was sincerely and earnestly interested in them. This applied not only to proper and unbiased rewarding of merit: it applied equally to the encouragement of those who wanted to engage in worthwhile activities beyond the call of official regulations. Remembering how discouraging it had been to him to find among his official superiors a complete lack of interest in his research, he went out of his way to let every would-be researcher know that he was behind him strongly. He also let it be known that he was prepared to help him in every practical way possible. One way in which he did so was to make the valuable books and bound medical journals in the Surgeon General's office readily available, by mail and express, to anyone in the service wishing to use them. Those interested in experimental work were not kept at isolated, scientifically arid posts, performing uncongenial tasks, as he had been. Instead, he saw to it that such men received assignments to duty in or near large cities. Then they were encouraged to make the fullest possible use of nearby laboratories and other research facilities. Many who served under him remarked that the morale of army medical officers all over the country had been kept high by the feeling that they had in the Surgeon General a personal advocate and friend at the seat of Government.

One of his first official acts after taking over his new responsibilities was to move vigorously for the establishment of an Army Medical School. As a scientific man, he had long felt and seen the need for special training, over and above that provided by civilian medical schools, for those beginning careers in military medicine. He saw a wide gap between the orthodox training given a civilian physician about to begin general practice in a typical American community and the particular, specialized work of a professional army doctor. So it is not surprising that he set as one of his major goals the establishment, as soon as possible, of a postgraduate school where medical officers might close that gap.

He was not the first chief of the Army Medical Corps to see the need for such a school. During the Civil War Surgeon General William Alexander Hammond had not only seen it but had done something about it. He seemed to be making excellent progress for a while too, obtaining classroom space, selecting his faculty, and drawing up his curriculum. Then, just as he was about to get the school under way, Secretary of War Stanton, who managed to oppose a good many worthwhile projects as well as some excellent men, began raising objections. His opposition, he claimed, was due to the fact that the classes would have to be held in the evenings: the students would find the Washington theaters more appealing than classrooms and would cut classes in favor of the lighter forms of entertainment. It apparently did not occur to him that attendance could be made compulsory and absenteeism punished like any other infractions of regulations: he seemed more interested in finding reasons for opposing than for aiding the plan. Well based or not, Stanton's opposition proved decisive. General Hammond had to call off his ambitious scheme. As a result, as George Worthington Adams points out in *Doctors in Blue*, "Army surgeons were forced to perfect their learning upon the battlefields."* About all the baffled and defeated Hamilton could do was to devote as much of his off-duty time as he could to the writing of a text on military hygiene and sanitation. This was full of excellent information for those who chose to read it. Unfortunately, very few did.

General Sternberg was more fortunate than his Civil War predecessor had been. This was due in large part to his having the good luck to serve under a different kind of Secretary of War. Secretary Lamont was one of his close personal friends and helped the project along in every way he could. Thanks to his friendly and powerful influence, the Army Medical School came into being on June 24, 1893, when the War Department issued General Order No. 31 creating it. Thus began the first of the many service schools which are now a part of all branches of the army. Except for a three-year period during and immediately after the Spanish-American War, this peculiar medical institution, which Dr. Welch once called "America's oldest school of preventive medicine," has been continuously giving army medical officers that valuable knowledge which they could not obtain anywhere else. Since that relatively humble beginning it has outgrown several buildings as one after another failed to keep up with its expanding curriculum and research activities. In his *History of the Medical Department of the U. S. Army*, Colonel Ashburn calls it "Sternberg's greatest monument."†

The Surgeon General referred to it with pride in his annual report for 1893-94. He had, he said, "recognized the possibility of improvising a school which, although adding nothing to the expense of the Army Medical Department, would afford all the advantages that could be derived from one costing heavily for its establishment and maintenance." Lecture rooms had been found in the Army Medical Library and Museum. The huge ac-

---

* *Doctors in Blue: The Medical History of the Union Army in the Civil War* (New York: Henry Schuman, 1952), p. 37. Permission to quote from this work here and elsewhere in the present volume has kindly been granted by the successor publisher, Abelard-Schuman, Ltd.

† *Op. cit.*, p. 150.

cumulation of specimens and similiar material at the Medical Museum had provided everything needed for experimental work. Army officers already on duty in Washington had been available, without extra cost, as instructors. A fortunate transfer of a Hospital Corps company had even provided, also without extra cost, "facilities for instruction in drill, company administration, first aid and battlefield management."

The regular faculty consisted of five instructors. A fortunate and wise selection for which Dr. Sternberg should be credited was that of Captain Walter Reed, who had been brought to Washington as professor of clinical and sanitary microscopy and director of the Pathological Laboratory, a post which gave the latter a chance to develop his bent for research after a long and arid period in the West. In addition to Reed and the other five regulars, there were six lecturers from the outside who addressed the students from time to time on their specialties.

Dr. Sternberg's fond hope of maintaining the Medical Department at top efficiency and in complete readiness at all times for any emergency was cruelly jolted less than a year after he became Surgeon General. The country was mired in one of the worst panics in its history. There were insistent and powerful demands that Federal expenditures be cut to the bone. Bowing to them, the House Appropriations Committee's Subcommittee on Military Affairs took mighty whacks at the budget and personnel requests submitted by the Secretary of War. While the recommended cuts were directed at the War Department as a whole, they struck a particularly heavy and crushing blow at the Medical Department. Dr. Sternberg was especially alarmed over the subcommittee's recommended reduction from 120 to 90 in the number of assistant surgeons, the Medical Department's workhorses, who carried on the day-to-day job of keeping soldiers healthy.

As soon as the proposed cuts were made public Dr. Sternberg appealed to Congress to make them less drastic. In that he was only partially successful. The measure as finally passed provided for 110 assistant surgeons—10 less than had formerly been provided for but 20 more than the subcommittee had recommended. He and the others of the War Department were less successful in other efforts to restrain the economy-minded committee. Like their brothers in other branches of the service, medical officers had to resign themselves to reduced pay and allowances for official travel, greatly retarded advancement, and even cuts in their retirement incomes. Dr. Sternberg greatly feared the closing of his pet project, the Army Medical School. This, however, he was able to avert.

Those Congressional slashes—which a newspaper writer likened to the work of "a keen broad-axe instead of a pruning knife"—actually hit the Medical Corps much harder than the cutting of its personnel would indicate. Congress also ended the practice of employing acting assistant surgeons on a contract basis. It forbade the employment of private physicians except by the visit. No longer could they be employed for extended service. No longer could they be placed in charge of army hospitals. They could not be trusted with government property. They could not enforce discipline among members of the Hospital Corps. They could not supervise the maintenance of proper sanitary conditions at army posts. The families of army personnel, enlisted men and officers alike, were forced to look elsewhere for the excellent medical care to which they had become accustomed. All of these things had a bad effect on morale and were later to cause great embarrassment to political leaders and add immeasurably to the grief of the men fighting the Spanish-American War.

This was indeed a severe blow for a conscientious, ambitious Surgeon General, eager to provide the best possible care for the nation's approximately twenty-eight thousand soldiers and their dependents.

In spite of the slashing of his staff, he went doggedly ahead, doing the best he could with what he had left. Alert to the possibilities of any new scientific development, he was one of the first to appreciate the revolutionary potentialities of the x-ray. As soon as possible after Professor Wilhelm Konrad Roentgen demonstrated this powerful force in 1895, he managed to obtain x-ray units for several of the larger post hospitals. Whenever possible, he also provided bacteriological laboratories. Physical disabilities which in the past had been regarded as incurable and therefore permanent were studied with a questioning mind. Thanks to his unwillingness to accept incurability without full investigation, many servicemen gladly gave up disability pensions in exchange for restored working capacity, and the taxpayers were saved huge sums. The army's tuberculous received new hope with the establishment at Fort Bayard, New Mexico, of a hospital devoted to the treatment of that disease alone. Better care of the tuberculous was also provided at other hospitals. Impelled by the same passion for the dissemination of scientific knowledge which had brought the Army Medical School into being, Dr. Sternberg organized additional training schools for the Hospital Corps. Seven new army hospitals were opened during his first two years as Surgeon General. Five of them, built according to his specifications, reflected his conception of the proper use of floor space, the proper utilization and arrangement of equipment, etc.

In spite of his close devotion to the details of his office, Dr. Sternberg managed to find a little time to do with as he pleased, and most of it he devoted to writing. In 1895 he completed a major work which he called *Immunity, Protective Inoculations in Infectious Disease and Serum Therapy*. It ran to some three hundred and twenty-five pages. The next year he revised his *Manual of Bacteriology*. The new edition also had a new name, *A Textbook of Bacteriology*. It too was favorably received, adding substantially to his reputation. In all, no fewer than forty-eight manuscripts were published during the approximately nine years between his appointment and retirement, an average of about one every ten weeks. Nor did his work appear only in scientific journals of limited public interest: such widely read general publications as *Popular Science Monthly*, the *Century Magazine,* and the *Youth's Companion* also welcomed and featured his contributions.

At times his enthusiasm wandered rather far afield. When the need for a public library for the nation's capital aroused the interest of public-spirited residents of that voteless municipality, he became one of the prime movers in the campaign to establish it. When it opened, its shelves were heavily loaded with volumes which he had been accumulating over the years, some of them highly prized. Attacking ignorance in another form, he began a one-man campaign against poor spelling, sloppy grammatical construction, and amateurish sentence structure in the written and spoken work of young doctors. Speaking on the authority of his membership on various army medical examining boards, he complained that a large proportion of the current crop of medical school graduates (except, of course, graduates of the Army Medical School, which took a serious view of such shortcomings) "would utterly fail to pass the civil service examinations required of clerks in the government service." No amount of medical knowledge, he said in an address at Georgetown University, "will enable an illiterate man to maintain the respect and confidence of educated people." A doctor with a limited knowledge of medicine may be able to conceal his deficiency if he has a pleasant manner and is otherwise acceptable, and such a doctor can win success in his profession. But a serious inability to use the English language properly "is something that reveals itself, sooner or later, to the educated classes, among whom a physician with a reasonable degree of ambition and self-esteem would naturally hope to practice." As an example of what he was talking about, he read a list of some one hundred and twenty misspelled words, "culled with exact spelling from the papers of those examined by the Board of Medical Examiners representing the State Medical Society of Pennsylvania." Among them were *apatite, assleep, alsow, boath, fatial, hedacke, jerms, ulser, suddent, skinn, and sower* (for sour).

The election of 1896 brought a new President and presidential family to the White House, but it had no effect upon the welcome General Sternberg received. Although a medical officer was assigned to full-time duty there, Mrs. McKinley's health was so poor that he could not care for her and discharge his other White House medical responsibilities alone. Dr. Sternberg was almost always the physician called upon to help out. As the White House's gracious hostess found it more and more difficult to stand up physically under the heavy strain of official and unofficial entertainment, the Surgeon General's calls became more and more frequent. At times he was there every day or oftener. As a result of that close and constant association of such a particularly personal nature, the relationship between the Sternbergs and the Mc-

Kinleys became fully as cordial as that between the Sternbergs and the Clevelands had been. During those years, Mrs. Sternberg wrote afterward, "we learned to love and esteem President Mc-Kinley and his wife very highly." The two couples were frequently together at informal family dinners and holiday gatherings. Especially pleasant to the Sternbergs in later years were recollections of winter evenings spent at the White House, sitting cozily around a big open fire brightly fueled by driftwood which had washed ashore on the Massachusetts coast—a gift from one of the President's New England admirers. Among their White House memories too was a Christmas dinner with the McKinleys at which the President did himself proud as a turkey carver and even prouder as a genial, delightful host relaxing in the cheerful warmth of his family and friends.

But perhaps the most memorable of the Sternbergs' White House associations came on January 1, 1898. As guests of the President, they were in the Blue Room during the New Year's reception at which the White House doors were opened wide to Washingtonians and visitors to the city. President McKinley shook thousands of hands and exchanged perfunctory but friendly greetings with thousands of well-wishers in the long line that serpented from the Blue Room out to Pennsylvania Avenue. At closing time several hundred who had been waiting in the cold were still in line. Tired as he was, the President could not refuse to see them. "Let them in," he ordered. "I don't want anyone to be shut out and disappointed." So the handshaking went on. It did not end until the last visitor had received his friendly handshake and cheerful greeting.

Notwithstanding his conscientious attention to his official duties and his medical writing, the Surgeon General found time to attend a great many medical and scientific meetings. And he invariably took an active and prominent part in them. This interest was rewarded at one time or another by his election to the presidency of a number of organizations, including the Association of Military Surgeons of the United States, the American Public Health Association, the Association for the Prevention of Tuberculosis of the District of Columbia, and the Cosmos Club. He was chairman of the Section on Military Medicine of the Pan

American Medical Congress and an honorary member of the
American Association of Physicians, the Association of American
Medical Colleges, the American Academy of Medicine, and the
French Society of Hygiene, as well as a fellow of the New York
Academy of Medicine and (as already indicated) a fellow of
Johns Hopkins University. The University of Michigan made
him an LL.D. in 1894, and Brown University did so three years
later. Dr. Sternberg also won limited fame in the nonmedical
field of ornithology. He was the first and, until his death, the
only president of the Audubon Society of the District of Columbia.

But the honor that brought him greater satisfaction than any
other was his election to the presidency of the American Medical Association. By a fortunate coincidence, that came at the
association's semicentennial meeting in 1897. During the en-
suing twelve months, and particularly in his presidential address
at the 1898 meeting, he used the influence of his office to help
bring about a number of improvements in medical practice. He
plugged for greater and ever greater emphasis upon the fostering
of the scientific spirit in the profession and in the public health
agencies. He worked for the elimination of smaller and, in his
view, inadequately staffed and equipped medical schools. He went
aggressively to war against medical quackery. He called for a militant defense against the active enemies of vaccination and animal experimentation. He did what he could, as he had been doing for years, to lift the level of public information regarding
medical matters. He sought especially to promote a wider dissemination of knowledge concerning medical developments and
their vast potentialities for improved health throughout the world.
He urged doctors to follow his example and become writers "for
the purpose of calling the attention of the non-medical portion of
the community to the recent achievements of scientific medicine."

The outbreak of the war with Spain prevented him from at-
tending that 1898 meeting and delivering his address in person.
It was read for him by a friend and fellow army officer, Colonel
Alfred A. Woodhull.

About six weeks after his election as AMA president, General Sternberg sailed for Hamburg on the first leg of the trip

to Moscow as an American delegate to the International Medical Congress. Mrs. Sternberg went with him. On the long swing by trains and small boats from Hamburg to the ancient Russian capital, they experienced two "firsts" which registered strongly on their memories: between Malmo and Stockholm they ate for the first time at a self-service restaurant, now familiar to Americans everywhere as the cafeteria; and, somewhere along their route, they went sight-seeing for the first time in broad daylight at 10 P.M.

A newly completed and super-luxurious Moscow hotel, not yet open to the general public, was placed at the disposal of those attending the Congress. The Sternbergs' share of this luxurious living consisted of two bedrooms, a dining room as large as a theater lobby, an entrance hall, and a reception room—more space, as well as elegance, than they had ever enjoyed or would enjoy again. Whenever they wanted a panoramic view of the city, it was right at hand; they had only to step out on their own private balcony. Mrs. Sternberg was especially impressed by all this. And she had a word for it—"charming."

Dr. Sternberg found unaccustomed luxury at the International Congress of Medicine too. The sessions were held at Moscow's leading theater, large, ornamental, and elegant. Attending every meeting of the eight-day gathering, he, as usual, found great stimulation in the formal papers and even more in the informal talks he had with leaders of world health from other countries. These were the things he reveled in.

He made an unpleasant discovery, however, one that disturbed him a little. He was the only Surgeon General or health official of corresponding rank and responsibility who did not hold the military rank of major general at least. His friends expressed surprise that his country had seen fit to advance him only to the rank of brigadier general. They did not, however, allow his subordinate rank to diminish their admiration for him or his achievements, or their eagerness to honor him whenever they had an opportunity to do so. Such an opportunity came just before adjournment, when the assembled medical men got together for a group photograph. Somewhat timid and retiring by nature, General Sternberg took a position, as inconspicuous as he could find, in a back row, well to one side. But the others would have none of that. That was no place for the outstanding personage at the Congress. Using whatever physical force was required, they made him move to the most conspicuous spot—the center of the front row. "That's where you belong," one of them said, "in the very front of medical science of the present day." And right there, in his bright new dress uniform, sword, and sash, they made him sit while the photographer snapped the picture.

The Sternbergs saw no midnight sun on their way back home. Taking a southerly route by way of Warsaw, Vienna, Paris, and Cherbourg, they were back in Washington in late September. Many matters that could not be handled by his subordinates were awaiting his attention, and he tackled them with zest.

CHAPTER XIV

Danger Signals

WHEN THE U. S. S. *Maine* was blown up in Havana Harbor on February 15, 1898, war feeling rose to fever heat all over the United States. Members of Congress, high-ranking officers of the army and navy, officials of the civil government, the ordinary man on the street and in the shop—practically everybody knew for a dead certainty that war with Spain was coming, and coming soon. And nobody had any other idea than that it would be an offensive war, to be taken aggressively to the enemy in Cuba, Puerto Rico, the Philippines, and anywhere else Spanish fighting men could be found and made to do battle.

That is, everybody reacted that way unofficially. Officially, the government took the position that war was an extremely unlikely possibility, and that, if it should come, it would be fought only defensively. All we would have to do would be to protect the North American continent against invasion. Acting on this self-delusive theory, Congress on March 9, after the post-*Maine* fever had been boiling for nearly three weeks, appropriated fifty million dollars for national defense. The President took that word *defense* with conscientious literalness. According to his interpretation of the purpose of the appropriation—which was the decisive interpretation, since the fifty million dollars was placed at his disposal—none of it could be used to ready the nation for possible warfare away from our own coastline. Not a dollar could be spent even for preparation for offensive war. There was generous provision for strengthening coast fortifications, but none for other types of guns and ammunition or for medical supplies. The Medical Department's share of the appropriation was a mere twenty thousand dollars. In his efforts to prepare for that war which everyone knew was coming, General Sternberg was further frustrated by similar restrictions placed upon the Quartermaster and Commissary Departments, which would have to keep the Medical Department, as well as other departments, supplied with vitally needed equipment after war came. All he could do was to draw up plans for the buying of medical and hospital supplies as quickly as possible. He only hoped there would be time enough to meet the emergency after it arrived.

War was declared on April 25, effective four days earlier when the American minister at Madrid had received his passports. President McKinley called for a volunteer army of 125,000 and an increase in the strength of the regular army. In August the latter had grown from 28,000 to about 58,500 officers and men, and the volunteers, as a result of a second presidential call, from nothing to more than 216,000. Thus, at its August peak, the country had approximately 275,000 men under arms, exclusive of those in the navy, or about ten times as many as in April. And the harried Surgeon General, like the harried Quartermaster General and the others caught in that surging tide of manpower, found himself facing the staggering problem of making supplies and equipment intended for one man suffice, by some miracle of administration, for ten.

From his long experience in the Civil War and Indian campaigns, General Sternberg knew, better than anybody else probably, that disease would very likely kill a great many more American soldiers than the Spaniards. But, from his years of toiling in laboratories and poring over scientific textbooks and medical journals, he had concluded that heavy sickness casualty rolls were not inevitable. He was sure illness could be greatly curbed by proper preventive measures—but they would have to be employed all along the line. Every man of every rank would have to observe certain rules of personal hygiene and camp sanitation. Any man who failed to do so would not only jeopardize his own health, he would also expose his whole regiment, or even his whole encampment, to epidemics. The Surgeon General's first blow in that campaign of preventive medicine came on the very day war was declared. The final vote on the war resolution had barely been taken when Circular No. 1 started on its way to camps and other military installations all over the country.

In time of war a great responsibility rests upon medical officers of the Army, for the result of a campaign may depend upon the sanitary measures adopted or neglected by commanding generals of armies in the field. The medical officer is responsible for proper recommendations relating to the protection of the health of troops in camp or in garrison, and it is to be believed that, as a rule, medical officers of the United States Army are well informed as to the necessary measures of prophylaxis and the serious results which infallibly follow a neglect of those measures especially when unacclimated troops are called upon for service in a tropical or semi-tropical country during the sickly season. In Cuba our armies will have to contend not only with malarial fevers and the usual camp diseases—typhoid fever, diarrhea and dysentery—but they will be more or less exposed in localities where yellow fever is endemic and under conditions extremely favorable for the development of an epidemic among unacclimated troops.

To meet this danger, General Sternberg listed a number of measures which he urged medical officers and contract surgeons to take or have taken by the proper military authorities:

Whenever practicable, campsites were to be on high, well-drained ground which had never before been used for that purpose. Sinks (latrines) were to be dug before a camp began receiving men, if possible; if not then, as soon as possible thereafter. All accumulations of fecal matter, or body discharges, were to be covered with fresh earth, quicklime, or ashes three times a day. New sinks were to be dug as soon as the old ones had been filled to within two feet of the surface, and the old ones covered with earth. Men depositing body discharges elsewhere than in the sinks were to be punished.

All refuse from the kitchen was to be buried immediately. Except when spring water of tested purity was available, only boiled or filtered water, hot tea, or hot coffee was to be drunk. Every fever case was to be promptly reported and treated. The discharges of fever patients were to be disinfected without delay. Special precautions were to be taken against flies. Whenever practicable, marches were to be scheduled for early morning or late afternoon, avoiding the heat of the day. Heavy eating or drinking when fatigued or overheated was inadvisable. Ripe fruit was to be eaten in moderation, but it was noted that green or overripe fruit would tend to upset the bowels. All food was to be cooked thoroughly. Quinine, from three to five grains, was to be taken early in the morning whenever malaria was especially prevalent in the community, but not otherwise. The men were to wear light woolen underwear, which was to be changed as quickly as possible, or dried in the sun or by the fire, whenever it became damp from rain, perspiration or any other cause.

Sanitary authorities are agreed that these were excellent instructions. There is no doubt that, had they been conscientiously carried out, there would have been little sickness among the troops. Unfortunately, they were not.

As it usually is in a time of emergency, Congress was generous to the Medical Department and other governmental agencies after the war began. It found, however, as earlier and later Congresses have done, that it takes more than money to outfit an army and protect it from the enemy and from disease. It takes time too. With those funds so generously provided by the war-excited legislators, it was possible to buy some medicines and supplies in the open market, though at a great deal more than their normal cost. But there were many others which even the magic of millions could not produce overnight. Such vital articles as medical chests, surgical instruments, hospital tents and furniture, certain drugs, and first-aid packs had to be ordered from the manufacturers. Their production was slow, no matter how feverishly a distraught Surgeon General might prod the manufacturers and beg them to turn them out in a hurry.

The assembling of Medical Department personnel also was enough to give the Surgeon General nightmares. On April 22 Congress authorized appointment of a chief surgeon to the staff of each corps, division, or brigade commander, and the President allocated a surgeon and two assistant surgeons for each regiment of volunteer infantry, engineers, or cavalry. Fifteen additional assistant surgeons were authorized on May 12, and permission was given General Sternberg to employ on a contract basis as many acting assistant surgeons as he considered necessary. He employed some six hundred and fifty of them. Unfortunately, hardly any of these newly added army doctors knew anything about environmental sanitation as General Sternberg thought of it. Hardly any had had any training or experience in caring for soldiers under war conditions. Very few indeed knew anything about observing military discipline themselves or enforcing it upon others. Some were not even good doctors in terms of general practice, and a few were pretty bad characters generally.

This was not General Sternberg's fault. With plenty of time, he could have made a careful investigation of every applicant and kept out the obviously unfit; but he did not have anything like that much time. He had to recruit doctors on an emergency basis, and the best he could do was to rely upon the recommendations of those whose opinions he considered trustworthy. Unfortunately, some proved unworthy of his confidence. Some were more interested in doing their friends favors than in protecting the high standards of the Medical Department or insuring the best possible care of the sick and wounded. This also applied to the approximately seventeen thousand contract nurses who were employed for service first in the general hospitals only and later in the field hospitals as well.

Congress forgot to make any provision for a Volunteer Hospital Corps. Thanks to that oversight, the corps had a staff of only six thousand to do work which normally required nearly four times that number. Unfortunately, the privates assigned to hospital duty often were even more deficient in training and adaptability to the work than they were in numbers.

General Sternberg turned to various emergency measures to provide the medical supplies and equipment he had been prevented from stockpiling. When regiments of the army were ordered to assemble at mobilization camps for merging into larger units, they were instructed to take with them all of the material of this kind they had. When they arrived at the mobilization points, it was found that they had brought very little, if any, medical equipment. Some had not had any in the small towns and cities where they had been playing at war at regimental strength. Others blamed inadequate transportation: it was all the men could do to get to the mobilization camps themselves with their essential equipment—and medical equipment was not considered essential.

General Sternberg appealed to the governors, asking them to

see that all troops from their states were amply supplied with medical equipment before leaving, but this did not help much. Sixteen governors could not comply with the request because their troops had no medical supplies. Those who were able to send some could not send anything like enough.

Meanwhile, the Surgeon General was doing everything he could to speed up the production of medical material. With those suddenly unfrozen millions, he let contracts for everything he would be likely to need and hoped deliveries would be made in time for the expected flood. When delivery of medical and surgical field chests was not made when promised, the supplies which were to have filled them were shipped in ordinary packing cases. Medical officers on active duty with troops were authorized to buy needed medicines wherever they could. Sometimes they were able to; often they were not.

A veteran of military service, General Sternberg had long known that the Medical Department would be dependent in time of war, as it had been in peace, upon other departments for its proper functioning. But this realization was impressed upon him with crushing potency when, for example, grave shortages of medical supplies showed up in numerous camps in the face of his personal knowledge that ample supplies had been shipped in ample time. The head of the Medical Department could not order the Quartermaster Department to ship badly needed medicines and hospital equipment by express when the economy-minded Quartermaster Department decided to save the taxpayers money by shipping by freight. Nor could he force the Quartermaster Department to pack all Medical Department material together so as to make carload lots of the same type of material going to the same destination. The Quartermaster Department, for reasons which it considered sound, wise, and economical, packed smaller shipments with those headed in the same general direction but destined for other branches of the army. Then, after their arrival at a camp siding, somebody desperately needing a surgical instrument or supply of drugs had to control his impatience while car after car was unloaded and its contents sorted. The complete equipment for a two-hundred-bed hospital could not be located for weeks.

Exasperating delays occurred when shipments were made by sea as well as by land. Medical supplies rated no priority or special consideration on shipboard either. In loading transports and freighters headed for Cuba and Puerto Rico, those in charge at the loading docks were as likely as not to pack medicines and hospitable furniture in inaccessible parts of the hold, where they would be the last to be unloaded. Even after they had been located, it was sometimes found that there were no lighters to take them ashore.

Notwithstanding all these things—the shortage of medical equipment and supplies, the delays in getting delivery of the limited stocks that were available, and the necessity of relying upon doctors who had their education in military medicine still ahead of them—the regulars and volunteers who crowded the mobilization and instruction camps enjoyed good health for several weeks. There was some sickness, of course, but it was easily controlled.

Then the picture changed radically. Epidemics began breaking out all over the country, especially in the South. The sickness rate was about twice as high in June as in May; it went higher in July, and still higher in August, when it stood at about four times the May rate. Illnesses of one kind and another caused nearly seven and a half men out of every thousand to be discharged for disability before they were able to strike a blow against the enemy.

Typhoid struck fastest and most furiously. It exploded in varying degrees of intensity in nine-tenths of the volunteer regiments within two months after they went into camp. There were more than twenty thousand cases in the United States alone. Nearly a fifth of the army's entire officer and enlisted personnel contracted it at some time or other. It caused more than 86 per cent of all deaths from all causes. It killed about one volunteer out of every sixty-one stationed in this country, nearly fifteen out of every thousand in the whole army, as more than seven and a half men out of every hundred it attacked died. Even the camps in the North, supposedly outside the "typhoid belt," did not escape. Other diseases also struck savage, quick, and quickly fatal

blows. Malaria added heavily to the sickness rolls, as did dysentery, measles, etc.

One of Dr. Sternberg's first acts after the outbreak of war
was to do away with the regimental hospitals which had proved
so unsatisfactory in the Civil War, replacing them with much
larger divisional hospitals. Unfortunately, the benefits of this
wise change were largely nullified by the typhoid outbreaks,
which crowded nearly all other types of cases out of the new
hospitals. Even the general hospitals were jammed with typhoid
patients.

The divisional and general hospitals also had other troubles.
The lack of properly trained doctors made it necessary to staff
them with those transferred from regimental duty. Some were
willing to be transferred; many were not. The latter often resisted with everything they had, including, in some instances,
powerful political and military influence. Governors and members of Congress did not hesitate to apply pressure to keep them
with their regiments. Sometimes fellow officers objected to their
being taken from the troops with whom they had been serving.
All of this created additional vexatious problems for the Surgeon
General.

The sick and wounded were sometimes as reluctant as the
doctors to leave their regiments. To avoid being removed, they
would keep their true condition secret as long as they could. Of
course, every hour they spent on active duty added dangerous
new links to the chain of infection. To relieve the pressure at
the divisional and general hospitals, many of the sick were sent
to civilian hospitals. Others jumped at the chance to go home
and be treated by their family doctors. Unfortunately, they were
more likely to leave a trail of typhoid and other diseases in their
home towns than to be benefited by the treatment they received.

Seeing the need for fast, safe, and comfortable transportation for the sick and wounded, General Sternberg fitted out three
hospital ships to carry medical supplies to the war areas and
bring back those incapable of further active service. A hospital
train, consisting of ten tourist sleepers, a dining car, a staff car,
and a combination car, shuttled between coastal terminals and

general hospitals. In all, it carried some two thousand patients. Only four of them died en route.

Two of the hospital ships—the *Missouri* and the *Relief*—were extensively remodeled to make them well suited to their new duties. The third—the *Olivette*—was converted with a minimum of change so as to make her ready for duty as soon as possible. Her conversion consisted for the most part of placing on board the equipment removed from a field division hospital. She performed entirely acceptably, though her career as a mercy ship was brief: while coaling in stormy weather on August 31 she began listing heavily and sank in twenty feet of water.

Dr. Sternberg was caused much vexation and discomfiture by the delays encountered in the much more extensive operation of converting the *Missouri* from a cattle boat to a hospital ship. Hoping to get her into service ten days after her acquisition in July, he was not able to do so until late August. It was not for lack of prodding on his part: under that constant prodding the colonel in charge of her conversion kept himself and his workmen—eight hundred in the daytime, half that many at night—on the job around the clock, in spite of the intense heat that seemed particularly oppressive at Pier 22, Brooklyn. Even that extreme effort was insufficient to get the *Missouri* ready by the time set for her delayed sailing after it was seen that the July target date was out of the question. She sailed a day late, still incompletely converted. As she put out to sea carpenters were still hammering, plumbers were still adjusting pipe joints, painters were still covering up cattle-boat rust with their brushes, electricians were still stretching wire and testing equipment, and other workmen were still at their tasks. Those men must have worked well, in spite of their difficulties, for the *Missouri* proved to be a good ship.

By the time she was at last at sea, General Sternberg found himself in much more serious trouble. Forgetting the years before the war when the Medical Department was on starvation rations, that strict prohibition against laying up a stockpile of materials and supplies, that drastic cut in the number of assistant surgeons, and the impossibility of any human's obtaining

overnight in huge quantities articles that had to be ordered, designed, and manufactured, editorial writers, reporters, politicians
—nearly everyone, it seemed to the harrassed Dr. Sternberg—
loosed a barrage of criticism and invective at the Surgeon General who could not produce miracles. He was not alone in this
shower of abuse, it is true. Secretary of War Russell A. Alger,
the Quartermaster General, and others were also bitterly criticized. General Sternberg and his friends felt that the criticism
heaped upon him was extremely unfair, extremely unjustified,
and, in many cases, extremely vicious.

His defense was not that there were no major epidemics in
army camps. That would have been silly. Nor did he deny that
sanitary conditions at many of the camps were far from what
they should be. He insisted, however, that he should not be held
responsible for conditions which he had no power to prevent.
For example, he did not see how he could properly be blamed
for the appointment of Dr. Rush Shippen Huidekoper as medical
director at Camp Chickamauga. Dr. Huidekoper caused him
great embarrassment and directed a storm of abuse at his head.
This appointee, it was revealed, was not a regular doctor at all
but a veterinarian. True, he was a graduate of the medical department of the University of Pennsylvania and had engaged in
general practice for a short time. But he had later been graduated
from the Veterinary School at Alfort, France, and had been associated with a New York animal hospital for some time. There
were other things about him that were not calculated to make
parents of army men feel any too pleased to have their sons in
his care. Some of them the New York *Herald,* one of Dr. Sternberg's most persistent critics, recounted under attention-attract-
ing headlines:

Dr. Huidekoper has been known in New York as a strong advocate
of horse meat as food. A few years ago he gave a dinner to a large
party of friends and after it was finished informed them that the roast
was cut from his favorite mare Pandora. He explained that Pandora
had broken her leg and that he had been compelled to shoot her. Dr.
Huidekoper has also figured in other sensational incidents.

At Chickamauga, returning soldiers say his preference for horses
was strongly exhibited. When a sick horse or mule was reported, Dr.
Huidekoper hastened to treat it, and, it is alleged, often neglected human
patients to do so.

Who had caused Dr. Huidekoper to be made an army doctor? Three senators had recommended him highly. In accordance with his necessity-imposed practice of not waiting to make a detailed check of every applicant, Dr. Sternberg had accepted him on their recommendation and put him to work.

Even more troublesome to General Sternberg than the unfortunate appointment of an ardent veterinarian to safeguard the health of thousands of troops were the ignorance and indifference of the men themselves. With few exceptions, they simply did not see the necessity of going to any trouble to keep themselves well. Even if it had been possible to hand-pick every medical officer or contract surgeon, the task of winning the troops' cooperation in the observance of rudimentary sanitary rules would have been baffling.

At Fort McPherson, Georgia, the sewers became choked with paper, sacks, handkerchiefs, and even the men's underwear. Latrines were ignored while the men relieved themselves in the nearby woods and fields. After the ground had been almost literally covered with excreta, the ordure was washed into the brook which supplied water for the camp's swimming pool. Many of the men also drank from that pool rather than from the water sources which were kept under sanitary supervision.

At Columbus Barracks, Ohio, where one hundred men were crowded into squad rooms intended for sixty-five and many slept on the floor because not enough bunks and mattresses had been provided, there were complaints that the men were repulsively dirty about their persons and clothing. Choked and over-running toilets were commonplace. Their contents stood in repulsive pools on the floors and filled whole buildings with odors that were enough to drive people outdoors. The very streets in front of the barracks were used as dumping lots for filth accumulated in the nearby civilian community.

At Fort Leavenworth, Kansas, the camp site became so honeycombed with abandoned latrines that it was almost impossible to find a site for a new one. General Sternberg mentioned an attempt to do so in which "six different holes were dug before a spot was found which had not previously been used for this purpose." Assistant Surgeon General Greenleaf reported to his official superior:

> I have never had a more trying time than during the past two weeks in efforts to keep the camps reasonably clean. . . . We have had to hire civilians to clean the latrines—remove their contents [and] the garbage— clean the camp streets and finally to stay on duty at the latrines and cover excrement as it was deposited. Orders, written and oral, requiring the soldiers to do anything in the way of police were repeatedly issued, but were totally disregarded, and the sinks and kitchens were soon infested with such swarms of flies that I felt sure there would be an outbreak of disease.

General Sternberg had high praise for America's fighting men, calling them "as a rule, intelligent, patriotic and brave." But, he added, they knew little and cared less about discipline:

> Each man was in the habit of judging for himself and of acting in accordance with his individual judgment. Discipline consists essentially in an unquestioning obedience of orders from those having proper authority to give them. Trained officers can not at once establish discipline among untrained troops, and when both officers and enlisted men are without military experience it is evident that with the best material time will be required for the establishment of discipline. And in the absence of discipline it is impracticable to enforce proper sanitary regulations in camp. The Surgeon General may formulate sanitary regulations and the general commanding an army corps or division may issue the necessary orders, but in the absence of discipline these orders will not be enforced. A reckless recruit will drink the water which has been condemned as unsafe and at night will defile the ground in the vicinity of his tent rather than visit the company sink, which possibly is in a disgusting and unsanitary condition because of a failure to carry existing orders into effect.

That lack of interest in sanitation was nothing new in American military history, as General Sternberg well knew. He had encountered it in the Civil War, just as other medical officers had encountered it in other wars. As a junior army doctor, the Surgeon General had seen how heavily that "don't care" attitude added to the sickness and mortality rolls of that earlier conflict. George Worthington Adams tells us about it and its effects in his *Doctors in Blue*:

> . . .when sinks were common, the principal problem was to persuade the men to use them. Some soldiers wandered off into the bushes because of modesty alone. More often they did so, and imperilled the health of the whole neighborhood, because of the disgusting condition of the latrines. The ordinary kind was simply a pit, surmounted by a

pole and possibly screened from view by a few pieces of brush. When its edges were clean, and earth was thrown into it once a day, it was considered adequate, even though it repelled its users, and would be condemned today.*

In another place he says:

But the sanitary crusaders ran headlong into the incorrigible "rugged individualism" of the American people. On reaching camp, recruits frequently let themselves go. Men who were so careless that they frequently shot themselves by accident could give little attention to the Sanitary Commission's ideas of camp cleanliness or to the advice of their medical officers. . . .

. . .most of the camps were dirty; clogged drains resulted in floods after each rain; and flies covered garbage left in the tents.

Most objectionable was the dearth of latrines and the reluctance of the men to use them. Some regiments had dug no latrines at all. The men of one such regiment had gone for eight days "relieving themselves anywhere within a few feet of their tents." The usual "sink," as the army called it, was a straddle trench thirty feet long, into which fresh earth was supposed to be thrown once a day, but frequently was not. It was usually so malodorous and so befouled at the edges that the soldiers often ignored it, despite orders. Dysentery and typhoid inevitably followed, and among the civil population as well. . . .†

It was little comfort to General Sternberg to know that the fathers of the men who were paying no attention to his sanitary instructions had paid no attention to the sanitary instructions of another Surgeon General in another war. He knew full well what these men's indifference to sanitation would almost certainly do to them and to him. And he realized how powerless he was to do anything about it.

* *Op. cit.*, p. 204.
† *Ibid.*, pp. 18-20.

CHAPTER XV

Soldier under Fire

UNFORTUNATELY for General Sternberg, his inability to perform overnight miracles with that money excitedly appropriated by Congress soon began to have repercussions in the fighting zones as well as at home. A small army of newspaper men, many of them with well trained noses for sensation as well as news, had a free hand to see and write about anything they wanted to. As Colonel Ashburn points out,* General Shafter's expedition against Santiago included, in addition to some seventeen thousand fighting men, seventy-one medical officers and eighty-nine newspaper correspondents, "the former to experience many troubles, the latter to cause many."

The newspaper correspondents found plenty of people, military and civilian, eager to furnish sensational statements for the waiting cables. One of the most eager was Colonel Theodore Roosevelt. The condition of the men at and near the front, he told them, was "appalling." Their treatment at the hospitals was so bad, he said, that the sick and wounded escaped as soon as they could and returned to the fighting lines. "There were no cots for the wounded," he charged. "After being operated upon, if they had blankets, they lay on the mud in their blankets."

Crew members of an army transport told startling stories of gross neglect at Ponce. Sixty-four sick soldiers, they said, had been compelled to remain on pontoons alongside the ship, "exposed to the broiling sun and powerless to keep off the flies and mosquitoes." These men's very faces were covered with flies and

* P. M. Ashburn, *The History of the Medical Department of the United States Army*, p. 185.

other insects, according to those sailors. All the time an army surgeon "was sitting on deck smoking a cigar without offering the least assistance to the suffering soldiers." The ship's captain finally ordered the pontoon's removal, "plainly informing the surgeon in charge that such a scene was a disgrace to the United States." Within an hour after a launch from the cruiser *Cincinnati* had towed the pontoon away, "four of the men died."

Reports were widely published of several hundred wounded men lying on the wet grass while a single army surgeon did his best to look after them. "The less severely wounded declined treatment, that those in more serious condition might be more quickly cared for," one correspondent wrote. "The whole story is too horrible to talk about, and there can be no possible excuse offered. . . ."

An emotional description of the home-coming of a regiment of volunteers—the 157th Indiana—was published in the Chicago *Times-Herald*:

> Several thousand people gathered at the Union Station to cheer the returning soldiers, but when they came out of their coaches the voices that would have been raised in gladsome shouts responded only to sighs and the smiles of welcome were changed into looks of inexpressible pity for the haggard and wan soldiers who left here [Indianapolis] only four months ago for the scene of war.
> So pathetic was the scene that many women burst into tears and many strong men turned away to hide their emotion. Two privates who left Indianapolis with the regiment were not with their comrades. They lay in long black boxes alongside the tracks, the objects of curiosity to the hundreds of people.

Those men in the long black boxes had not died heroically on the field of battle or from battle-won wounds, the newspaper writer emphasized, but from illness that should have been prevented or cured. And the plight of many of their comrades was only a shade better than theirs:

> The arrival of the hospital train was most pathetic. Several cars in the forward part of the train were filled with soldiers suffering from attacks of fever and malaria. They lay in bunks in two tiers and paid little attention to the people about them.
> Here and there a pale blue-coated young man thrust his head out of the window and feebly waved a battered campaign hat as the train passed, and then sank exhausted on his bed. Others too sick to rise smiled feebly

at their comrades. Occasionally, a thin hand stretched from a window and slowly waved a greeting.

A personal reunion tragedy was described:

As the hospital train stopped at the station Mr. and Mrs. Darling of Elkhart made their way to the car. They were looking for their son Robert, who was a private in Company E. They knew he was sick and had come here to meet him and nurse him.

The father and mother entered the car and were advancing to the bunk in which Robert lay when a friendly hand checked them. The boy had breathed his last as the train entered the station, and the parents were stopped as they approached the corpse that the news might be broken as gently as possible to them. Young Darling was unconscious from the time he was taken into the car, and, though comrades worked with him all night in the effort to keep him alive to see his parents, fate seemed to be against them.

The men got off. Those able to do so marched through the downtown streets to another station, where they got on another train for the short ride to their next camp. "The streets were lined with people," the correspondent wrote, "but few had the heart to cheer the emaciated and travel worn marchers." Their colonel told that newspaper writer:

This is not the same regiment I took away with me last May. The personality is the same, but it is made up of a different lot of men. They have fever in their very bones, they are hungry and their strength is wasted. It is all due to the cesspools in which they lived in the South. When the men left Indianapolis they were strong and showed their hardness.

Newspaper editors, correspondents, and politicians all over the country held General Sternberg responsible for the conditions which had brought illness and death to Private Darling and those thousands of others. He was blamed for the typhoid epidemics, for the conduct of every callous, indifferent, dissipating medical officer or contract doctor, and for everything else that was not right about the troops' medical care. One correspondent cabled his paper that the Medical Department had "failed absolutely" to send hospital supplies for the troops wounded at Siboney. This failure, he charged, was due purely to "negligence that could have been the result only of incompetence." The *Medical Record* declared editorially:

The lessons to be learned from the Cuban campaign center more around the neglect of the sick and wounded than any other features of the battlefield. This aspect is all the more deplorable in that there are no evident reasons why the sick or wounded should not have had the best of care. This was at least his due, and it was impliedly guaranteed to him by the Government.

The *Medical Record* called for a thoroughgoing inquiry into the operation of the Medical Department. Referring to that suggestion, the New York *Times* commented that "the Surgeon General cannot demand such an investigation too quickly." The author of "Topics of the Times" column went on:

It may well be that others—and especially another whose name leaps to every tongue *—should share the Surgeon General's burden, but this fact does not clear him of the charge of high plain duty wilfully neglected. His difficulties in any case would have been many and severe, but the very worst of them have been of a sort from which he could instantly have escaped. The plea that incompetent subordinates were imposed upon him by a higher authority cannot be even considered. He could and should have protested against that foul crime at the very beginning and by taking pains to see that his protest reached the public ear, as did Gen. Merritt, Gen. Miles and the officers under Gen. Shafter, he would have forced instant remedial action. They say that Dr. Sternberg is a great surgeon. It may be but he has made an utter and disgraceful failure as an executive officer.

A Brooklyn *Daily Eagle* editorial charged:

...the trouble with the Surgeon General's Department has been the Surgeon General. He is not an executive officer by nature, by inclination or by habit of mind, and neither title nor experience has succeeded in making one out of him. Not being an executive officer, his selections or assignments for executive positions under him have been failures. Even when the men under him have been competent, their competency has been useless to the soldiers or to the government, because incompetents have been above and incompetents have been below these men of competency, and competency itself has been rendered impotent by that fact....The people will give to the Secretary [of War], but only for a little while longer, a chance to clean out these two departments† of failure, and, if he does not do that, then the people will turn on him and insist that the President of the United States shall clean them out.

The New York *Times* said in a leading editorial:

There has been much in recent weeks to impress the country with a painful lack of confidence in the efficiency of the chief medical officer of the United States Army, Surgeon-General Sternberg....In private business the most unprofitable and exasperating of employes is the employe in whose department blunders are constantly occurring and who is al-

* Presumably Secretary of War Alger.
† Medical and Commissary Departments.

ways prepared with complete evidence that the blunder was not his fault.
Surgeon-General Sternberg seems to be that sort of employe of Uncle
Sam. . . .This last exploit * will strengthen the painful impression that
Surgeon-General Sternberg is unfit for the position he holds and that to
his inefficiency is chiefly due the complete breakdown of the medical
department in this war. Indeed it suggests the reflection that it is within
the bounds of possibility that the country has had about enough of Surgeon-General Sternberg.

Adding greatly to Sternberg's troubles were the surgeons general attached to volunteer units from the various states. He was
entirely without say-so as to their selection. Usually appointed by
their governors, they showed up at the training camps with the
troops. Primarily responsible, not to the Surgeon General, but to
their political mentors back at home, they were not averse to
megaphoning complaints without taking the trouble to look into
their justification or justice.

One of these was Dr. J. M. Keeler, of the Arkansas State
Guard. In a report to his governor, which made big headlines,
he called the hospital at St. Thomas "a veritable death's hole."
Chickamauga Park he called "a veritable pest hole." The water
in Chickamauga Creek was "as muddy as any farmer's stock
pond," and "totally unfit for the use of man or beast, unless
boiled or filtered." Chickamauga Creek itself was "a river of
death." There were no facilities whatever for bathing, he said.
Garbage and human feces were deposited in pits just outside the
regimental lines and covered with earth "from day to day." Because of continuous rains, water had oozed up through those
filled pits until a large part of the camp ground, "I am told is infected with maggots." Dr. Keeler's report was conspicuously
sprinkled with such expressions as "I am told," "I have no doubt,"
etc., indicating that many of the charges he was so willing to hurl
were based upon nothing more substantial than uninvestigated
rumors. But they hurt.

An honest man, an official motivated by a high sense of
duty, a realist, and a sensitive person, Dr. Sternberg winced under
them and the many others like them. Willing to concede that
there had been shortages of badly needed medical supplies and
material and that some medical officers and contract doctors

* Sternberg's recommendation that troops be kept in the interior of Cuba,
where, he said, they would be more healthy than in camps in the U.S.

had failed to do their duty, he, nevertheless, insisted again and again that he was not to blame. The country, he protested, was being given an altogether unfair and incorrect picture of what was being done for the men. In their eagerness to dig up and expose the scandalous and the sensational, he said, the newspaper men were overlooking the good and even the remarkably good. Stung to vigorous self-defense by the appearance of denunciatory editorials and letters to newspaper editors, he set himself to the task of clearing away the "widespread misapprehension with reference to the responsibility of the Surgeon General of the Army."

It would require superhuman power to meet the expectation of many of those who have criticized the Surgeon General for his administration of the affairs of the Medical Department of the Army [he declared in a statement to the press]. His responsibility is great and to properly perform the duties incumbent upon him he must devote his entire time and energies to the administration of affairs pertaining to his office. But it is quite impossible for him personally to administer or even to supervise the medical administration of armies in the field. For this purpose there is a Chief Surgeon for every army corps, for each division and for each brigade. These Chief Surgeons are directly responsible to the Commanding Generals of the troops with which they are serving. The Surgeon General has no direct authority over them.

To hold him responsible for the conduct or professional competence of regimental surgeons, appointed by their governors, or contract doctors, appointed by himself under the exigencies of a state of war which ruled out personal inquiries into the qualifications and character of every applicant, was, the statement said, "absurd." "In short," it emphasized, "the Surgeon General of the Army is not personally responsible for the neglect or incompetency of medical officers, whether regular or volunteer."

What of the Surgeon General's responsibility when the sick and wounded failed to receive the supplies they ought to have? His statement went into that too:

The Surgeon General is responsible for the purchase and issue of medical supplies for the army; but it is the duty of medical officers on duty with troops to make timely requisitions for supplies, as it is quite impossible for the Surgeon General to foresee what the requirements may be for troops located at various posts and camps in our own country and in the islands now in our possession.

So far as possible, the Surgeon General has endeavored to anticipate the wants of the army in the field, and at each of the larger camps a branch supply depot has been established. The war has been largely conducted by telegraph, and telegraphic requisitions for supplies are constantly being received. These are at once transmitted to the proper supply depot, with orders for issue; but there is often unavoidable delay at the supply depot in getting the supplies packed and shipped, and unexpected delays frequently occur in securing transportation of these supplies to the point where they are needed. These are matters for which the Surgeon General is in no way responsible.

If General Sternberg hoped that this statement would quiet his critics, he was disappointed. The New York *World* shot back at him with an editorial titled "NOT 'PERSONALLY' RESPONSIBLE":

Surgeon-General Sternberg has felt called upon at last—his feelings must have been deeply overlaid—to make a public statement which he evidently expects will serve as his exoneration for the breakdown in the Medical Department of the army, which was first brought to public attention in the Santiago campaign.

The crucial assertion in his plea for mercy is this:

"The Surgeon-General of the Army is not personally responsible for the neglect or incompetence of medical officers, whether regulars or volunteers."

Certainly not. Mr.* Sternberg, private citizen, has never been held "personally" responsible for any of the grievous faults of his department.

But he is "officially" responsible, by usage, by common practice, by ethics, by law, by any rule he may ask to be applied to the measuring of his conduct.

If not, if every contract doctor hired to accompany the troops is to be held responsible for the blunders and cruelties of the department, why have a Surgeon-General? If a Surgeon-General may employ or appoint any friend's protégé to attend a regiment and not be held responsible for his efficiency, then no official, civil or military, has any responsibility; no one can be held responsible for anything and there is no such thing as responsibility.

A New York *Times* editorial appearing about this time also showed marked impatience with General Sternberg's defense of his handling of the Medical Department. Calling him "an earnest officer and an unquestionably accomplished scientist," it nevertheless severely blamed him for "conditions which he and his subordinates appear to have lacked the foresight and the executive force successfully to meet."

The admissions of General Sternberg justify some earlier convictions that we had formed of his earnestness, but appear to make plainer the

* *Sic.* This may have been due to a typographical error.

lack of executive force in the head of the Medical Corps. It was not enough that the Surgeon General, observing the development in each new camp of typhoid fever, should issue orders to his subordinates, some of whom were more concerned with asserting authority over volunteer surgeons than they were in the correction of unsanitary conditions and the neglect of the commonest rules of decency, cleanliness and order in camp. There was needed at the head of the Medical Corps a man of force, not only intelligent, skillful and highly educated, but also not afraid to insist that the advice he gave should be heeded and the orders he made not be thrown in the waste basket.

The editorial ended on this caustic note:

. . .being one of the most accomplished of investigators, an authority on many medical subjects, it must be apparent that he lacked nerve, the force of character that carries authority, the general executive ability to put his knowledge to effective use. The story of failing supply or inadequate supply for troops in the field or in camp seems all the more exasperating and inexcusable in the light of the report of Surgeon General Van Reypen of the navy that he has yet to learn of the first instance of any failure of that kind in the navy during the entire campaign.

The *New York Medical Journal* rose to General Sternberg's defense against this adverse comparison:

It is forgotten that the Navy is a standing, permanent institution, always in service. Should stores therefore be requisitioned in advance and subsequently be found unnecessary for the particular purpose for which they were requisitioned, the money would not have been wasted, but the country would merely have paid in advance for what it would sooner or later inevitably have had to pay for. The Army, however, was on a different footing altogether. . . .

We said from the first and we repeat it more emphatically as fresh evidence comes to light that the administrative part of the army medical department accomplished all that could have been accomplished under existing conditions.

A great deal was said about the supposed shortage of doctors with the Santiago campaign. General Sternberg cited official figures showing that there were seventy-one with the Fifth Army Corps when it sailed from Tampa. That was an average of more than four doctors for every thousand men. Moreover, he said, twenty additional doctors had been sent to Santiago a short time later on the hospital ship *Relief*. That should have been enough, he insisted. His critics, he charged, were demanding a great deal more in the way of medical care of the troops than could reasonably be expected:

It has not been the expectation of the Medical Department that wounded men would immediately receive the attention of the Surgeon. No modern army makes provision for so large a number of medical officers as this would require. But attached to our army is a corps of non-combatants known as the Hospital Corps, which is the organized and authorized Red Cross of the army. At the outbreak of the war we had 800 hospital corpsmen in service. At present there are more than 6,000. We have done our best to instruct them in giving first aid to the wounded, and in a majority of the cases a first aid dressing properly applied by one of these men is all that is required.

To the many demands that he resign or be removed, General Sternberg made no reply at all. To his less violent critics who merely called for an immediate investigation of the Medical Department, he said, in a statement to the press:

I am ready at any moment for a complete investigation with reference to my administration of the affairs of the Medical Department; but the War Department is not disposed to make such an investigation as the result of sensational newspaper articles. There is at present an evident craze to criticise without regard to truth or justice. I have no doubt there will be a Congressional investigation into the conduct of the War; but I do not feel at liberty at present to insist upon an investigation for my own vindication, because it would be contrary to the general interests of the service.

It would make it necessary for me to give up all the important work which at present almost overwhelms me, for the purpose of devoting myself to a presentation of the facts relating to my administration. It would make it necessary to take clerks away from their daily tasks in order to look up the documentary evidence on file in my office, and, in the meantime, important matters would necessarily be neglected and the sick in all parts of the country would suffer. It would make it necessary to call upon the medical officers, who are now urgently needed for the care of the sick in our various camps and hospitals, to come to Washington as witnesses; and all this to satisfy the clamor of irresponsible newspaper reporters. There has been no official complaint with reference to my administration of the Medical Department.

Dr. Sternberg's statement that he was too busy to participate in an official investigation of the Medical Department certainly was no exaggeration. Even his sternest critics conceded that he was giving himself unsparingly to his work. But nobody except Martha Sternberg knew how long and how hard he worked. Only she realized how devotedly he applied himself to his crushing responsibilities. As she wrote after the storm had subsided:

Our home became as busy as any office. Telegrams came at all hours, the telephone rang almost constantly, and wives and mothers in great numbers sought information regarding husbands and sons. Our evenings at home were no longer for rest and recuperation. My sympathetic husband would see all people who came in distress and he tried to answer all the questions as best he could.

Among the many who took their troubles to the overburdened Surgeon General was a Mrs. Tanner, otherwise unidentified, except that she was active in Red Cross work. A Red Cross nurse went through every troop train immediately after its arrival in Washington, doing everything she could for the men and removing any who appeared not to be in condition to continue on to their destinations. The invalids appreciated this service: some of their officers, healthy and callous, did not.

"In numerous instances," Mrs. Tanner complained, "we could not get the boys off because, the moment the train stopped, the officers had disappeared—probably to fortify themselves with such refreshments as we do not furnish—and no one had power to give them into our hands."

She took the matter up with the Acting Secretary of War. He called General Sternberg. The Surgeon General told her to remove from the trains any men considered unfit to travel, with or without permission from their officers. If it was not to be had, she was to call a certain major he named, who would approve the removals.

This seemed to be all she needed. But, when she tried to remove the sick and wounded, there was a demand for written authority. That she did not have, so "I was not much better off." Back she went to the War Building. She asked General Sternberg to put in writing authority to remove those sick and wounded soldiers. He told her he would do even better than that: he would assign a surgeon on his staff to meet all incoming troop trains, with full authority to remove anyone who ought to be removed. That solved the problem. There were no more complaints about soldiers' having to travel when they were in no condition to do so.

Meanwhile, that fire of criticism kept up unabated. It even affected for a time the pleasant relations between the McKinleys and the Sternbergs. As Mrs. Sternberg said later:

The kindness of President McKinley is one circumstance which stands out in bold relief against the difficulties of those trying days. One day

he inquired of General Sternberg why I had not made my usual visits
to Mrs. McKinley, and he was informed that I was all broken up over
the adverse criticism of the conduct of the war. He told General Sternberg to bring me over, as I evidently needed a lesson in politics. When
we met the following Sunday, he expressed regret that I should have
worried over the newspaper accounts, remarking at the same time that I
did not understand that much of the criticism was for political effect and
that history would reveal that we had all done our duty, and in the
meantime we had at least the approval of our consciences.

The attacks did not let up with victory. Indeed, many who
had formerly been devoting their main energies to the war itself
turned their fire upon General Sternberg with increased fervor as
soon as the Spaniards had been safely disposed of. Typical of
those postvictory blasts was this editorial in the New York
World:

Never did a successful war have a sadder ending than that which
marks the close of our war with Spain. As the troops come home—
those who are able to come—the story is everywhere the same: a story
of official neglect, incompetence and blundering, with the natural results of sickness, starvation, debility and every form of suffering among
the men.
   ...It is not one of the "horrors of war." War had nothing to do
with it. The majority of them have had no experience of war. Not one
in ten has been within a hundred miles of an armed enemy. They have
been in camp, in their own country, in the midst of plenty, within reach
of the National Treasury, into which the people have poured more than
$200,000,000 to support this war, with the railroad, the telegraph, the
post-office, the farm, the garden, the market near at hand, and the loving
care and tenderness of a whole nation watching over them as a mother
watches over her children. And yet the battlefield itself would have been
mercy compared with what they have had to endure and are still en-
during.

To get at the truth regarding the conditions mentioned in
these attacks, General Sternberg launched an investigation of the
epidemics in army camps, with special attention to typhoid fever.
It was conducted by a three-man commission headed by Major
Walter Reed. The other members were Major Victor C. Vaughan
and Major Edward O. Shakespeare. The Reed-Vaughan-Shake-
speare Commission disclosed some things which were already generally known and some that had not yet been revealed. Typhoid
had become rampant among both regulars and volunteers, but
especially among the latter. Not a single regiment in seven army
corps had been free from the disease. More than 90 per cent of

all volunteer regiments had developed typhoid within the first eight weeks after going into camp. Both large and small encampments had had epidemics. The disease had appeared in epidemic form in the North as well as in the South. The danger that isolated cases would explode into epidemics had been greater in military camps than in civilian communities because of the greater difficulty of disposing of human excreta. Because typhoid was widely prevalent in every part of the country, "chances are that, if a regiment of 1,300 men should be assembled in any section and kept in a camp the sanitary conditions of which were perfect, one or more cases of typhoid would develop." A soldier with beginning typhoid fever might scatter his germs into every latrine in his regiment before finding out he had it. Some camps had not been wisely located; some had not been allocated enough space. "Many commands were allowed to remain on one site too long." "Requests for changes in location made by medical officers were not always granted." High-ranking line officers (nonmedical) were at least partly responsible for the insanitary condition of the encampments: "Greater authority should be given medical officers in questions relating to the hygiene of camps." Approved water supplies had played no significant part in the outbreaks. In some of the encampments there had been serious overcrowding: not only had the tents been too close together, there had also been too many men to a tent. The cases officially reported as typhoid had represented only a fraction of the total: many cases diagnosed as malaria had actually been typhoid. The typhoid situation had not been affected by what the men had eaten.

The report contained nothing reflecting upon the Sternberg administration of the Medical Department. The selection of camp sites was normally not his responsibility. He found it pleasant reading.

CHAPTER XVI

Counterattack

GENERAL STERNBERG was as confident as President McKinley that time and the telling of the complete story of the war would bring a complete vindication of himself and the Medical Department. Generally speaking, his confidence was justified. Although all his critics were never silenced, most of them were. The predominant opinion that crystallized after the war fevers and political passions subsided was that he had done an excellent job under teriffic handicaps.

That judgment was greatly strengthened by the report of the Dodge Commission, published in 1900. This commission, headed by General Grenville M. Dodge and consisting of nine army officers, in addition to himself, and three civilians, was appointed by President McKinley to investigate the conduct of the whole war. Its report substantiated what General Sternberg had been contending all along—that the Medical Department's freely admitted unpreparedness for war had been due to policies and practices over which it had no control. It pointed out, for example, how drastically Congress had reduced the number of assistant surgeons and how it had forbidden the continued employment of contract doctors. The lawmakers, not the Medical Department or the Surgeon General, it explained, had failed to provide for a Volunteer Hospital Corps. The shortages of medical equipment and supplies the Commission laid to "lack of appropriations by Congress, except for the annual needs of the Army." As a result, "No contracts, even provisional, had been made during the months of March and April, . . .funds not being available."

Many complaints of shortages were without justification, the report said, because the shortages complained of had not existed in fact. When there had been actual shortages, there often had been sound practical reasons why they could not be prevented. The report commented upon the arbitrary decision—made by the Quartermaster Department, not the Medical Department— to save money by shipping by freight. It mentioned a shipment which left St. Louis on May 17 and had not arrived in Chicka- mauga at the end of the month. As had also been pointed out by others, shipments by water, also the responsibility of the Quartermaster Department, were even more uncertain and un- satisfactory generally:

> Bad as conditions were on land, they were worse when the transporta- tion was across the sea. Medicines, stores, and hospital furniture were often put in holds of transports for Cuba and Puerto Rico under all sorts of freight. At Siboney and Daiquiri, because of the lack of proper landing facilities and the difficulties of finding ships and getting at their contents, perhaps a full third of the supplies taken aboard at Tampa early in June were not put ashore until the middle of July, after the surrender of Santiago and the opening of the harbor, and some of these stores were carried north to be later brought back undisturbed.

Colonel Dodge and his fellow commission members left no doubt as to where they thought the blame lay:

> The loading, shipping, and unloading of medical stores are not done under the orders of the Medical but of the Quartermaster's Department, and the Medical Department is not responsible therefor. The blame for so much of the lack of medical supplies as was the result of slow trans- portation and failure to deliver, and it is no small portion thereof, must rest with the Quartermaster's Department, the system it follows, and the officers belonging to it.

The commission's findings with regard to the typhoid epi- demics were like an echo of many of Sternberg's own statements:

> The outbreak and prevalence of this disease may properly be at- tributed to the combined operations of many causes. Large bodies of men who are not soldiers, under officers who have had little or no mili- tary training, can not be brought together and held for many weeks in camp and remain healthy. If the water supply is not abundant or is not good; if the thoroughly well-established rules of sanitation are not ob- served; if the discipline of the camp puts little restriction on drunkenness and immorality; if the soldier does not know how to live and his officers do not watch him and teach him; if his food is poorly cared for and badly cooked; and if he is permitted to eat and drink anything and every- thing that he can find, sickness certainly will prevail. If, as at Camp

Thomas, a regiment can go ten days without digging sinks; if the sinks dug are not used or they quickly overflow and pollute the ground; if practically no protection is afforded against the liquor sellers and prostitutes of neighboring places; if commands are crowded together and tents are seldom struck, or even never, during the occupation of the camp; if no one is called to account for repeated violations of sanitary orders, it can not but be that typhoid fever once introduced will spread, rapidly and widely.

Strict enforcement of sanitary regulations did, in some instances, keep infectious diseases at a minimum, the commission emphasized, giving an example: the Eighth Massachusetts Volunteer Infantry remained "very healthy" for many weeks at Camp Thomas, although during those same weeks there was much sickness in other regiments encamped nearby and getting water from the same sources.

There had been many complaints that the dressings of the wounded had not been changed often enough. There was "no good basis" for such charges, the commission said, because "it is the established rule of modern treatment that inspection and re-dressing are to be postponed until there is observed to be staining of the dressing or rise of temperature." In wound cases, it averred, "the less it [the dressing] is disturbed the more quickly and kindly a wound heals."

Colonel Dodge and the others of the commission were equally unsympathetic with the charge that hospital patients had not had enough to eat. It simply was not true, they averred. This did not mean that the sick and wounded got as much as they wanted of exactly what they wanted. For one thing, the funds available for the purchase of food did not permit unlimited variety. That limitation also prevented purchases in unrestricted quantities. Nevertheless, the commission insisted, these limitations did not prevent anyone from getting all the food—good food—he needed.

It had been charged that the hospital ship *Relief* had sailed from Siboney with considerably less than a capacity passenger list, leaving a great many sick behind. The Dodge Commission found that this had indeed been done. It also found out why: some of those left behind had yellow fever; others had illnesses which had not yet been diagnosed; the rest had been exposed to yellow fever. A large proportion of the last group would almost certainly develop cases. To take either group aboard would have resulted in an epidemic among the wounded. "To prevent such a condition occurring, the surgeon in charge decided, and wisely too, that in view of an existing uncertainty of diagnosis he would not take any cases of fever of any kind, and therefore sailed with only a limited number of patients, all wounded."

What of the alleged overcrowding on hospital ships and among the sick and wounded on transports? That undoubtedly had existed, the commission agreed. But here again the blame belonged elsewhere than on the shoulders of the Medical Department and its Surgeon General. Many who had been convalescent, or apparently even entirely well, upon going aboard had become seriously sick during the voyage, and required care and facilities which, for understandable reasons, had not been provided for them. Another complication was also mentioned: after the ships had been loaded with the troops and cargoes they were expected to carry, civilians with influence had managed to obtain permission to go along. Others, lacking such influence, had managed to get aboard just before sailing and avoid discovery until it was too late to send them back.

In Cuba, where ambulances were "really needed," they had been "almost wholly wanting." But the Dodge Commission did not blame their absence upon the Medical Department or its chief. Forty of them, fully equipped, had been ready to leave Tampa with General Shafter's Fifth Corps. The General had ordered thirty-seven left behind. As a result, "a large number of wounded were subjected to unnecessary hardship and suffering."

Favorable though the report generally was to General Sternberg and the Medical Department, they did not escape criticism altogether. The commission "regretted" that women nurses had not been used more extensively. The medical supply table was considered too restricted. The Surgeon General, it said, should have kept in closer touch with health conditions in camp and in the field. There had been actual shortages of foods and medicines, and at times there had not been enough doctors and nurses to meet immediate needs, the report averred, adding that not all of these personnel and material shortages could be regarded as unavoidable.

These minor criticisms and blame-placings were unpleasant, of course. General Sternberg would have been happier if the Dodge Commission had stated unequivocally that the Medical Department had met all situations in superb style and was entitled only to unalloyed praise from beginning to end. But Sternberg had no real reason to complain. The report as a whole was regarded generally as an exoneration of his handling of the army's medical affairs. To him and his sturdy friends, it was an excellent answer to his critics. They found particular pleasure in its general summing up: ". . .notwithstanding all the manifest errors, of omission rather than of commission, a vast deal of good work was done by the medical officers, high and low, regular and volunteer, and there were unusually few deaths among the wounded and sick."

This last statement, surprising to most people even today, gave strong support to one of General Sternberg's favorite contentions: in spite of those widely publicized epidemics, the men of the Spanish-American War had fared much better healthwise than those of any other major war in which this country had ever participated. He took particular delight in setting people right on this. At the 1899 meeting of the American Medical Association, he said:

As compared with the Civil War and other great wars during the present century, the mortality from wounds and disease among our troops during our war with Spain has been low. Our wounded have had, to a large extent, the advantage of prompt treatment with antiseptic dressings and a very considerable portion of those who were not killed outright have recovered without any mutilating operation or septic complication. The mortality from disease has been comparatively low. . . .The total number of deaths reported in our enlarged army, including regulars and volunteers, from May 1, 1898, to April 30, 1899, is 6,406. Of these 5,438 died of disease and 968 were killed in battle or died of wounds, injuries or accidents. During the Civil War the number of deaths from disease was 186,216.* The number who were killed in battle or died of wounds was 93,969, or about one-half of the deaths from disease.

Dr. Sternberg quoted official figures showing that the army's

* Medical military authorities say this figure really should be close to 210,400, as 24,184 deaths believed to be due to disease were attributed to unknown causes.

disease death rate during eight of the first twelve months of the Spanish-American War had been lower than during the corresponding months of the Civil War. (The four months in which it had been higher, of course, included the epidemic period from July to September, inclusive.) The disease death rate for the entire first twelve months of the Civil War, he pointed out, was actually nearly 70 per cent higher than that for the corresponding period of the Spanish-American War. (The fighting phase of the Spanish-American War ended, of course, in August, 1898. But the Army was still large, and while on occupation duty in tropical countries continued to be exposed to virtually the same diseases as before.) Moreover, General Sternberg went on, in spite of those early epidemics, it took the Army Medical Department only about half as long to gain control of epidemic diseases in the Spanish-American War as in the Civil War. In the earlier conflict, he said on the authority of those official figures, the peak of disease mortality was not reached until February, 1863, some twenty-two months after the outbreak of war. In the Spanish-American War, on the other hand, that peak was reached and passed in September, 1898, the fifth month after the declaration of war. The disease death rate for the twelfth month after the outbreak of the Spanish-American War was less than a fifth of the rate for the twelfth month of the Civil War.

Dr. Sternberg had even more surprising news regarding typhoid. Epidemics had sent the 1898-99 fiscal year typhoid death rate to more than twenty-two times the average for the previous ten-year period. But even they, he said in that AMA address, had not prevented the average American soldier from having a much better chance of escaping death from typhoid during the first year after the outbreak of the Spanish-American War than he had had in the first year of the Civil War. Sternberg quoted records which showed that an average of 1,971 men per 100,000 succumbed to this disease during the first year of the earlier war. The year that followed the declaration of war against Spain brought an average of only 1,237 typhoid deaths per 100,000. As was true of disease generally, the peak of typhoid mortality had been reached many months earlier in the Spanish-American War than in the Civil War. Moreover, the Medical Department's curbing of that disease in the later war was powerful as well as prompt: during the last half of that twelve-month period the typhoid death rate was "remarkably low." Indeed, the speaker declared with pride, "in the history of large armies the record has never before been equaled."

Dr. Sternberg also had potent facts and figures relieving the Medical Department of responsibility for delays in getting medical supplies and equipment to the fighting areas of Cuba, and used them at times. But the most effective presentation of the Medical Department's side of the controversy was made by others, whose testimony carried greater weight from their not being parties to the dispute. One who did much to set the record straight was Lieutenant Colonel Nicholas Senn, in charge of the operating staff in the field. There had unquestionably been delays, perhaps even inexcusable delays, he said. But the fault was not the Medical Department's:

The hospital ship *Relief* brought an immense amount of medical supplies, delicacies, cots, pillows and blankets. When we arrived at Siboney we knew our presence was much needed, and looked in vain for some one to inform us where and how to land. The precipitous and rocky nature of the shore and the great depth of the ocean made it unfavorable to secure an anchorage for several days. A single lighter attended to the demands of numerous transport ships. I am sure no one can blame the Medical Department for the unavoidable delay in unloading the supplies. The little steam launches did what could be done in bringing to the shore what was most needed. Major Torrey* worked night and day in supplying the requisitions made by the surgeons in the field and hospitals. There was no red tape here; all they had to do was to inform him what was wanted and it was delivered as soon as it could be brought ashore. The lack of proper transportation facilities from the landing to the front cannot be charged to the Medical Department. It took more than a week of the hardest kind of work to land the supplies.

Colonel Senn contended that it was true "only to a certain extent" that the sick and wounded lacked medical supplies. Shortages "owing to the unexpected enormous demands" were "supplied as quickly as could be done under the existing circumstances." Operating in all the hospitals in the Cuban war zone, he "was always able to find the essential antiseptics and dressing materials required in military practice." That was true, he said, even when supplies were at their lowest. There was "no lack at

* Commander of the *Relief*.

any time of stimulants and antiseptics." Immediately after the battle, it is true, there was a shortage of tents and blankets, but it was promptly corrected. In spite of monumental difficulties of supply and transportation, the men had fared much better than soldiers normally do:

> War always has had its hardships and discomforts; it can not be prosecuted in parlor cars and clubhouses. Our soldiers expected deprivations and unavoidable discomforts, but on the whole they were subjected to less actual suffering than they had reason to look for. To the credit of the medical officers it must be said they shared the inevitable hardships with the soldiers. They lived on the same food, drank the same water, and made the moist ground their beds. . . .Among the thousands of sick and wounded with whom I have been brought in contact during the Cuban campaign I have seldom heard a complaint; on the contrary, I have heard nothing but words of praise for the hard-working, self-sacrificing medical officers and the department they represented in the field.

Captain Edward L. Munson, in charge of an ambulance company in Cuba and adjutant to the Chief Surgeon of the Fifth Corps, also made his contribution to what he considered the pursuit of truth. Like others, he blamed shortages of medical equipment and supplies upon inadequacies and blunders at the points of debarkation. Ships about to sail for the Santiago expedition had been loaded with all the drugs, medicines, instruments, hospital tentage and other medical supplies that were likely to be needed for such an operation, he said. When they reached Cuban waters, there had been no launches or other small boats to get the stuff ashore. Time after time, Captain Munson declared, he had appealed to the Quartermaster Department for a lighter or small steamer. Time after time he had received the same answer: the Quartermaster Department could do nothing. As a result, "the Medical Department was compelled to rely entirely upon its own energies and improvise its own transportation." Unfortunately, there was little it could do either. He stated that:

> I feel justified in saying that at the time of my departure large quantities of medical supplies urgently needed on shore still remained on transports, a number of which were under orders to return to the United States. Had the Medical Department carried along double the amount of supplies, it is difficult to see how, with the totally inadequate land and water transportation provided by the Quartermaster's Department, the lamentable conditions on shore could have been in any way improved.

A number of medical officers, as well as others, also rallied to the defense of General Sternberg and the Medical Department against charges of neglect of the sick and wounded. One of them was Dr. Frank Donaldson, Assistant Surgeon, U. S. Volunteers. He was especially anxious to choke off the rumors about Camp Wickoff, with which he was most familiar. Writing from that camp at the tip of Long Island to the editor of *Medical News,* he called the charges "little short of mendacious." They not only were spiteful and untrue, he said, they also were bringing distress to thousands of parents. Thanks to these rumormongers, "families all over the country are in panic, and terrible and unnecessary suffering has been caused." He told about poor people who had spent their last dollar and even gone into debt to go to the camp and "rescue their sons from the death and starvation which they had read was encompassing the boys here."

General Joe Wheeler had told him about an incident of this kind. An aged couple traveled thousands of miles bringing with them a little bag of food for their son. When they reached Camp Wickoff, they were surprised and delighted beyond expression to find the "starving" youngster getting along quite all right, eating well, and making a good recovery.

Since state officials had been among the most strident of General Sternberg's critics and the most eager to trumpet unsupported charges, he had learned not to expect praise from them. But the Governor of Oregon gave him a pleasant surprise. Concerned over reports about Oregon troops in San Francisco, he went there for a personal, on-the-spot investigation. His conclusion was this: " . . .the whole trouble had been caused by a handful of malcontent privates who manufactured the stories out of their imaginations or distorted facts in a shameless manner. . . as a whole, the soldiers give testimony to good treatment by the government and their superior officers."

Brigadier General H. V. Boynton told about another on-the-spot investigation inspired by similar malcontents. Governor Frank S. Black of New York heard reports of mistreatment and neglect of men in the Eighth New York Regiment. Unlike his Oregon counterpart, he did not run them down himself but sent his surgeon general. The latter arrived in the evening, and the news spread fast. During the night trouble-makers passed the word along: "All those who want to go home report at sick call in the morning." And they did, some four hundred of them. One was on a cot, carried by his buddies. His eyes had a most unnatural stare, the result, the visiting surgeon general was told, of paralysis. In spite of this condition, his companions said, he had had to spend the night out in the open: there was not enough room for him in the hospital. The surgeon general eventually learned that he was not paralyzed at all. There was nothing the matter with him. He had a regular bed in the hospital. The glassy stare had been produced by belladona which the others had put in his eyes.

The slow revelation of incidents of this kind contributed mightily to the swing of public opinion in General Sternberg's favor. Another great help was the unwillingness of many of his critics to back up the statements they had so glibly made. One of these was the Rev. Teunis S. Hamlin, pastor of Washington's Church of the Covenant. Called upon to substantiate some serious charges he had made in a sermon, he declined to do so. Admitting that he had had no personal knowledge of the conditions about which he had complained, he took refuge in the lame statement that he had spoken "upon information found in reputable papers and statements issued from officials of the War Department and found in the public press."

The minister may have been satisfied with this explanation, but many others were not, including members of his own church. One of them, Vice President Garrett A. Hobart, became so angry that he moved his church membership.

CHAPTER XVII

Four Men on a Mission

WHEN, IN 1897, Giuseppe Sanarelli, a highly reputable Italian bacteriologist, announced at Montivideo, Uruguay, that he had found the yellow fever germ, General Sternberg naturally read the announcement with a great deal of interest, if also with a great deal of skepticism. His first reaction was to think that the Sanarelli bacillus (*Bacillus icteroides*) was his own *Bacillus X*, upon which he had built such strong but unfounded hopes some years before. Tests at the Army Medical Museum's bacteriological laboratory, however, showed that the two organisms were entirely different.

General Sternberg's skepticism was, he was sure, fully justified. If the Sanarelli germ was actually the yellow fever bacillus, then it certainly would be present, and therefore observable, in all cases of yellow fever. But General Sternberg had not been able to find anything like it in significant numbers in the many yellow fever cases he had examined. Therefore, he reasoned, whatever it was that Sanarelli had found was not the yellow fever organism. "If it (the Sanarelli bacillus) were constantly found in the blood and tissues of yellow fever cadavers, there would be little reason to doubt its specific character," he said in a paper read at that Twelfth International Medical Congress in Moscow in August, 1897. "But both my researches and those of Sanarelli show that, notwithstanding the most painstaking investigations, this bacillus has not been found in a considerable proportion of the typical cases of yellow fever examined."

The doubting Surgeon General also had other reasons for questioning the Sanarelli claims. If the Sanarelli bacillus were really the yellow fever germ, then a serum made from it would give people protection against the disease, But he was convinced that it would not. "The serum of M. Sanarelli has failed here in Brazil," a friend of his had written him from Rio de Janeiro. "The results of the experiments which we made at São Paulo have not recommended the employment of this serum. It is neither preventive nor curative."

The Surgeon General had also read in a prominent medical publication a paper in which the author, Dr. P. E. Archinard, told about his own and others' unsatisfactory experience with the Sanarelli serum: ". . . we are forced to conclude that this agent, in our hands, has shown no curative powers whatsoever, none of the important and dangerous symptoms of the disease having been in any way mitigated or prevented by its administration."*

As firm in his disbelief in the Sanarelli claims as Dr. Sternberg was Dr. Aristides Agramonte, a well-known Cuban bacteriologist, then an army contract surgeon. The Cuban was as certain as the American that in time the falsity of those claims would be fully exposed and hoped to have a part in their exposure. In December, 1898, Dr. Sternberg sent Agramonte back to Cuba, where the latter had made some yellow fever investigations during the war, to carry on exhaustive experimental tests of the validity of the Sanarelli claims. In Havana, Agramonte found himself working alongside two physicians of the U. S. Public Health and Marine Hospital Service, both of whom had given unqualified support to the Sanarelli claims. Drs. Eugene Wasdin and Henry D. Geddins were still "finding" proof that the Sanarelli bacillus caused yellow fever. ". . .we frequently investigated the same cases," Dr. Agramonte wrote later in a magazine article. "I often autopsied bodies from which we took the same specimens and made the same cultures in, generally, the same kind of media, and, finally, we rendered our reports to our respective departments, Wasdin and Geddins affirming that Sanarelli's bacillus was present in almost all cases, while I denied that it had any specific

* P. E. Archinard, "Experiments Performed at the Charity Hospital of New Orleans and Elsewhere with Sanarelli's Anti-Amarylic Serum in the Fall of 1898," *New Orleans Medical and Surgical Journal*, LII (Aug., 1899), 79-86.

character and showed its occurrence in cases not yellow fever."*

For about two years Sanarelli was, as Dr. Agramonte said of him, "the hero of the hour." General Sternberg, Dr. Agramonte, and a few others in a tight little group of doubters received scant support. But their day finally came. It was shown beyond question that the Sanarelli bacillus had nothing at all to do with causing yellow fever, and was, instead, identified as the hog cholera bacillus.

With American troops still stationed in Cuba, although the war had been over several months, there gradually took shape in General Sternberg's mind a plan to carry on and greatly enlarge the yellow fever investigations which the tireless Dr. Agramonte had been carrying on since his return to the island. What was needed, he decided, was a board of medical investigators devoting their full time for an indefinite period to a broad exploration of yellow fever's cause and control. He talked the scheme over with some of his official advisers. Then he dictated the following letter:

WAR DEPARTMENT SURGEON GENERAL'S OFFICE

WASHINGTON, May 23, 1900

To the Adjutant General of the Army

SIR:

I have the honor to recommend that Major Walter Reed, Surgeon, U. S. Army, and Contract Surgeon James Carroll, U. S. Army, be ordered to proceed from this city to Camp Columbia, Cuba, reporting their arrival and instructions to the commanding officer of the post, the commanding general, Department of Havana, and Pinar del Rio, and the commanding general, Division of Cuba.

I also recommend the organization of a medical board with headquarters at Camp Columbia, for the purpose of pursuing scientific investigations with reference to the infectious diseases prevalent on the island of Cuba and especially of yellow fever.

The board to be constituted as follows:

Major Walter Reed, U. S. Army; Contract Surgeon James Carroll, U. S. Army; Contract Surgeon Aristides Agramonte, U. S. Army; and Contract Surgeon Jesse W. Lazear, U. S. Army.

* Aristides Agramonte, "The Inside Story of a Great Medical Discovery," *Scientific Monthly*, I (Dec., 1915), 209-239.

Contract Surgeon Agramonte is now on duty in the city of Havana and Contract Surgeon Jesse W. Lazear at Camp Columbia. It is not considered necessary to relieve them from the duties to which they are at present assigned.

The board should act under general instructions which will be communicated to Major Walter Reed by the Surgeon General of the Army.

Very respectfully,
GEORGE M. STERNBERG,
Surgeon General, U. S. Army

Major Reed was an inspired choice for the chairmanship. A man of charming manner, he caused anybody who knew him even slightly to become an ardent admirer. He and General Sternberg were close personal friends and had been for years. Each had a warm regard for the other's character and capabilities. There is good reason to believe General Sternberg had had his eye on him for some time for an especially important assignment, even before he knew that he would send him on this epochal yellow fever mission of discovery.

Before leaving for Havana, Reed received both written and verbal instructions from his chief. The former, dated May 29, 1900, reached him at the Army Medical Museum, where he was serving as curator. The letter read in part:

You will naturally give special attention to questions relating to the etiology and prevention of yellow fever. As you are familiar with what has already been done by other bacteriologists in this field of investigation, I do not consider it necessary to give you any suggestions or detailed instructions. But it is evident that the most important question which will occupy your attention is that which relates to the etiology of this disease.

Reed's verbal instructions, of course, were off the record. As far as is known, they were heard by no one but these two men, so that there is no way of knowing exactly what they were. However, we have it on the authority of Dr. Sternberg himself that he instructed Reed to work on the theory that the mosquito might be the agency of yellow fever transmission. "Having for years given much thought to the subject," he wrote a few years later in a magazine article, "I became sometime since impressed with the view that probably in yellow fever, as in the malarial fevers, there was an 'intermediate host.' . . .I therefore suggested to Dr. Reed, president of the board appointed upon my recommendation for the study of the disease in the Island of Cuba, that he should give special attention to the possibility of transmission by some insect."*

The mosquito-transmission theory—as a theory—was more than fifty years old and had its origin even earlier: General Sternberg was not in any way its originator. Dr. Benjamin Rush, who struggled valiantly with Philadelphia's worst yellow fever epidemic after exposing himself to even greater dangers by signing the Declaration of Independence, had commented upon the large number of mosquitoes during the 1793 outbreak. Noah Webster had made similar observations during New York's unhappy experience with the disease two years later; however, neither he nor Rush had suggested a cause and effect relationship. As early as 1809, Dr. John Crawford had stated positively that man contracted numerous forms of illness by taking into his body minutely tiny particles formerly in the bodies of other types of animal life. In 1848 Dr. Josiah Nott of Mobile, Alabama, had indicated his belief that mosquitoes transmitted yellow fever. In 1854 Beauperthuys had flatly proclaimed the mosquito-transmission theory. On August 14, 1881, Dr. Carlos Finlay, a prominent Cuban physician, had told the Academy of Sciences in Havana that the mosquito was unquestionably that all-important link in the chain of infection. He did not indict mosquitoes generally, however. Most of them he regarded as harmless as far as yellow fever was concerned. He contended, then, and at every opportunity thereafter, that the disease was transmitted by a single mosquito species, known then as the *Culex*, later as the *Stegomyia fasciata,* and now as the *Aedes aegypti.* He had won very few converts to his theory during the intervening years, however, both his fellow doctors and the general public having remained unconvinced.

Their skepticism is understandable. It was readily conceded that Dr. Finlay had built up a strong theoretical case. It was quite true, the skeptics admitted, that yellow fever epidemics and swarms of *Stegomyia fasciata* mosquitoes appeared in the same places at the same times. The yellow fever belt was also,

* "Preventive Medicine," *Popular Science Monthly,* LXII (Feb., 1903), 348-358.

generally speaking, the *Stegomyia fasciata* belt. True too, yellow fever often raged out of control in seacoast communities in tropical countries, while in the mountains, a comparatively short distance away (where this mosquito species could not survive the cold), yellow fever outbreaks were unknown. Guayaquil, for example, a seaport, never knew when another epidemic would strike. Yet Quito, in the same country but at a much higher elevation, had as little to fear from yellow fever as Chicago or Montreal. The same was true of sea-level Vera Cruz and mountain-high Mexico City. Dr. Finlay called attention to all these things. He also reminded those who would listen to him that Ronald Ross had recently identified the mosquito as the malaria vector.

This array of evidence was certainly impressive. Finlay's logic was sound enough. But, if the *Stegomyia fasciata* were really the yellow fever vector, why had he not been able to produce at least one case of yellow fever which had demonstrably been transmitted in that way? The question had him baffled. Strong and airtight as his theory was, he had never been able to demonstrate it in practice. Time after time—a hundred times or more—he had placed *Stegomyia fasciata* mosquitoes on the arm of a yellow fever patient. Time after time he had watched them bite deeply into the flesh. Time after time he had later watched them bite arms, legs, and other parts of the bodies of well people. Time after time he had watched hopefully for the well to become sick with yellow fever. And time after time he had seen those people stay completely well, as free from yellow fever signs and symptoms as if they had received injections of distilled water or nothing at all.

It is not surprising, then, that Dr. Sternberg was not completely convinced that the mosquito—the *Stegomyia fasciata* or any other—was that vital link in yellow fever transmission. Nor is it surprising that very few other people gave the mosquito-transmission theory even the partial acceptance that he gave it. Along with possible mosquito transmission of yellow fever from the sick to the well, Dr. Sternberg's verbal instructons to Reed alluded to the likelihood that the disease was centered in some organism which neither he nor anyone else had yet been able to isolate or identify. Sternberg himself had toiled long and hard to find such an organism and had refused to admit, in spite of his failure, that it did not exist. There was a possibility, he insisted, that the yellow fever organism had escaped his and others' observation because of its extremely small size, too small to be seen under the microscope or to be stopped by the usual laboratory filters. That possibility had been greatly strengthened, he thought, by the experiments of the German bacteriologist Friedrich A. J. Löffler. Löffler had taken material from animals sick with foot and mouth disease, passed it through filters capable of stopping any organism then known, and injected it into other animals, which had subsequently developed the illness. If a tiny organism could transmit foot and mouth disease, why could one not also transmit yellow fever?*

That question apparently had already been answered in the negative. Dr. Sternberg himself had tried to induce yellow fever in animals—dogs, rabbits, and guinea pigs—by injecting into them blood taken from yellow fever patients. The attempts had been uniformly unsuccessful. However, the outcome might have been different with human beings. Possibly "these animals were not susceptible to the disease." Their failure to develop yellow fever "could not be accepted as showing that the germ of yellow fever was not present in the blood." Unfortunately for Sternberg's confidence in that point, at least one experiment with which he was familiar had proved fruitless, in spite of the use of a human subject. During his visit to Vera Cruz Dr. Daniel Ruiz, in charge of one of the city's largest hospital's, had, at his request, injected blood from a yellow fever patient into a nonimmune, who had remained completely well.

Nevertheless, to Dr. Sternberg's way of thinking, that experiment too might have told an untrue story. The yellow fever patient giving the blood had already had the disease eight days. Perhaps, the dissatisfied Dr. Sternberg reasoned questioningly, that was too long. It was "quite possible that the specific germ

* Although, as stated, Dr. Sternberg's belief in the existence of a submicroscopic causative agent for yellow fever was based largely upon the results of Löffler's studies, he presumably did not specifically discuss them in his verbal instructions to Reed. In their paper on "The Etiology of Yellow Fever," Reed and Carroll state that this was done by Dr. William H. Welch, who, they say, suggested that they also try filtration experiments.

might have been present at an earlier period and that after a certain number of days the natural resources of the body are sufficient to affect its destruction, or in some way cause its disappearance from the circulation." Sternberg's reasoning of 1887 was to be proved in later years to be thoroughly sound.

General Sternberg was "especially anxious that this experiment should be repeated with blood taken from a case in the early stage of the disease." It was no easy matter to persuade people to take this risk: he could not serve, being an immune. So it is not surprising that he included blood inoculations on human volunteers among the tasks he assigned the Reed Board.

In addition to those written instructions [he wrote later *], I talked freely with Major Reed, President of the Commission, and gave him my views as to the most promising lines of experiment relating to the etiology of yellow fever. . . .I urged that efforts should be made to ascertain definitely whether the disease can be communicated from man to man by blood inoculations. Evidently if this is the case the blood must contain the living infectious agent upon which the propagation of the disease depends, notwithstanding the fact that all attempts to demonstrate the presence of such a germ in the blood, by means of the microscope and culture methods, had proved unavailing.

Dr. Agramonte was still at Military Hospital No. 1, in Havana, when he received his first intimation of the board's existence. The news came in a letter from Major Reed written in the office of General Sternberg and dated May 25, 1900:

An order issued yesterday from the War Department calls for a board of medical officers for the investigation of acute infectious diseases occurring on the Island of Cuba The board consists of Carroll, yourself, Lazear and the writer. It will be our duty, under verbal instructions from the Surgeon General, to continue the investigation of the causation of yellow fever. The Surgeon General expects us to make use of your laboratory at Military Hospital No. 1 and Lazear's laboratory at Camp Columbia.

Reed and Carroll, the letter continued, planned to leave New York on a transport between June 15 and 20. They "are looking forward with much pleasure to our association with you and Lazear in this interesting work." It appeared to him that there was "a year or two of work before us."

These four men, setting out on one of the most epochal ex-

* "Researches Relating to the Etiology of Yellow Fever," *Pan-American Surgical and Medical Journal*, XXI (April, 1916), 16-20.

periments in medical history, had their first meeting as a board on Monday afternoon, June 25, just a few hours after Reed's and Carroll's arrival. Their meeting place was the veranda of the Columbia Barracks Hospital's officers' quarters. Dr. Agramonte wrote of it:

We were fully appreciative of the trust and aware of the responsibility placed upon us and with a feeling akin to reverence heard the instructions which Major Reed had brought from the Surgeon General; they comprised the investigation also of malaria, leprosy and unclassified febrile conditions and were given with such detail and precision as only a man of General Sternberg's experience and knowledge in such matters could have prepared.*

Either Dr. Agramonte or Dr. Lazear told the new arrivals about what Dr. Agramonte called a "particularly interesting" case. Exactly a week before the meeting a soldier-prisoner whose identity was not revealed had died of yellow fever. In the guardhouse since June 6, he had shown the initial symptoms on the twelfth. Eight other soldier-prisoners had shared this man's cell, staying with him in those close quarters during the six days he was sick. One of them had even moved into his bunk after his death and slept there. None of them had developed yellow fever. Another incident was called to the board members' attention: three men, presumably not prisoners, had handled the clothing and washed the linen of those who had died from yellow fever while in prison. None of them had developed yellow fever either.

These incidents made a strong impression upon those four medical scientists. If yellow fever was contracted by close physical association with its victims and by handling their clothing, why had all those men escaped it? Maybe Dr. Sternberg, Dr. Finlay, and those few others were right after all. Maybe the causative organism really was transmitted by an intermediate host. And maybe that intermediate host was a mosquito. So "it was decided that, although discredited by the repeated failure of Dr. Carlos J. Finlay, of Havana, to demonstrate it, the matter should be taken up by the board and thoroughly sifted."

* See "The Inside Story of a Great Medical Discovery," *loc. cit.*

CHAPTER XVIII

Mission Accomplished

MEANWHILE, a yellow fever epidemic in a tiny Mississippi community had been adding substance to the mosquito-transmission theory. This outbreak was different from others in that the houses in which cases were occurring were at some distance from each other and from all other houses. That made it possible for Dr. Henry Rose Carter, yellow fever expert of the U. S. Public Health and Marine Hospital Service, to study the case, or cases, in every house separately. Although he was transferred to another part of the country while this study was still under way, he arranged with two local physicians to continue the record-keeping.

When the records were assembled and evaluated, three important facts stood out: (a) although many people had entered those houses during the first ten or fourteen days after those patients became sick, not one had developed yellow fever; (b) a large proportion of those who entered those houses after that time soon began showing the characteristic yellow fever symptoms; and (c) some of those who developed yellow fever had not been near the patients at all during their illness, but had waited until after they had died or recovered before entering the houses.

Following those clearly marked trails, Dr. Carter arrived at these conclusions: (a) neither the yellow fever patient nor anything he had handled or soiled was capable of giving the disease to others by direct contact; (b) like malaria, yellow fever had to depend upon a third agency for transmission to others; (c) that agency had to wait about ten days or two weeks after biting a yellow fever patient (during which time the disease developed in its own body) before it could pass it on to human beings.

As it happened, Dr. Carter was on duty in Havana for some time after the Reed Board (known officially as the Yellow Fever Commission) began its studies. Naturally enough, men so greatly interested in the same thing got to know each other well and spent considerable time in consultation. In spite of General Sternberg's interest in the mosquito as a possible yellow fever vector and the continued good health of the cellmates of the prisoner who had died of the disease, Major Reed had shared the widespread doubts regarding this insect's role in yellow fever transmission. Dr. Carter's records now gave him something to think about. His doubts began to weaken: could the mosquito be the answer to the yellow fever-transmission problem after all? Deciding to find out, he ordered the experiments tailored to reflect his new interest in this phase of the subject. However, he could not personally supervise them for a while, having been called back temporarily to Washington. He ordered the experiments to go ahead in his absence; Dr. Lazear was designated to act for him until he returned.

Dr. Finlay was, of course, delighted to co-operate. Here seemed to be the promise of complete vindication for himself and his theories. At last, he was convinced, the mosquito—the *Stegomyia*—would be definitely identified as the link between old and new yellow fever cases. Eagerly he turned over to Dr. Lazear the mosquito eggs he had been so carefully incubating. But Finlay, who had known so much disappointment, was destined to know even more. Eleven persons were bitten by the Finlay *Stegomyia* mosquitoes. One of them was Dr. Carroll, who, with another volunteer, developed the disease. The remaining nine remained perfectly well, enough to leave serious doubt as to whether the *Stegomyia* was the long-sought link. Dr. Lazear was not a man to give up easily. Unconvinced though he was, he was determined to pursue the trail to its ultimate end. The cultivation of *Stegomyia* mosquitoes went on. And so did the experiments. And so did the failures and disappointments.

Then that trail took a sudden turn. Dr. Lazear himself developed yellow fever after allowing himself to be bitten a second time, the first having failed to produce the disease. Unlike Dr. Carroll, he did not get off with a relatively light case but became steadily worse, dying on September 25. A message went at once to the absent Reed. He hastily rearranged his plans and started back to Havana as soon as possible.

A scientist to the last, Dr. Lazear had told the intimates who gathered at his bedside as much as he could about his illness and what had caused it. He positively identified the mosquito as a *Stegomyia,* of course. It had bitten a yellow fever patient at least ten days before biting him, thus following the pattern set in that rural Mississippi community. But there was also something else about Lazear's illness which Dr. Carter had not noticed about that Mississippi epidemic: the biting of that yellow fever patient had occurred within the first three days after he became sick.

This last bit of information struck Reed with particular force. Was that the missing factor which had blocked success in those earlier experiments? If these three conditions—using the *Stegomyia* mosquito, having it bite a yellow fever patient during the first three days of illness, and preventing it from biting a non-immune volunteer until at least ten days thereafter—should be met, would the experimenters be able to produce yellow fever cases virtually at will? Only more tests upon human beings would tell. Reed sent out a call for volunteers. The response was accelerated by a promise of two hundred and fifty dollars for each person accepted. That sum had a particularly strong appeal to Americans drawing army pay.

Not all of them were interested in money alone. John J. Moran and John R. Kissinger were interested solely in making this contribution to science's eventual victory over Yellow Jack. Neither would accept a cent. Some say Reed touched his hat and said, "Gentlemen, I salute you." Others say he did no such thing. Be that as it may, he was touched by their youthful eagerness to help.

The experiments soon got under way in earnest. *Stegomyia* mosquitoes began biting volunteers from ten to fourteen days after biting newly diagnosed yellow fever patients. And this time it was a case's failure to develop, and not the appearance of those characteristic symptoms, which proved the exception to the rule. The pattern set in those initial tests continued as the experiments were repeated over a period of several weeks. Before they were brought to an end the *Stegomyia* had been clearly pinpointed as the yellow fever villain.

While these experiments were bringing such sweet satisfaction to the long-suffering Dr. Finlay, others were making their own contributions to the unearthing of Yellow Jack's deadly secrets. A wire-net partition was strung from wall to wall and from floor to ceiling of a room, splitting it into sections of approximately the same size. Fifteen *Stegomyia* mosquitoes that ten or twelve days before had bitten some yellow fever patients newly admitted to one of the Havana hospitals were loosed on one side of that screen. Then a nonimmune walked in, and the door was closed. At the same time two other nonimmunes entered the other side. During the next thirty minutes the first man was bitten seven times. Reed wanted him to be certain to receive an infection strong enough to insure his getting yellow fever. So he returned him to the mosquito-inhabited side of that partition a few hours later. The insects pounced upon him again, biting him five times. The next day he returned and was bitten three times. On the fourth day he began showing the symptoms that told Reed and the other yellow fever experts that he had the disease. The other two men, just a few feet away from those mosquitoes but with the wire net between, showed no signs of illness.

Meanwhile, Reed had run into trouble of another sort. A considerable segment of the Havana press began howling about his use of human subjects. Some of the local papers "have abused us soundly and have charged us with all kinds of inhumanity and barbarity," he wrote General Sternberg. However, the Spanish consul, "a most courteous and intelligent gentleman," supported him solidly in his use of Spanish civilians and promised to continue to do so "as long as we do not use minors and the individual gives his written consent." The board chairman assured his chief that "I am not at all disturbed by these newspaper attacks." Nevertheless, he took a very wise step to minimize them. He felt he had little to fear as long as no deaths occurred among his volunteers. But, should even one of them die, the protests—in the newspapers, on speakers' platforms, and perhaps even in the halls of Congress—might quickly reach such fury that it would be impossible to go on. It was essential, therefore, that nobody die, if possible.

To bring about that feat of medical miracle-working (yellow fever is one of the most fatal of diseases, with deaths often ending from a third to a half of the cases), Major Reed turned to Dr. Roger Post Ames, placing him in charge of those who developed the disease. Dr. Ames, an army surgeon, was probably better qualified for that task than any other person of his time. He was fortunate enough to have as his chief nurse Gust Lambert, a young Norwegian whom he had trained to care for yellow fever patients. This team worked so well that not one of his volunteers succumbed. Reed indeed had chosen wisely. It is probably no exaggeration to say that we are indebted to that wise choice for the continuation of the experiments and for the knowledge they produced.*

Keeping his eye anxiously on Dr. Ames, Gust Lambert, and their patients, Reed went ahead steadily with this experiment, as well as the others he had launched. Other volunteers went into that tight little screen-bisected shack. Those on the mosquitoless end continued as free from yellow fever as if they had been in Labrador or Greenland. Bites by the infected mosquitoes upon those in the other portion of the building brought the characteristic symptoms, some of them violent, seemingly presaging death. Reed had much reason to worry as it seemed to take even greater magic than the Ames-Lambert team possessed to save them and the whole enterprise. As one crisis after another arrived and passed, he developed a tremendous admiration for these two.

Having demonstrated so convincingly that one section of that building was safe and the other dangerous, as far as yellow fever was concerned, Major Reed put on another demonstration to prove it was the infected *Stegomyia*, and nothing else, which made all that difference. The infected area was disinfected, not in the orthodox way, by spraying powerful germ-killers about the place, but by merely capturing and removing the mosquitoes.

* Dr. Ames has been called "the forgotten man of the Yellow Fever Commission." Some of his admirers have tried to obtain for him the same official recognition received by others participating in the experiments, but their efforts have been unsuccessful.

Afterward a nonimmune spent some time in each end of the building. Each remained perfectly well.

While some volunteers were being bitten by infected mosquitoes (and usually getting yellow fever) and others were proving that one could spend hours and days in an infected building without getting the disease, provided he did not allow one of the mosquitoes to bite him, still others were finding answers to some other vital questions: Was the *Stegomyia* the only agency of infection? Or could a person also get yellow fever by handling the clothing and other articles used by yellow fever patients?

Not far from the building used in those mosquito experiments Major Reed supervised the construction of another one. It was much smaller. Its tight little windows, carefully screened to keep out vagrant mosquitoes that might fly in and distort the picture, almost kept out the air as well. And then from the nearby Los Animas yellow fever hospital began a parade of orderlies carrying a repulsive, stomach-stirring assortment of articles used by those who had recently died of, or recovered from, yellow fever. Mattresses still carried the shallow concavities outlined by one human body after another engaged in a life-and-death struggle with Yellow Jack. Some of them were foul-smelling with human excreta. Others carried the moist stains of the black vomit which, as much as anything else, is the mark and symbol of yellow fever. Bed linen contained similiar stains and odors. If anything from a patient's body could give anybody yellow fever, this weird collection certainly should. But to Reed it was not quite enough. He asked the hospital superintendent to have attendants collect basinfuls of fresh excreta and black vomit. This was poured over the stuff until it was soggy through and through.

Volunteers went into that ill-smelling room, undressed, put on soggy pajamas and slept, under ill-smelling, damp sheets, on those ill-smelling mattresses, pillows, and pillow cases. They were allowed to leave the building the next morning and stay away all day, lest the inadequate ventilation affect their general health, but they returned at night for twenty successive nights. Not one of them developed yellow fever.

Even the most stubborn skeptic could not ask for any more conclusive or dramatic proof than these experiments had yielded.

The mosquito-transmission theory which had interested Dr. Nott in 1848 and which had become a virtual passion with Dr. Finlay in 1881 was as firmly established as the law of gravity or the process of human reproduction. General Sternberg, eagerly watching the experiments from far-off Washington, was justified in his belief that an "intermediate host"—probably a mosquito— was in reality the answer to the mystery and the terror of yellow fever.

But Reed and his doughty warriors were not yet ready to pack up their equipment and go back to their prosaic duties as orthodox Army doctors. Obviously, the *Stegomyia* got from the yellow fever patient an organism which, after it had undergone certain changes in its body, was passed on to someone else. Dr. Sternberg and numerous others, of course, had tried in vain to find it, but their failure did not mean that it did not exist. Reed and his associates resolved to find out as much as they could about it and to find it, if possible.

Blood was taken from a newly diagnosed yellow fever patient. It was then injected into the arm of a nonimmune. The latter began showing the yellow fever symptoms after the usual incubation period. Here was another epochal demonstration in the exciting parade of progress against Yellow Jack: while the *Stegomyia* was the normal agency of transmission, that organsim could also be transferred directly in the blood.

Reed and his two surviving fellow Board members then began looking for the answer to another question: Is it a parasite or a toxin that passes in the yellow fever patient's blood from him to the other person? The patient who had contracted the disease by that transfer of blood was asked to give the experimenters a specimen of his own blood. This they injected into another nonimmune. A few days later he also developed yellow fever. That answered the Board's question: the yellow fever virus is a living organism, not just a toxin or chemical body, for only a living organism is capable of multiplying. And, had the original virus not multiplied, that second person would not have been able to transmit the disease to the third.

There was still another job left for the Reed Board to do, and this it did in short order. Taking blood from a newly diagnosed yellow fever patient, someone passed it through a Pasteur filter, capable of stopping anything large enough to be seen under the most powerful microscope. Then that filtered blood was injected into the arm of a nonimmune. He too developed yellow fever, proving that the yellow fever organism is, as the scientific men say, "submicroscopic," just as General Sternberg had suggested and just as the organism causing foot and mouth disease in animals had been found to be.

At last the Board was able to start packing. Reed could begin working on his report. It actually contained very little, except details, which General Sternberg did not already know, for the Surgeon General had been in correspondence with Reed all along. A considerable number of the Reed letters are in the Sternberg family files which were made available to the present writer.

Reed wrote on June 27, two days after his arrival, that he and the others "have already organized as a board and have begun work." He had a few words of praise for Dr. Agramonte's earlier work in yellow fever research in Havana. He asked Dr. Sternberg to try to locate his and others' "baggage"—actually, their laboratory equipment, which had failed to arrive on their ship. In a letter dated October 22 he suggested some changes in the phraseology of a progress report which he intended making at the 1900 meeting of the American Public Health Association and which he, properly enough, had submitted to his official superior for approval. He complained on November 13 of being seasick, "as usual," on his return voyage to Havana after being informed of Dr. Lazear's death. He was worried about the cold weather, which he knew would greatly reduce the island's mosquito population. However, he was prepared to heat the buildings, if necessary, and hoped in that way "to counteract the outside temperature." On November 26 the small screened building for the mosquito tests was "nearly completed," and he and the others "have already begun our observations." Several persons, American and Spanish, had volunteered for the experiments, and "we hope to be able to decide some of the vexing problems in the etiology of this disease." That cold weather, with its almost certain effect upon mosquito survival, was still a problem in spite of the heated buildings.

On December 14 he was able to tell Dr. Sternberg about two cases of yellow fever "brought about by the bites of infected mosquitoes." To answer in advance the charge that they might not be authentic, he had had his patients examined by some of the best known yellow fever experts in the world, including Dr. Finlay and Major William C. Gorgas. A third case, which had not yet had time to develop fully since the mosquito-biting occurred, was beginning to look like yellow fever. Indeed, "his symptoms point plainly in that direction." A fourth case, bitten only three days before, was still in the incubation stage. Meanwhile, the three nonimmunes who had then spent fourteen nights in that building "horribly infected with clothing and bedding" had not shown "any symptoms whatever." Still, perhaps "it is yet too early to pronounce an opinion as to the probability of their escape." (They did escape, of course, every one of them.) On the whole, "we feel very much pleased with the results." He inquired whether "you consider it necessary that we should try blood injections, as you suggested when I last saw you."

Two days later Reed was able to tell his chief that those two cases about which he had been uncertain had been definitely diagnosed as yellow fever. That gave four cases out of five inoculations. This he termed "quite satisfactory, I think." Thanks to the excellent treatment and care the men had received from Dr. Ames and Nurse Lambert, the first three cases "we consider out of danger." Actually, the third case had been extremely mild. The last patient was still quite sick, and he could not say what the outcome would be. (The patient survived.) In a few days he was planning to turn loose the infected mosquitoes in one of the structures—the one he called "our building No. 2"—in order "to demonstrate conclusively how a building becomes infected." The volunteers on the mosquitoless side of the wire-screen partition, he pointed out, would breathe "the same atmosphere" as those on the other side, proving, if proof was needed, that nothing in the air had anything to do with causing yellow fever.

He had important news on the new year's first day. The attempt to infect a building solely by loosing infected *Stegomyia* mosquitoes therein "has met with complete success." The volunteer who had entered one end of the structure soon after the insects were turned loose and had been bitten several times had developed an unmistakable case of yellow fever four days later. However, he "will make a good recovery." Meanwhile, "the two nonimmunes who have slept each night in the non-infected end of the same room, only protected by a wire screen partition, are still well and healthy." The same was true of those sleeping in beds and using articles contaminated by yellow fever patients.

On January 13, Major Reed wrote General Sternberg about another experiment which has already been mentioned—taking blood from a patient and injecting it into the arm of a nonimmune. This had produced "a pretty infection," and it had taken just two and a half days to do so. "The parasite," he explained "is therefore in the general circulation, and yellow fever thus follows exactly the modes of conveyance found in malarial fever."

In perhaps the last letter Reed wrote to General Sternberg— the last among the Sternberg papers—he mentioned the strain which he had been under and the terribly heavy responsibility he had carried in directing experiments on human beings. One of the last volunteers to go into the shacks where medical history had been made those last few months was not doing at all well when he wrote on January 31. The man had "a very serious infection." His temperature had been hovering around 104 degrees for three days. Reed was afraid Dr. Ames and Nurse Lambert would not be able to pull him through. If they should fail, the sweet fruits of victory would turn bitter:

Should he die, I shall regret that I ever undertook this work. The responsibility for the life of a human being weighs upon me very heavily just at present, and I am dreadfully melancholic. Everything is being done for him that we know how to do.

Fortunately, that "everything" was enough. Before Reed sailed northward on the S. S. *McPherson* a little over a week later, he was freed from this crushing burden. Dr. Ames and Nurse Lambert had not failed him.

General Sternberg was as eager as anybody to shower praise upon Reed and his fellow workers for what they had accomplished—a task he would have given his right arm to accomplish himself. There was no disposition on his part to show or feel jealousy or envy that others had done what he had tried for so many years to do. However, he did take great satisfaction in the knowledge that, over a period of many years, he had tediously laid the groundwork for the Reed Board experiments, had conceived and suggested the creation of such a board, had personally selected Reed and the others who had performed so gallantly, and had had much to say about how it would carry on. Those contributions of his, his friends insisted, entitled him to a major share in the glory of the over-all victory.

Some, however, have shown a disposition to minimize Sternberg's contribution. It has even been suggested that he was not responsible for the creation of the Reed Board at all—that it was somebody else's idea, rather than his. The *Journal of the American Medical Association*, for example, said in an editorial in praise of Dr. Welch: "It is said that his advice led to the creation of the Yellow Fever Commission of the U. S. Army, which, with the lamented Reed at its head, accomplished the epochal discovery of the role of the mosquito in the spread of yellow fever."*

Dr. Welch was a particular admirer of General Sternberg. He was also a man of the greatest fairness and unselfishness. Nothing was more distasteful to him than to be praised for something for which someone else deserved the credit. The next issue of the *Journal* carried this letter:

To the Editor: In the all too generous appreciation of my work in the *Journal*, April 9, it is intimated that my advice may have led to the creation of the Yellow Fever Commission. As all that relates to the history and work of this Commission is highly important, permit me to say that the credit for the creation of this Commission belongs solely to General Sternberg, who had previously so completely exhausted the purely bacteriologic study of yellow fever that it was possible for the Commission to follow the new direction which proved so fruitful in results.
                                        WILLIAM H. WELCH

Even before the issue of the *Journal* containing this letter appeared, Dr. Sternberg received a black-bordered letter (Dr. Welch's sister had recently died) stating that he had just seen

* "William Henry Welch," *Journal of the American Medical Association*, LIV (April 9, 1910), 1212-1213.

the *Journal* editorial, "which involved such injustice to you that I have sent a letter of correction to the editor."

> Of course I was not concerned in the creation of the Yellow Fever Commission [he wrote], and I do not recall that you consulted me about it. Even if you did, the whole credit for the creation of the Commission belongs solely to you, and so I stated in my letter. I added, although it was not necessary to do so, that you had previously explored the purely bacteriological study of yellow fever, so that it was open to the Commission to traverse new paths. Without your previous work, which cleared the way, I do not doubt that the Commission would have spent most of their time going over the same ground which you had traveled.

The medical sage of Baltimore's 807 Saint Paul Street ended his letter with a warm tribute to his friend:

> I regard you as the real pioneer of modern bacteriological work in this country, and I have always admired the way in which you mastered the technique and the literature of the subject, and made yourself an important contributor to the development of the new science, by sheer perseverance and native ability under circumstances which would have discouraged one of less force and aptitude for the study of nature.
>
> Our friendship and former close association have been a source of unmixed pleasure, and you need no assurance of my continued affectionate regard.

There has also been some question as to whether General Sternberg actually suggested to Reed the use of human volunteers. Some of Reed's admirers claim the idea originated with him. It certainly is not mentioned in Reed's written instructions. But such a delicate matter, full of potential controversy that might have stopped the whole enterprise at the beginning, would hardly have been mentioned in a letter under any circumstances. It was the sort of thing to be discussed in man-to-man conversation. And we have the evidence of no less an authority than Dr. Agramonte that it actually was—that General Sternberg did mention it to Reed, a fact to which Reed himself alluded in his letter of December 14. The only then-surviving member of the Reed Board wrote to Dr. G. M. Kober, prominent Washington physician, on January 3, 1916:

> With regard to our own work I may say that General Sternberg's instructions to Major Reed were so precise yet so complete that they embraced even human experimentation, a thing until then considered well-nigh impossible, and, without the moral support which his reputation as a scientist of the highest order and his official position rendered

us, I am sure we would never have undertaken the method of investigation with which you are familiar.

In that same letter Dr. Agramonte gave General Sternberg credit for another important contribution to the final victory at Havana:

I feel in my heart that in the greatest achievement of modern medicine, the almost total extinction of yellow fever in our hemisphere, he took an important part that has not been generally recognized, in spite of your pointing it out in your speech [June 8, 1908]. I say an important part and I would be tempted to say the most important part, since by the elimination of many confusing and erroneous ideas with reference to the cause of the disease, obtained by his indefatigable work in South and Central America, he cleared the way for us who came after him, laboring in the same field of investigation; he saved us the work, and thus the waste of effort and time which it would have entailed, by dealing with the fallacies in vogue during the last quarter of the Nineteenth Century, elucidating the question of yellow fever in a manner nearly complete.

In the address Dr. Agramonte mentioned, Dr. Kober gave General Sternberg full credit not only for originating the idea of organizing the Reed Board and selecting its membership but also for outlining its basic procedures. He also referred to statements by three other outstanding men in praise of Sternberg's contribution to the victory of 1900-1901. Dr. Welch, he said, regarded Dr. Sternberg's earlier research in yellow fever as a necesasry preliminary to the Reed Board experiments, a statement which Dr. Welch is known to have confirmed on more than one occasion. Secretary of War Elihu Root believed that Sternberg's policies as Surgeon General had made the accomplishments of the Reed Board possible. And Dr. William Osler thought that Sternberg's contribution to the conquest of yellow fever assured him a high place among the benefactors of his time.

CHAPTER XIX

Housing and Health

AT BREAKFAST one morning soon after her husband became Surgeon General, Mrs. Sternberg noticed that he was unaccustomedly depressed. Concerned, she asked him what the trouble was. It was nothing he assured her, and attempted to divert the conversation in another direction. She knew there was something on his mind and demanded to be told what it was. He admitted that there was a problem which disturbed him. The stenographers in his office were showing up for work looking tired, listless, and even hungry. Their home conditions were not what they should be. In some instances several families were using the same kitchen. One young woman had been coming to work without breakfast because the others using a common kitchen did not get out in time for her to cook her meal and get to work. High rents, added to other expenses, left little money for food. If workers in the Surgeon General's office were living like that, so must many others in the other government offices and in stores and offices of business concerns.

Some time after that his good friend Dr. Kober and some others organized a nonpartisan group known as the Civic Center, aimed at making Washington a more pleasant place to live and work. Dr. Kober was made chairman of its Committee on Housing of the People, which in 1895 made a survey of several residential areas.

The committee's report focused attention upon what a few Washingtonians already knew and had known for a long time. Former Negro slaves who had escaped to the Federal capital during the Civil War were still living in the shanties they had occupied in the crowded city of war time, made more hovel-like by some forty years of physical deterioration and the years' accumulation of filth and debris. Conditions in the white sections were little, if any, better.

Two hundred and forty-eight people were found to be living in the fifty dwellings visited—nearly five to a building. Ninety-two of them were young, under eighteen. The thirteen alleys on which those fifty houses hung haphazardly varied from ten to thirty feet in width. Seven of them were blind alleys, each forming, as Dr. Kober said, "a cul-de-sac, winding and turning in the middle of blocks of buildings, and undiscoverable, almost, except by the initiated." Nearly three-fifths of these wretched structures were "hidden away in the rear of other structures, with only one approach, and that sometimes disguised." They were "difficult, even dangerous, of access, off the policeman's beat, inviting lawlessness and crime." More than a third of those tired old structures were of frame construction, "a constant menace in thickly settled residence and business districts."

With few exceptions, they had neither attics nor cellars, the floors almost touching the ground and the sun beating down relentlessly upon the roofs just above the occupants' heads. Nearly half of them had no sewer connections of any kind, the occupants relying for their toilet needs upon twenty-four extremely insanitary privies. Six dwellings were near stables. In fact "one or two of the houses were located over stables." Those long, winding, endless alleys stank of long-dead rats and cats. Fewer than half of the houses had piped water, the other families getting what they required from hydrants. Some of these were in their own yards, some in neighbors' yards, some a block or more away. Only half of those fifty dwellings were in a satisfactory state of repair, the others having been found "in various stages of decrepitude and decay." One building had been in use a century or longer, part of that time as the District of Columbia jail: four—including that one—were "unfit to live in."

For those wretched accommodations, Washington's ultra-poor paid far too much, as the poor usually do. An investigator observed sardonically that one family was having to pay more per room than it ought to pay for the whole dirty, rat-infested building. But the investigators wandering about in those slums found not only poverty, filth, and congestion, they also found disease and crime. Here were some of the nation's worst "lung blocks." In those cold, waterless, insanitary structures the germs of many diseases found ideal conditions under which to grow, multiply, and kill.

Miss Clara de Graffenreid, a special agent of the U. S. Department of Labor, told about the committee's findings and their implications. The effects of such living conditions upon morals she called "often disastrous." For, she said:

It is no secret that many of the alleys hide criminals. Our records reveal three openly disreputable houses. In one dwelling resides a woman with a jail history. Other houses are tainted with the suspicion of being "fast," and men in them are supported by women who have no visible income. Tenants, not immoral themselves, profit by the traffic in sin. In another family the oldest unmarried daughter has two illegitimate children. Three cases of drunkenness are chronicled. One woman, upright herself as far as the evidence goes, besides her own numerous offspring, cares for the two youngest children of a sister in the penitentiary, whose three daughters and two sons are in prison, while still another son is at the reform school—seven out of nine in that family behind bars.

Meanwhile, General Sternberg, who had been following the work of this committee with great interest, had become chairman of a subcommittee—the Subcommittee on Permanent Relief and Sanitary Dwellings for the Poor—of the Central Relief Committee, appointed by the District of Columbia Commissioners. Preferring to do his own investigating instead of turning the work over to professionals, he made visit after visit to Washington's slum areas to find out for himself "how the other half lives." In a preliminary report dated January 27, 1897, he described conditions strikingly similar to those found by Dr. Kober and his investigators. A large proportion of the city's poor lived in alley basements, many of which were "unfit for human habitation." Fewer than half had either running water or sewer connections. Many of those alley shacks, their yards, and the box privies in those yards were in a "very insanitary condition," which resulted in an abnormally high mortality from typhoid fever and other infectious diseases.

This state of affairs is a disgrace to the Nation's capital [the Surgeon General told the District Commissioners], and in our opinion calls for legislation by the Congress of the United States by which the District Commissioners may be enabled to condemn and destroy tenements which are unfit for human occupation, to condemn and pay for buildings and grounds required for the purpose of widening alleys and opening blind alleys conformably to existing laws, to construct branch sewers, and to introduce water and gas, so that sanitary tenements may be erected on these minor streets or alleys which can be rented to the poor at rates as low [as] or lower than are the insanitary dwellings now occupied by many of them.

These two reports, coming within three weeks of each other, stirred the city's civic leaders to a determination to do something about the conditions they had exposed. The best plan of attack, it was decided, was the direct one, to start building decent houses which poor people could afford. A meeting to get a home-building program started was called by the Civic Center, the Washington Board of Trade, the Central Relief Committee, and other organizations. General Sternberg as the principal speaker emphasized that the building of such dwellings could be made not only good philanthropy but also good business. He urged the organization of a stock company for this purpose, and the others present voted to go ahead with the sale of stock. This was so successful that the new concern, the Washington Sanitary Improvement Company, was soon filing incorporation papers. General Sternberg was named a member of the board of directors, and, at the board's first meeting, was elected president. He held the office, serving without pay, until his death.

The Washington Sanitary Improvement Company, he said at the first meeting of the executive committee, would have two primary objectives: first, to pay stockholders 5 per cent on their investment; and, second, to "supply to wage-earners improved, wholesome homes at reasonable rents." The houses it would build would provide "the very best accommodations from the standpoint of hygiene" and the utmost in comfort that could possibly be provided at the rentals charged. No building would be erected until there was a clear need for it, to avoid real estate speculation. The buildings, though "simple in their exterior and economical in construction," would provide ample ventilation, space, and sunlight. Every unit would include a bathroom with hot and cold running water, commode, etc. It would also be furnished with a cellar, a kitchen sink with hot and cold running water, and a kitchen range. There would be a separate entrance for each apartment, and every family would have a small but attractive back yard. General Sternberg himself drew the plans. At his suggestion, one month's rent was refunded to families that had not required any inside repairs during the previous year. This was regarded as a wise provision, since it gave the tenants an incentive to take care of the property and make minor repairs themselves.

It may be wondered how these homes, erected for middle-class workers, would help do away with the slum dwellings that had aroused the pity and indignation of both committees. It is true they were not intended to strike at the slums directly. But they were expected to, and did, hit at them indirectly by providing more comfortable living quarters for the middle class and thus causing them to vacate the quarters they had been occupying. These would be occupied, in turn, by slum dwellers, leaving the slum structures without occupants. Then the owners would be forced by grim economic stress to destroy them, either replacing them with decent structures or turning the land to other uses. General Sternberg was pleased with the prospect of helping both groups: both, he felt, needed helping.

Under General Sternberg's skilful guidance, the Washington Sanitary Improvement Company succeeded in both of its objectives. Its assets and surplus increased steadily from year to year, and, when World War I building restrictions brought this type of construction to a halt temporarily, it had built 320 dwellings, providing twice that many housing units. Attracted by its financial success, other concerns in Washington and elsewhere emulated it. It thus had an indirect effect upon housing in many parts of the country, and even in other countries. In 1900 it received a gold medal at the Paris Exposition, the only American concern to do so. A gold medal was also awarded to General Sternberg personally.

In spite of the Washington Sanitary Improvement Company's undoubted success in helping Washingtonians on the lowest economic levels, albeit indirectly, General Sternberg was not satisfied. They needed more direct help. So, early in 1904, he bestirred himself in behalf of another type of housing concern, to build homes for the most poorly paid of Washington's workers— "the day laborers, laundresses and other humble wage-earners," Dr. Kober called them. The Washington Sanitary Housing Company was chartered by act of Congress on April 23, 1904. One of General Sternberg's fellow incorporators was Alexander Graham Bell.

General Sternberg was again elected president, and most of the procedures he had introduced in the operation of the Washington Sanitary Improvement Company were adopted, including the refunding of the twelfth month's rent to a tenant who had not called upon the company for inside repairs during the previous year. He also drew the house plans, as he had done before. In order to cut construction costs without affecting the health of the occupants, the houses were built on cheaper land. Certain features found in the other concern's structures, such as cellars and bay windows, were dispensed with. Rentals were fixed at substantially lower levels than those charged for the other units. The "day laborers, laundresses and other humble people," General Sternberg decided, could not pay enough to return 5 per cent on the capital investment if clean, sanitary, and comfortable housing was to be provided. So, with his fellow directors' approval, he set the dividend rate at 4 per cent, asking prospective stockholders to make that concession to philanthropy. Unfortunately, many of them were unwilling to do so. The Washington Sanitary Housing Company's financial success did not match its success in slum-clearing. Dr. Sternberg and the others found that that difference between 4 and 5 per cent made a great deal of difference to those with money to invest. At the 1906 meeting of stockholders, after the company had been in operation about two years, he was obliged to tell them that the sale of stock had practically come to a standstill after reaching slightly less than forty-seven thousand dollars. Six of the stockholders present promised to do their best to raise thirty thousand dollars in additional capital. The records do not say whether they were successful, but General Sternberg was able to announce about five weeks later that these six, "with commendable zeal," had received "a number of respectable subscriptions." Under this stimulus, the company went ahead with the construction of twenty additional two-story flats, each accommodating two families.

The stimulant proved only temporary. The sale of stock again struck a snag, and the only way out became plain to everyone: the dividend rate would have to be increased. General Sternberg recommended a boost to 5 per cent, and this was approved by the stockholders. After it became effective early in 1911 there was no lack of capital. The company was able to build fifty-seven two-family houses between then and 1915, which brought the total to ninety-seven.

Heading these two large housing projects did not by any means constitute all of General Sternberg's activities in behalf of better homes for the poor and the near-poor. In one way and another he is credited with having done more to make living decent and comfortable than any other Washington resident of his time. As early as 1897 he drafted a measure authorizing the District of Columbia health authorities to condemn structures found to be unfit for human beings to live in. As Washington had had legislation of this kind before (and had allowed it to lapse), its prompt passage seemed certain. But owners of such property, enjoying the lush incomes it brought them, were powerful politically, and their opposition was made more effective by the indifference of members of Congress who favored Sternberg's proposal but did not work energetically enough to push it through. The measure dragged on from session to session for six years. Finally, on May 1, 1903, its supporters rallied their forces and got a favorable vote on it.

Dr. Sternberg and the others leading the drive for better housing won a powerful ally when Theodore Roosevelt moved to Washington as Vice-President. He had heard about the city's hovels, but it was not until Washington became his home that he realized how wretched they really were. The sordid picture painted for him by many friends, and particularly by Jacob A. Riis, who had done so much in exposing New York's slums, strengthened Roosevelt's interest in decent housing. After Roosevelt succeeded to the Presidency, he was able to do more about it. In his message to Congress in December, 1904, he called upon that body to begin "a systematic investigation into and improvement of housing conditions in Washington." The city's labyrinthine alleys he called "breeding grounds of vice and disease." The festering illnesses in those slum areas, he said, tended to offset the "exceptional wholesomeness" of the capital's better sections. He called for a special "Commission on Housing and Health Conditions in the National Capital." Such a commission, he told the lawmakers, "would not only bring about a reformation of existing evils, but would also formulate an appropriate building code to protect the city from mammoth tenements and other evils which threaten to develop here as they have in other cities."

About a year later the President again appealed to Congress to do something about housing. As a step in that direction, he ordered a study to be made of the living conditions of Federal and District employees. He named his friend, James B. Reynolds, who had had a great deal of experience with the University Settlement in New York, to take charge of it. The Reynolds report fully confirmed the unsavory findings of the earlier ones. Typical was the remark of a colored woman whom he interviewed. Pointing to her filthy yard and its ill-smelling box-type privy, she commented: "Why, my old massa wouldn't ha' kept his horses stabled in such a place."

At Mr. Reynolds's urging, Roosevelt created a group known as the President's Homes Commission, each member being requested to serve without compensation as a public service. General Sternberg was one of the fifteen asked to participate in this "large field of usefulness." At the Commission's first meeting he was unanimously elected chairman. The commission made its own study and turned in its own report, which was in reality General Sternberg's handiwork. It told about finding nine persons sleeping in two bedrooms. At another place eight were sleeping in a single room. Four, five, and six sleepers in a room were not unusual. Many of the rooms were poorly ventilated: in any number of cases, "the occupants are obliged to rebreathe this vitiated air until it is absolutely fetid and poisonous."

Although General Sternberg's sensitive mind and sympathetic understanding did not by any means miss the other tragic implications of shabby, squalid housing—the vice it incubated, the families it dissolved, and the misery it created—this man of medicine was especially impressed by the tie-up between poor housing and poor health. Hovels and high death rates went hand in hand, he knew. To lower the one, you would have to eliminate, or at least greatly improve, the other. While this was true of disease generally, it was particularly true of tuberculosis. Not only did Washington's slums give the national capital, which ought to be a light of health for the rest of the country, a tuberculosis death rate higher than that for any state in the U. S. Death Registration Area, but Washington had also the "disgraceful preeminence" of reporting more tuberculosis cases per thousand of its residents than any other city of the United States except Denver and Los Angeles, to which tuberculosis patients from all over the country flocked in a desperate, last-chance hope that some miracle of western climate would help them after everything else had failed.

Better housing alone, however, could not solve Washington's tuberculosis problem, or even make satisfactory headway against it. It was also necessary to provide treatment for those who had the disease, and that Washington had failed to do. True, the city had a charity tuberculosis hospital which took care of the indigent. But it did nothing for those government employees, white-collar workers in business offices, and others of the great middle class whose slightly better economic situation closed that institution's doors to them or whose pride prevented them from accepting treatment on a charity basis. Providing institutional care for them became another job for the man who was one of the first, if not the first, to demonstrate the tubercle bacillus in the United States; who, as Surgeon General, had caused the establishment of the Army's first all-tuberculosis hospital; and who, as Washington's most eager apostle of health, had successfully promoted legislation to require the registration of all tuberculosis cases and to establish a free tuberculosis hospital. He worked with influential and wealthy friends in behalf of the needed institution as assiduously as he had been working for better housing and other projects for the community good. The Washington Sanatorium Company, pledged to provide the best possible treatment at rates lower than those charged at privately owned sanatoriums but without the taint of charity, was incorporated in

1906. General Sternberg was named president, and Starmont Sanatorium threw open its doors a few months later.

Like those houses General Sternberg had caused to be erected for so many of Washington's middle-class families, Starmont was built and operated with simplicity and efficiency in mind, with a minimum of frills and ornamentation for ornamentation's sake. That did not prevent it from having a beauty and stateliness which impressed patients and visitors alike; its seventy-six-acre site was a gently sloping, well-wooded hill about eighteen miles from Washington, in the neighboring state of Maryland. Its one large permanent building, formerly used as a residence, housed the offices and residential quarters of doctors and other members of the staff and their families, as well as the laboratory, recreation rooms, and kitchen and dining rooms for both staff and patients. The broad porch that all but surrounded the pleasant structure contained cots, recliners, and comfortable chairs, where ambulatory patients rested and amused themselves during the day. Much emphasis was placed upon their getting lots of fresh air, thanks to the teachings of General Sternberg's friend, Dr. Trudeau, whose open-air sanatorium at Saranac Lake was bringing about revolutionary changes in the treatment of the disease. The patients slept in tents of the latest design, providing ventilation through the roofs. The flooring was solid, substantial, and comfortable. The furnishings were simple but adequate.

Starmont did its job well. There is no telling how many government workers and others with small incomes found their lost health there. It soon took a prominent place among the institutions of its kind. But in another and sternly realistic sense it failed. Like so many other nobly conceived institutions, it died of financial starvation. Ironically enough, those who caused Starmont to fail were those whom it was intended to help. Contributions, many of them generous, were received from philanthropically minded individuals and organizations up to the last. But they were not intended to carry more than a relatively small part of the load, at best to close the gap between patients' payments and the cost of operation. Unfortunately for the institution, many prospective patients were swayed by the still-strong but discredited belief that the best way to get well of tuberculosis was to go west. They raised as much money as they could and bought tickets for California, Colorado, Arizona and the other states that were supposed to heal sick lungs with huge dosages of sunshine and dry air. Most of them, of course, never returned. The beds they would have occupied at Starmont, had they not been lured westward by that false hope, remained unoccupied, and the money they would have paid Starmont for treatment, but didn't, widened the gap between income and outgo.

It hurt General Sternberg to see those empty white beds and the growing red-ink figures on the account books. He made appeal after appeal to the doctors and to wealthy friends not to let Starmont close its doors, asking the former to advise their patients against going west and the latter to increase their gifts. Somehow, he felt, those who needed it and their well-wishers would keep it going. "The people will not let such an undertaking fail," he would say to his intimates. "They do not know its work and its needs. When they know, they will support it."

But they disappointed him. They either never learned about Starmont or were not sufficiently interested in it after they learned. With growing sadness, he saw it drift rapidly toward insolvency, as that gap between income and outgo became wider and wider. In the end he had to admit that indifference, ignorance, and false ideas about the curative powers of western sunshine had won their tragic victory. That was one of the bitterest defeats of his life.

CHAPTER XX

Soldier at Rest

On June 23, 1901, General and Mrs. Sternberg sailed from San Francisco on the U.S.S *General Hancock* for Manila on his last major assignment as Surgeon General. President McKinley had asked him to make the trip to get first-hand information on the health of the troops on Philippine occupation duty. The fast troop transport, swinging far north of Hawaii, made the run in the quickest time ever made by a ship of that kind up to then. His mission accomplished—he was well pleased with what he had found out about the men's health and the facilities provided for maintaining it—they again boarded the *General Hancock* for the homeward trip. Putting in at Kobe for fueling, they learned that President McKinley had been shot and was in serious condition, though he was expected to recover. While they were still there other cables arrived with less hopeful news. At Nagasaki, their next stop, the news was even more somber. But it was not until they were about to land in San Francisco that they learned of their friend's death from the pilot and the ship news reporters, who told them about it just before the *General Hancock* docked.

They had scarcely unpacked at their Washington home when a message came from Mrs. McKinley, who had already moved from the White House to her old home in Canton, Ohio. She wanted them to visit her there. A few days later the three of them made a sad pilgrimage to McKinley's grave.

One of President McKinley's last official acts was to sign a bill creating two new corps of the Army Medical Department. Surgeon General after Surgeon General had been working for an Army Nurse Corps. But all previous Congresses had paid no attention to their pleading—or at least not enough. However, General Sternberg was successful in 1901. The same legislation also created the Army Dental Corps. This double accomplishment brought great satisfaction to the man who, since soon after becoming Surgeon General, had been known as the father of the Army Medical School.

As June 8, 1902, the date on which General Sternberg would automatically retire for age, approached, some of his friends began a campaign to enable him to do so with the rank of major general. That, they felt, would be only a just reward for his long and honorable military service and a fitting tribute to his rank as America's most distinguished bacteriologist. In a more practical sense, the promotion would add substantially to General Sternberg's retirement income, which at best would be considerably less than his active-duty pay. Secretary of War Elihu Root readily fell in line and promised to do all he could. The *Journal of the American Medical Association* gave the proposal hearty endorsement, calling upon the nation's lawmakers to show this honor to "one who has been an honor to his country as well as a faithful public servant for forty-one years, much of it in arduous and perilous service in the field and on the frontier."

The Senate passed the bill in short order, and it received a favorable report from the Military Affairs Committee of the House. However, when it reached the House floor, just four days before General Sternberg's retirement, it ran into difficulties. Those who opposed it went to great pains to point out that their objections were not due to any lack of admiration for General Sternberg or to a reluctance to show him every consideration and honor. Such legislation would, they said, set a precedent which might do harm in the future. Friendly and impersonal as it was, their opposition was effective. The bill's supporters were unable to rally the votes they needed when the final test of strength came, and a brigadier general he remained. A similar attempt made some time after his retirement was also unsuccessful.

But unsympathetic Congressmen could not keep his friends from honoring him in another way, and this they did. A number of them—Dr. Welch, Dr. Simon Flexner, Dr. Kober, Dr. Victor C. Vaughan, the Surgeons General of the Navy and the U. S.

Public Health and Marine Hospital Service, Dr. Hermann M. Biggs, and others—formed themselves into a committee to make Sternberg's retirement a gala occasion. The person most concerned in all their planning did not know what was in the wind until he received a letter from Dr. Biggs asking him to select a banquet date that would best suit his convenience.

The date selected was June 13. The place was Delmonico's in New York. Many messages came from those who could not attend. There was a flood of laudatory oratory. Then the recipient of all this praise arose in a burst of applause to respond to these expressions of good will. Almost inevitably at such a time, he took a long look back through the misty years to the time when he was getting started as an army medical officer, and before. He found it "hard to realize that the country boy of my name who came to this city as a student of medicine in 1858 is here today as the honored guest of leading members of the medical profession of the United States." He remembered how, "when the war tocsins sounded, my future career was determined by the favorable verdict of an army medical examining board as to my qualifications as an army surgeon." He told of having had, in his early days as an army doctor, to furnish his own microscope and whatever other research equipment he used. He spoke with pride of his efforts as Surgeon General to encourage medical officers interested in research. He mentioned the "thoroughly equipped laboratory in connection with our Army Medical School in the city of Washington, at all of our general hospitals in this country and in the Philippines, and also at every military post of any importance throughout the United States." He described the almost complete elimination of smallpox among the native population of the Philippines, Cuba, and Puerto Rico. He reminded his assembled friends that it was a group of army medical scientists, picked for the work by the Surgeon General of the army, who had taken Yellow Jack's measure at Havana and an army doctor who had put the Yellow Fever Commission's knowledge to effective use by practically wiping out yellow fever in Cuba, its ancient stronghold, and by showing how it could also be wiped out in other places. Bubonic plague had been held in check in the Philippines and had all but disappeared from the city of Manila, where it had long raged out of control. All of these accomplishments had brought him great satisfaction, the speaker declared, and had made him proud to have had "a small share in promoting the advancement of scientific medicine and the interests of our beloved and humane profession."

Secretary Root was not at the banquet, not being a doctor. But he wrote Dr. Sternberg, calling him "an officer whose scientific attainments and devotion to the public service entitle him to grateful recognition." He would, he said, "always be proud of the achievements of the Medical Corps of the United States Army under your administration."

Soon after his retirement General and Mrs. Sternberg moved from Sixteenth Street, N.W., where they had been living for some time, to a new home they had selected on California Avenue. The main difference between the old place and the new was that the latter had a great deal more room, enough for a garden. There for hours at a time the famed enemy of germs warred relentlessly on bugs and other insects that attacked his favorite flowers, shrubs, and vegetables. Barren ground came beautifully alive with a burst of rose bushes. When the weather was bad or he felt the pull of authorship, he worked on his book, *Infection and Immunity*, the enlarged, more comprehensive and up-to-date version of his earlier work on that same general subject, which still held a place of honor on the library shelves of medical schools and doctors' offices throughout the world.

But in those years of retirement it was not the flowering shrubs or the writing of *Infection and Immunity* that gave him the greatest satisfaction. His most pleasant employment was doing what he could for the people of the city he and Mrs. Sternberg had adopted as their own. Although his work in behalf of decent housing for Washington's working people, for its tuberculous, and for its other unfortunates began some time before he retired, it was not until after retirement that he found all the time he wanted to give to it. Even his appointment to the chair of preventive medicine at the George Washington University Graduate School did not interfere with his whole-hearted devotion to his work of making life better for those whom fortune had overlooked. In those busy, happy postretirement years he gave his experience, his labor, and his eager enthusiasm to numerous tasks in addition to those which have been mentioned. He was, for example, president of the Citizens' Relief Association, of the board of directors of the Garfield Hospital, and of the board of visitors of St. Elizabeth's Hospital, chairman of the Committee on the Prevention of Tuberculosis, and a founder, director, honorary member, and treasurer of the National Association for the Study and Prevention of Tuberculosis. His honorary membership in the last-mentioned organization was a distinction he shared with only one person, Dr. Trudeau.

As June 8, 1908, approached, his friends, in the main those who had staged the banquet to commemorate his retirement from the Army six years earlier, decided to celebrate his seventieth birthday even more elaborately. The letter of invitation pointed out that the birthday banquet would not only mark the attainment of three-score years and ten but also "testify in a slight manner the high appreciation which each and every one of us feels for you, and for the splendid achievements contributed by you to the Country, to Philanthropy, to Friendship."

Another event of great importance to General Sternberg which also occurred in 1908 was the Sixth International Congress on Tuberculosis, which attracted to Washington outstanding tuberculosis workers from all over the world. At a dinner which he and Mrs. Sternberg gave in honor of Dr. Koch, the discoverer of the tubercle bacillus placed his arm on Sternberg's shoulder, called him "my brother in the work" and "one whom I especially admire among the men of the world," spoke of their friendship since that first meeting in Rome some twenty-three years earlier, and saluted him as the father of American bacteriology.

"The sight of these two men, one of whom first isolated the bacillus of pneumonia and the other of whom discovered the tubercle bacillus a year or two later, clasping hands and smiling at each other in this happy way was inspiring," William H. Baldwin, one of the guests, commented later, "and nothing could better indicate General Sternberg's international standing in the field in which Dr. Koch was so renowned than the hearty recognition of it by Dr. Koch on this occasion."

This would not have been such a happy occasion to General and Mrs. Sternberg if they had known how much the physical strain to which he was subjecting himself would affect his health. As chairman of the Committee on Local Affairs, he had found himself enmeshed in multitudinous details of a trying nature. Then, too, there were many other duties, normally belonging to others, which he willingly assumed in preparing for the gathering. His heart had never been right since his attack of yellow fever, in spite of his unwillingness to concede that he was not in first-rate health. Climbing stairs was something he should not have done, but the building selected for the Sixth International Congress on Tuberculosis, a new one, was not completed by opening day or, for that matter, until some time afterward. Unfortunately, the elevators were among the installations that were not ready, and Dr. Sternberg had to do a good deal of stair-climbing. The others, or most of them at any rate, had stout hearts, and this extra strain did not hurt them, but Mrs. Sternberg was certain as long as she lived that Dr. Sternberg's heart suffered serious damage from that extra strain and that it contributed directly to his death. Nevertheless, he refused to take to the sidelines because of his age, his ailing heart, or anything else. Some of the hardest work he did in behalf of his two housing projects, Starmont Sanatorium, and the other enterprises that had aroused his enthusiasm was done during the next several years.

In late October, 1915, he suffered a severe heart attack that sent him to bed. He never left it. His tired, weakened heart stopped beating at 2:30 on the morning of November 3, just twelve days before the death of his friend and fellow tuberculosis pioneer, Dr. Trudeau. The attending physician called a cerebral hemorrhage the immediate cause of death. The secondary, or contributing, cause, he wrote on the death certificate, was chronic myocarditis (inflammation of the heart muscles).

A young physician who had met General Sternberg soon after opening his office in Washington told later of standing on the sidewalk when the flag-draped coffin was placed on an army caisson for the journey to the soldiers' final camping ground at Arlington. Near him, also watching the sad procession, stood one of his patients, a middle-aged woman who had had tuberculosis but had regained her health at Starmont. Her niece had also started the fight for restored health there. And, as he stood on the wind-swept pavement and watched the sad procession start moving, "my mind went to another little family in my circle of patients, which, although struggling with poverty, was enabled to live comfortably and to raise the children in sanitary surroundings in one of the homes provided by General Sternberg's labors."

Those humble people Dr. H. C. Macatee told about had innumerable counterparts not only in Washington but throughout the world. For millions of people were indeed under heavy debt to this white-haired, soft-spoken soldier in white who, on the battlefield, in the laboratory, and in the broad field of human helpfulness had spent a long lifetime making life a great deal easier and happier for all of us. And they still are.

Bibliography

In addition to the sources cited below, considerable use has been made of contemporary newspaper accounts, most particularly from the New York *Times*, the Washington *Post*, the Washington *Star*, and the New York *Daily Tribune*, and, to a lesser extent, from the New York *World*, the Kansas City *Star*, the Montgomery *Advertiser*, the New York *Herald*, the Burlington *Democrat-Journal*, the Washington *Evening Times*, the Boston *Herald*, and the Brooklyn *Daily Eagle*.

General Sternberg, one of the most prolific doctor-authors of his time, wrote voluminously in numerous medical, military, and other fields. It would be impracticable to list all of his published writings, but an attempt has been made to include his most important and significant work.

BOOKS, ARTICLES, AND PAMPHLETS

ABBE, CLEVELAND. "Treatise on Meteorological Apparatus and Methods," in *Chief Signal Officer of the Army, Annual Report to the Secretary of War for the Year 1887*. Washington: Government Printing Office, 1888.

ABBOTT, A. C. *Transactions of the College of Physicians of Philadelphia*. Philadelphia: College of Physicians of Philadelphia, 1918.

ADAMS, GEORGE WORTHINGTON. *Doctors in Blue: Medical History of the Union Army in the Civil War*. New York: Henry Schuman, 1952.

Addresses Delivered at the Complimentary Banquet to General George M. Sternberg on His Seventieth Birthday, 1908. Washington, D. C.: privately printed.

AGRAMONTE, ARISTIDES. "The Inside Story of a Great Medical Discovery," *Scientific Monthly*, I (December, 1915), 209-39.

Alabama State Department of Health, Annual Report, 1888. Montgomery: Alabama State Department of Health, 1889.

ALGER, RUSSELL A. *The Spanish-American War*. New York: Harper and Brothers, 1901.

ARCHINARD, P. E. "Experiments Performed at the Charity Hospital of New Orleans and Elsewhere, with Sanarelli's Anti-Amarylic Serum in the Fall of 1898," *New Orleans Medical and Surgical Journal*, LII (August, 1899), 79-86.

————, WOODSON, R. S., and ARCHINARD, JOHN J. "The Serum Diagnosis of Yellow Fever," *New Orleans Medical and Surgical Journal*, L (February, 1898), 455-70.

ASHBURN, P. M. *A History of the Medical Department of the United States Army.* Boston and New York: Houghton Mifflin Co., 1929.

ASHFORD, BAILEY K. *A Soldier in Science.* New York: William Morrow and Co., 1934.

Association for the Prevention of Tuberculosis in the District of Columbia. Seventh Annual Report (Year ending September 30, 1915). Washington, D. C., 1915.

BALDWIN, E. R. "History of Tuberculosis Research in America," *Yale Journal of Biology and Medicine*, XV (January, 1943), 301-9.

BALDWIN, WILLIAM H. "General George M. Sternberg, An Appreciation," *Journal of the Outdoor Life*, XII (December, 1915), 388-89.

BARTHOLAW, ROBERTO. "Dr. Sternberg's View of the Action of Potassium as an Antiseptic" (letter), *Medical News*, LXVI (January 17, 1885), 3.

Battles and Leaders of the Civil War. (Grant-Lee Edition.) New York: The Century Co., 1894.

BEARDSLEY, LEVI. *Reminiscences, Personal and Other Incidents, Early Settlements of Otsego County.* New York: C. E. Vinten, 1852.

BELFIELD, WILLIAM T. Letters from Vienna regarding Koch's announcement of the discovery of the tubercle bacillus, in *Chicago Medical Journal and Examiner*, XLIV (June, 1882), 613-17; XLV (July, 1882), 37-39; XLV (August, 1882), 170-73.

————. "On the Relations of Micro-Organisms to Disease" (The Cartwright Lectures), *Medical Record*, XXIII (February 24, March 3, 10, 17, 24, 1883), 197, 225, 253, 281, 309.

————. Untitled article on demonstration of tubercle bacillus, in *Chicago Medical Journal and Examiner*, XLV (November, 1882), 516-18.

Biographical Review, Containing Biographical Sketches of the Leading Citizens of Otsego County. New York: E. C. Vinten, 1852.

Biographical Sketch of Dr. G. M. Sternberg. (Reprinted from *Physicians and Surgeons of America.*) Concord, N. H.: Republican Press Association, 1896.

BLAKE, J. L. *A Biographical Dictionary*, 13th ed. Philadelphia: H. Cowperthwait, 1856.

BORDEN, W. C. *The Use of the Roentgen Ray by the Medical Department of the United States Army in the War with Spain.* Washington: Government Printing Office, 1900.

BRADLEY, G. H., KING, H. V., and McNEEL, T. E. *The Mosquitoes of the Southeastern United States.* (Miscellaneous Publications, No. 236, U. S. Department of Agriculture.) Washington: Government Printing Office, 1939.

BROWN, JOHN HOWARD (ed.). *Lamb's Biographical Dictionary of the United States.* Boston: Federal Book Co., 1903.

CARMER, CARL. *The Susquehanna.* New York: Rinehart and Co., 1955.

CARTER, HENRY ROSE. *The Early History of Yellow Fever.* Baltimore: The Williams and Wilkins Co., 1931.

Chief Joseph's Own Story. (Reprinted from the *North American Review,* CXXVIII [April, 1879], 415-33.) Great Northern Railroad Company, n.p., n.d.

CLAXTON, CHARLES. "Virulence of Normal Human Saliva" (Abstract from thesis presented for the degree of Doctor of Medicine at the University of Pennsylvania), *Medical Times,* June 17, 1882, pp. 627-31.

COBB, SANFORD H. *The Story of the Palatines: An Episode in Colonial History.* New York: G. P. Putnam's Sons, 1948.

COOPER, WILLIAM. A Guide in the Wilderness. Dublin, N. Y.: Gilbert and Hodges, 1810.

CUGLE, FRANCES. *A Brief History of the Spanish-American War.* Harrisburg, Pa.: Kurzenknabe Press, 1898.

EGGLESTON, GEORGE CARY. *The History of the Confederate War, Its Causes and Its Conduct.* New York: Sturges and Walton Co., 1910.

EISENSCHIML, OTTO, and NEWMAN, RALPH. *The American Iliad: The Epic Story of the Civil War, As Narrated by Eye Witnesses and Contemporaries.* Indianapolis: The Bobbs-Merrill Co., 1947.

FISHBEIN, MORRIS, BIERRING, WALTER L., and others. *A History of the American Medical Association, 1847 to 1947.* Philadelphia and London: W. B. Saunders Co., 1947.

FLIKKE, JULIO O. *Nurses in Action: The Story of the Army Nurse Corps.* Philadelphia and New York: J. B. Lippincott Co., 1943.

GARRISON, FIELDING HUDSON. *An Introduction to the History of Medicine.* New York and London: W. B. Saunders Co., 1929.

"George M. Sternberg," New York *Times Magazine,* July 4, 1897, p. 24.

"George Miller Sternberg" (editorial), *American Journal of Public Health,* XXVIII (June, 1938), 774-75.

GESSNER, F. E. "Sternberg, George Miller," *Southwestern Medicine,* VIII (November, 1924), 530-34.

GIBSON, JOHN M. "Curtains for a Killer," *Today's Health,* XXVIII (May, 1950), 34, 35, 50, 51.

————. "Fingers of Death," *Hygeia,* XXVIII (February, 1950), 38,39, 57.

GIRARD, A. C. "The Management of Camp Alger and Camp Meade" (letter), *New York Medical Journal,* LXVIII (September 24, 1898), 457-59.

"Good Homes in Washington" (editorial), *Housing Betterment* (National Housing Association), V (January, 1916), 2.

GRADLE, HENRY. *Bacteria and the Germ Theory of Disease.* Chicago: W. T. Keener, 1883.

————, and WOLTMAN, H. "The Diagnosis of Consumption by Means of the Microscope." *Medical News,* XLII (February 17, 1883), 184-86.

HACKETT, L. W. *Malaria in Europe.* New York: Oxford University Press, 1937.

HAMILTON, DUANE. *History of Otsego County, N. Y.* Philadelphia: Everts and Fariss, 1878.

HAY, JAMES. "Medical Marvels in Our Army," *Munsey's Magazine,* LIX (November, 1916), 259-64.

HEINS, HENRY HARDY. *Throughout All the Years: The Bicentennial Story of Hartwick in America, 1746-1946.* Oneonta, N. Y.: Board of Trustees of Hartwick College, 1946.

HOLMES, B. "Medical Education in Chicago in 1882 and After," *Medical Life,* XXVIII (January, 1921), 7-12.

HONEYMAN, DOREN. *History of Union County, New Jersey, 1664-1923.* New York and Chicago: Lewis Historical Publishing Co., 1923.

HUME, EDGAR ERSKINE. *Ornithologists of the United States Army Medical Corps: Thirty-six Biographies.* Baltimore: Johns Hopkins University Press, 1942.

———. "Purification of Drinking Water in the Field," *Military Engineer,* XXIV (November-December, 1932), 609-15.

———. "Sternberg's Centenary, 1838-1938," *Army Medical Bulletin,* No. 46 (October, 1938), 69-78; *Annals of Medical History,* X (May, 1938), 266-72; *The Military Surgeon,* LXXXIV (May, 1939), 420-28.

———. *Victories of Army Medicine.* Philadelphia and London: J. B. Lippincott Co., 1923.

IRELAND, MERRITTE W. "Army Medical Plans and Needs Outlined by Surgeon General," *Comeback,* August 21, 1920, pp. 1-2.

KEAN, JEFFERSON RANDOLPH. *The Scientific Work and Discoveries of the Late Walter Reed.* Washington: Government Printing Office, 1903.

KELLY, HOWARD A. "George Miller Sternberg," *Johns Hopkins Hospital Bulletin,* XXXII (January, 1921), 1-5.

———. *Walter Reed and Yellow Fever.* Baltimore: The Normal Remington Co., 1906.

———, and BURRAGE, WALTER L. *Dictionary of American Medical Biography.* New York and London: D. Appleton and Co., 1928.

KOBER, GEORGE. *The History and Development of the Housing Movement in the City of Washington, D. C.* Washington: Washington Sanitary Housing Companies, 1927.

LOSSING, BLUSON J. *A History of the Civil War, 1861-65, and the Causes That Led Up to the Great Conflict.* New York: The War Memorial Association, 1912.

LOUNSBURY, THOMAS R. *James Fenimore Cooper.* Boston: Houghton Mifflin Co., 1882.

MCCAW, W. D. *Memoir of Walter Reed.* Washington: Walter Reed Memorial Association, 1904.

MCGEE, ANITA N. "Women Nurses in the American Army," *Proceedings of Military Surgeons of the U. S., 1899.* Columbus, Ohio: Berlin Printing Co., 1900.

MAXY, KENNETH F. *Rosenau Preventive Medicine and Hygiene.* (7th ed.) New York: Appleton-Century-Crofts, 1951.

"The Medical Department at Santiago, Report of Surgeon General," *Army and Navy Journal*, August 13, 1898.

MELENEY, HENRY E. "Tropical Medicine in United States Military History," *Bulletin of New York Academy of Medicine*, XVIII (May, 1942), 329-37.

Memorial Volume of the Semi-Centennial Anniversary of Hartwick Seminary, Held August 21, 1866. Albany: John Munsell, 1867.

MORRIS, CHARLES. *The War With Spain: A Complete History of the War of 1898 between the United States and Spain.* Philadelphia: J. B. Lippincott Co., 1899.

MORRISON, ELTING E. (ed.). *The Letters of Theodore Roosevelt. The Years of Preparation, 1898-1900*, Vols. I and II. Cambridge: Harvard University Press, 1951.

"The Official Summary of the Annual Report of the Surgeon General of the Army," supplement to *New York Medical Journal*, LXVIII (November 26, 1898), 793-98.

Otsego County, N. Y., Geographical and Historical, from the Earliest Settlement to the Present Time. Oneonta, N. Y.: Oneonta *Herald*, 1902.

"Pasteur's Method for the Prevention of Hydrophobia," *Medical News*, XLVIII (April 24, 1886), 449-53.

PHELAN, J. M. "George Miller Sternberg," *Army Medical Bulletin*, No. 52 (April, 1940), 70-74.

President's Homes Commission, Report. (U. S. Senate Document No. 644.) Washington: Government Printing Office, 1909.

PRITCHARD, WILLIAM BROADDUS. "A True Pen Picture of Camp Wickoff," *Medical News*, LXXIII (September 10, 1898).

Proceedings, Sixth International Congress on Tuberculosis, Washington, D. C., September 28 to October 5, 1908. 6 vols. Philadelphia: William F. Fell Co., 1908.

RAVENEL, MAZYCK P. (ed.). *A Half Century of Public Health.* New York: American Public Health Association, 1921, 331-34.

Record of Engagements with Hostile Indians Within the Military Division of the Missouri, from 1818 to 1882, Lieutenant General P. H. Sheridan, Commanding, Compiled from Official Records. Chicago: Headquarters, Military Division of the Misouri, 1882.

REED, WALTER. "Recent Research Concerning the Etiology, Propagation and Prevention of Yellow Fever by the U. S. Army Commission," in *U. S. Senate Documents*, Vol. IX. Washington: Government Printing Office, 1903.

————, CARROLL, JAMES, and AGRAMONTE, ARISTIDES. "The Etiology of Yellow Fever, An Additional Note," *Journal of the American Medical Association*, XXXVI (February 16, 1901), 431-40.

————, VAUGHN, VICTOR C., and SHAKESPEARE, EDWARD O. *Report of the Origin and Spread of Typhoid Fever in U. S. Military Camps during the Spanish War of 1898.* Washington: Government Printing Office, 1904.

RICHARDSON, JAMES D. (ed.). *Messages and Papers of the Presidents.* Washington: Government Printing Office, 1910.

ROBACK, HENRY (ed.). *The Veteran Volunteers of Herkimer and Otsego Counties in the War of the Rebellion.* Utica, N. Y.: L. C. Childs and Son, 1888.

ROOSEVELT, THEODORE. "Military Preparedness and Unpreparedness," *Century Magazine,* LIX (new series, XXXVII) (November, 1899), 149-53.

————. "Personal Letter Book, from September 20, 1901, to December 2, 1903." Manuscript in Library of Congress, Washington, D. C.

SCHNECK, JEROME M. "Sternberg and the Fort Harker Cholera Epidemic," *Journal of the Kansas Medical Society,* LV (May, 1944), 160-63.

SCOTT, HAROLD. *A History of Tropical Medicine.* 2 vols. Baltimore: Williams and Wilkins Co., 1939.

SCOTT, HUGH L. *Some Memories of a Soldier.* New York: Century Co., 1928.

SEIFFERT, GUSTAV. *Virus Diseases in Man, Animal and Plant.* New York: Philosophical Library, 1944.

SIMMONS, JAMES S. "Progress in the Army's Fight against Malaria," *Journal of the American Medical Association,* CXX (September 5, 1942), 30-34.

SMITH, GEDDES. *Plague on Us.* New York: Oxford University Press, 1941.

STERNBERG, MARTHA L. *George Miller Sternberg, A Biography.* Chicago: American Medical Association, 1920.

STRODE, GEORGE K. (ed.). *Yellow Fever.* New York: McGraw-Hill Book Co., 1951.

SUPERVISING SURGEON GENERAL, Marine Hospital Service. *Annual Report.* Washington, D. C.: Government Printing Office, 1889.

SURGEON GENERAL OF THE ARMY. *Annual Reports to the Secretary of War* for fiscal years ending June 30, 1894-1902. Washington, D. C.: Government Printing Office, 1894-1902.

"The Surgeon General of the Army and His Critics," *New York Medical Journal,* LXVIII (December 3, 1898), 820-22.

"Surgeon General Sternberg" (editorial), *Journal of the American Medical Association,* XXXVIII (April 19, 1902), 1011-12.

TORNEY, GEORGE H. Letter on Yellow Fever Commission, to Senator Robert L. Owen, dated April 29, 1910. (Senate Document No. 520.)

TRENT, JOSIAH C. "George Miller Sternberg," *North Carolina Medical Journal,* VII (June, 1946), 259-61.

TRUBY, ALBERT E. *Memoir of Walter Reed.* New York and London: Paul B. Hoeber, Inc. [1943].

TRUDEAU, EDWARD LIVINGSTON. *An Autobiography.* Garden City: Doubleday, Doran and Co., 1928.

VAUGHAN, VICTOR C. *Epidemiology and Public Health.* St. Louis: C. V. Mosby Co., 1923.

WELCH, WILLIAM H. "President Welch, General Sternberg and the Yellow Fever Commission" (letter), *Journal of the American Medical Association,* LIV (April 16, 1910), 1326.

WENTZ, ABDEL ROSS. *The Lutheran Church in American History.* (2nd ed., revised.) Philadelphia: United Lutheran Publishing House, 1933.

WHITE, BENJAMIN, ROBINSON, ELLIOT STERLING, and BARNES, LAVERNE
ALMON. *The Biology of the Pneumococcus.* New York: Oxford
University Press, 1938.

WILSON, CHARLES MORROW. *Ambassadors in White.* New York: Henry
Holt and Co., 1942.

WINSLOW, CHARLES-EDWARD AMORY. *The Conquest of Epidemic Diseases.* Princeton: Princeton University Press, 1944.

————. *The Life of Hermann M. Biggs.* Philadelphia: Lea and Febiger,
1929.

————. *Man and Epidemics.* Princeton: Princeton University Press,
1952.

WINTER, FRANCIS A. "The Romantic Side of the Conquest of Yellow
Fever," *Military Surgeon,* LXI (October, 1927), 438-52.

WOLD, LAURA N. *Walter Reed: Doctor in Uniform.* New York: Julian
Messner, 1943.

WOLFE, EDMUND J. *The Lutherans in America.* New York: J. A. Hill
and Co., 1889.

Yellow Fever: A Compilation of Various Publications. (Senate Document
No. 822.) Washington, D. C.: Government Printing Office, 1911.

GENERAL STERNBERG'S OWN WRITINGS

Books and Pamphlets

Bacteria (translated, with revisions and addenda, from the French of
Dr. Antoine Magnin). New York: William Wood and Co., 1884.

The Diagnosis of Yellow Fever: Yellow Fever and Quarantine. New
Orleans: L. Graham and Son, 1880.

*Immunity: Protective Inoculations in Infectious Diseases and Serum-
Therapy.* New York: William Wood and Company, 1895.

*Infection and Immunity, with Special Reference to the Prevention of In-
fectious Diseases.* New York and London: G. P. Putnam's Sons,
1903.

Malaria and Malarial Diseases. New York: William Wood and Co., 1884.

A Manual of Bacteriology. New York: William Wood and Co., 1892.

Photomicrographs. Washington, D. C.: Government Printing Office,
1879.

Photomicrographs and How to Make Them. Boston: J. R. Osgood and
Co., 1883.

*Report of the President of the Washington Sanatorium Company for the
Year Ending December 31, 1913.* Washington, D. C.: Washington
Sanatorium Co., 1914.

Report on the Etiology and Prevention of Yellow Fever. Washington,
D. C.: Government Printing Office, 1890.

Sanitary Lessons of the War and Other Papers. Washington, D. C.:
Press of Byron S. Adams, 1912.

Small Houses within the City Limits for Unskilled Wage Earners (2nd
ed.). New York: National Housing Association, n.d.

A Textbook of Bacteriology. New York: William Wood and Co., 1896.
(2nd ed., revised) 1901.

Contributions to Popular Publications

"Etiology and Geographic Distribution of Infectious Diseases," *Popular Science Monthly*, LII (January, 1898), 289-304.

"Home Treatment of Pulmonary Tuberculosis," *Journal of the Outdoor Life*, X (April, 1914), 97-127.

"Housing Conditions in the National Capital," *Charities Review*, XII (July 23, 1904), 762-64.

"Housing of the Working Classes, a Factor in the Prevention of Tuberculosis," *Journal of the Outdoor Life*, X (November, 1910), 319-26.

"Hygiene of the Farmhouse," *Youth's Companion*, LXXVII (April 16, 1903), 187.

"Importance of Laboratory Work in Medicine" (excerpt), *Review of Reviews*, XII (November, 1895), 581-82.

"Infectious Diseases, Causation and Immunity," *Popular Science Monthly*, XLI (September, 1892), 616-35.

"The Malarial Parasite," *Youth's Companion*, LXXII (April 28, 1898), 204.

"Malarial Parasite and Other Pathogenic Protozoa," *Popular Science Monthly*, L (March, 1897), 628-41.

"National Health Bureau," *North American Review*, CLVIII (May, 1894), 529-33.

"The Practical Results of Bacteriological Researches," *Popular Science Monthly*, XLVIII (April, 1896), 735-50.

"Preventive Medicine," *Popular Science Monthly*, LXII (February, 1903), 348-58.

"Progress in Bacteriology," *Youth's Companion*, LXXVIII (May 5, 1904), 219-20.

"Rational Treatment of Tuberculosis," *Journal of the Outdoor Life*, X (December, 1913), 352-82.

"Sanitary Problems Connected with the Construction of the Isthmian Canal," *North American Review*, CLXXV (September, 1902), 378-87.

"Sanitary Regeneration of Havana," *Century Magazine*, LVI (new series XXXIV) (August, 1898), 578-83.

"The Transmission of Yellow Fever by Mosquitoes," *Popular Science Monthly*, LIX (July, 1901), 225-41.

Contributions to Technical and Medical Publications

"The Action of Sunlight on Micro-Organisms" (with J. T. Dezendorf), *Medical Record*, XLVI (November 10, 1894), 607-8.

"Antivivisection in the District of Columbia: A Reply from Surgeon General Sternberg," *Boston Medical and Surgical Journal*, CXL (February 23, 1899), 198.

"Bacillus Diptheriae (Loeffler)," *Brooklyn Medical Journal*, III (March, 1889), 145-53.

"The Bacillus Icteroides as the Cause of Yellow Fever: A Reply to Professor Sanarelli," *Medical News*, LXXV (August 19, December 9, 1899), 225-28, 767.

"Bacillus Icteroides (Sanarelli) and Bacillus X (Sternberg)," *Journal of the American Medical Association*, XXX (January 29, 1898), 233-34; *Transactions of the Association of American Physicians* (Philadelphia), XIII (1898), 61-72.

"Bacteria and the Germ Theory of Disease," *Transactions of the Medical Society of California*, XII (1882), 193-98.

"Bacteriological Researches in Yellow Fever," *Transactions of the New York Academy of Medicine*, 2nd series, VII (1890), 313-16.

"Bicarbonate of Sodium and Bichloride of Mercury in the Treatment of Yellow Fever," *Therapeutic Gazette*, 3rd series, V (May 15, 1889), 298-304.

"The Biological Characteristics of the Cholera Spirillum—Spirillum Cholerae Asiaticae (Comma Bacillus of Koch)—and Disinfection in Cholera," *Medical Record*, XLII (October 1, 1892), 387-91.

"A Contribution to the Study of the Bacterial Organisms Commonly Found on Exposed Mucous Surfaces and in the Alimentary Canal of Healthy Individuals," *Studies from the Biological Laboratory* (Johns Hopkins University, Baltimore), II (March, 1882), 157-81; *Proceedings of the American Association for the Advancement of Science* (Salem, Mass.), XXX (August, 1881), 83-94.

"Deodorants," in *Reference Handbook of the Medical Sciences*, 1st ed. (New York: William Wood and Co., 1889), II, 405-6.

"The Destruction of Cholera Germs," in E. C. Wendt (ed.), *A Treatise on Asiatic Cholera Germs* (New York: William Wood and Co., 1885), pp. 325-35.

"Disinfectants," in *Reference Handbook of the Medical Sciences*, 1st ed. (New York: William Wood and Co., 1889), II, 478-80.

"Disinfection," in Hobart Amory Hare (ed.), *A System of Practical Therapeutics* (Philadelphia: Lea Brothers and Co., 1891-1897), I, 573-98.

"Disinfection and Individual Prophylaxis against Infectious Diseases," *Ninth Biennial Report, California Board of Health* (Sacramento, 1886), pp. 241-70; *The Lomb Prize Essays* (Concord, N. H.: American Public Health Association, 1886), pp. 99-136.

"The Disinfection of Human Excreta," *Journal of the American Medical Association*, XVII (August 22, 1891), 290-94.

"Dr. Finlay's Mosquito Inoculations," *American Journal of Medical Science,* new series, CII (December, 1891), 627-30.

"Dr. Freire's Protective Inoculations: Facts Versus Figures," *Medical Record*, XXXVII (May 10, 1890), 524-26; Science, XV (May 30, 1890), 328-29.

"Dr. Klebs' Ameba of Yellow Fever" (letter), *Journal of the American Medical Association*, XXX (April 30, 1898), 1054-55.

"The Etiology of Croupous Pneumonia," *Medical Record*, XXXV (March 16, 23, 1889), 281, 309; *Lancet*, I (February 23, March 2, 9, 1889), 370, 420, 474; *Transactions of the Medical Society of New York* (Albany, N. Y., 1889), pp. 53-80; *National Medical Review*, VII (December, 1897), 175-77; *Journal of Practical Medicine*, VIII (January, 1898), 306.

"Experimental Investigations Relating to the Etiology of the Malarial

Fevers," *National Board of Health Bulletin*, III (July 23, 1881), Supplement No. 14, pp. 1-11; *National Board of Health Reports* (Washington, D. C.: Government Printing Office, 1882), III, Appendix II, pp. 65-86.

"Experiments with Disinfectants," *National Board of Health Bulletin*, III (July 23, 1881), 21-22, 68; *Studies from the Biological Laboratory* (Johns Hopkins University, Baltimore), II (March, 1882), 201-12.

"Explanation of Acquired Immunity from Infectious Diseases," *Science*, new series, I (March 29, 1895), 346-49.

"Facts Versus Figures, Yellow Fever Inoculation," *Journal of the American Medical Association*, XV (July 26, 1890), 142-44.

"A Fatal Form of Septicemia in the Rabbit, Produced by the Subcutaneous Injection of Human Saliva," *National Board of Health Bulletin*, II (April 30, 1881), 781-83; *Studies from the Biological Laboratory* (Johns Hopkins University, Baltimore), II (March, 1882), 183-200.

"The Function of the Army Medical School," *American Medicine*, III (April 5, 1902), 547-51.

"Further Experiments with the Micrococcus of Gonorrheal Pus, 'Gonococcus' of Neiser," *Medical News*, XLV (October 18, 1884), 426-29.

"General Sternberg's Answer to His Critics" (letter), *Medical News*, LXXIII (September 10, 1898), 335-37.

"Germicide," in *Reference Handbook of the Medical Sciences*, 1st ed. (New York: William Wood and Co., 1889), III, 321-27.

"The 'Gonococcus' of Neiser, Bacteriological Notes," *Medical News*, L (February 26, 1887), 231.

"Historical Resumé of the Investigations of Yellow Fever Leading up to the Findings of the Reed Board," in *Proceedings of the Second Pan-American Scientific Congress, December 27, 1915-January 8, 1916* (Washington, D. C.: Government Printing Office, 1917), pp. 645-52.

"The History and Etiology of Bubonic Plague" (Toner Lecture), *Philadelphia Medical Journal*, V (April 7, 1900), 809-15.

"Hunting Yellow Fever Germs," *Medical News*, LIV (March 9, 1889), 253-56; *Proceedings, Quarantine Conference, March 5-7, 1889* (Montgomery, Ala.: Brown Printing Co., 1889), pp. 90-102.

"Induced Septicaemia in the Rabbit," *American Journal of Medical Science*, LXXXIV (July, 1882), 69-76.

"Injection of Finely Powdered Inorganic Material into the Abdominal Cavity of Rabbits Does Not Induce Tuberculosis; An Experimental Research" (with pathological notes by W. T. Councilman), *American Journal of Medical Science*, new series, LXXXIX (January, 1885), 17-30.

"An Inquiry into the Modus Operandi of the Yellow Fever Poison," *New Orleans Medical and Surgical Journal*, new series, III (July, 1875), 1-23.

"Investigations Relating to the Etiology and Prophylaxis of Yellow Fever," *Transactions, College of Physicians of Philadelphia*, 3rd series, X

(1888), 339-65; (abstract) *Medical News*, LII (April 28, 1888), 449-56.

"Is Tuberculosis a Parasitic Disease?" *Medical News*, XLI (July 1, 22, September 16, November 18, December 30, 1882), 6, 87, 311, 564, 730.

"Malaria," *American Public Health Association Public Health Papers and Reports*, IX (1883), 31-54.

"The Malarial 'Germ' of Laveran," *Science*, VII (April 2, 1886), 297-99; *Medical Record*, XXIX (May 1, 8, 1886), 487, 517.

"The Medical Department of the Army," *Medical Record*, LIV (August 6, 1898), 213-14.

"The Metchnikoff Theory" (letter), *Journal of the American Medical Association*, LXIII (November 14, 1914), 1779-80.

"Micrococcus Pasteuri," *American Journal of Medical Science*, new series, XCII (July, 1886), 123-31; *Journal of the Royal Microscopical Society*, 2nd series, VI (June, 1886), 391-96.

"Micrococcus Pneumoniae Crouposae," *Medical News*, LX (February 6, 1892), 153-54; *Lancet*, I (March 26, 1892), 682-83.

"The Microscopical Investigations of the Havana Yellow Fever Commission," *New Orleans Medical and Surgical Journal*, new series, VII (May, 1880), 1017-24; *Proceedings, American Association for the Advancement of Science*, XXIX (1881), 381-86.

"On Yellow Fever" (abstract), *Transactions, Epidemiological Society of London, Sessions 1875-76 to 1880-81* (London: David Bogue, 1882), IV, 39-52.

"Pasteur," *Science*, new series, III (February 7, 1896), 185-89.

"Pasteur's Method for the Prevention of Hydrophobia," *Medical News*, XLVIII (April 24, 1886), 449-53.

"The Pneumonia Coccus of Friedlander (Micrococcus Pasteuri, Sternberg)," *American Journal of Medical Science*, new series, XC (July, 1885), 106-23; XC (October, 1885), 435-38.

"Poisonous Effects of Saliva," (letter), *Medical News*, XLI (July 8, 1882), 53.

"Preliminary Notes upon a New Method of Treating Yellow Fever," *Therapeutic Gazette*, 3rd series, IV (August 15, 1888), 524-26.

"Preliminary Report of the Havana Yellow Fever Commission of the National Board of Health, Submitted November 18, 1879" (with S. E. Chaille'), National Board of Health Bulletin, Supplement No. 1 (n.d.), 1-19.

"Preventive Medicine," *Sanitarian*, XXXVIII (March, 1897), 193-94.

"Protective Inoculations in Infectious Diseases," in *Public Health Papers and Reports Presented at the Twentieth Annual Meeting of the American Public Health Association, 1892* (Concord, N. H.: Republican Press Association, 1893), pp. 273-91; *Boston Medical and Surgical Journal*, CXXVIII (January 5, 1893), 29, 56.

"Recent Researches Relating to the Etiology and Specific Treatment of Yellow Fever," *American Public Health Association Public Health Papers and Reports*, XXIII (1897), 426-36; *Medical News*, LXXI (November 13, 1897), 613-18.

"Recent Researches Relating to the Etiology of Yellow Fever," *Transactions of the Association of American Physicians* (Philadelphia), III (1888), 321-29; (abstracts) *Journal of the American Medical Association*, XIII (November 30, 1889), 771-73; *American Public Health Association Public Health Papers and Reports*, XV (1889), 170-72.

"The Recognition of Micrococci," *Medical Record*, XXI (April 1, 1882), 368-70; XXII (October 7, 1882), 429-30.

"Relapsing Fever," in *Reference Handbook of the Medical Sciences*, 1st ed. (New York: William Wood and Co., 1889), III, 70-78.

"Report on Epidemic Cholera at Fort Harker, Kansas, during the Summer of 1867," in Circular No. 1, Surgeon General's Office, pp. 29-31.

"Report on the Prevention of Yellow Fever by Inoculation," *Report of Supervising Surgeon, Marine Hospital Service, for the Fiscal Year 1889* (Washington, D. C.: Government Printing Office, 1889), pp. 135-239.

"Report on the Sanitation of Ships and Quarantine," *Operations of the United States Marine-Hospital Service for the Fiscal Year 1890* (Washington, D. C.: Government Printing Office, 1890), pp. 85-95; U. S. Senate Document No. 58, 51st Congress, 1st session (Washington, D. C.: Government Printing Office, 1890), pp. 5-18.

"Report on Yellow Fever Cases" (letter), *New Orleans Medical and Surgical Journal*, VIII (November, 1880), 482-87.

"Researches Relating to the Etiology of Yellow Fever," *Pan-American Surgical and Medical Journal*, XXI (April, 1916), 16-20.

"The Results of Treatment at the Starmont Sanatorium," *Washington Medical Annals*, X (May, 1911), 50-56.

"Sanitary Lessons of the War," *Journal of the American Medical Association*, XXXII (June 10, 1899), 1287-94.

"Science and Pseudo-science in Medicine," *Science*, new series, V (February, 1897), 199-206.

"The Thermal Death Point of Pathogenic Organisms," *American Journal of Medical Science*, new series, XCIV (July, 1887), 146-60.

"The Treatment of Yellow Fever with Sodium Bicarbonate and Mercuric Chloride," *Johns Hopkins Hospital Bulletin*, I (July, 1890), 68.

"Typho, Malarial Fever," in *Reference Handbook of the Medical Sciences*, 1st ed. (New York: William Wood and Co., 1889), III, 93-95.

"The Value of Carbolic Acid as a Germicide, as Established by Experimental Data," *Medical Record*, XXII (September 9, 1882), 314-17.

"Virulence of Normal Human Saliva" (letter), *Philadelphia Medical Times*, XII (September 9, 1882), 836-39; XIII (November 4, 1882), 80-82; *Medical News*, XLI (September 16, 1882), 332-34.

"What Is the Explanation of Acquired Immunity from Infectious Diseases?" *Lancet*, I (April 11, 18, 1885), 655, 696.

"What Is the Explanation of the Protection from Subsequent Attacks Resulting from an Attack of Certain Diseases, and the Protective Influence of Vaccination against Smallpox?" *American Journal of Medical Science*, new series, LXXXI (April, 1881), 373-78.

"The Work of the Army Medical Department during the Spanish War," *Journal of the American Medical Association*, XXXI (December 3, 1898), 1356-60.

"Yellow Fever," in *System of Practical Medicine* (New York and Philadelphia: Loomis and Thomson, 1897), I, 267-300.

"Yellow Fever," in *The Cyclopedia of Practical Medicine* (Philadelphia: Blanchard and Lea, 1881), Supplement, pp. 45-73.

"Yellow Fever," in *Twentieth Century Practice* (New York: William Wood and Co., 1903), XXI, Supplement 80, pp. 574-635.

"Yellow Fever and Mosquitoes," *British Medical Journal*, II (November 10, 1900), 1391.

"Yellow Fever and Quarantine," *Public Health Papers and Reports Presented at the Eighth Annual Meeting of the American Public Health Association, 1880* (Boston: Franklin Press; Rand, Avery and Co., 1881), VI, 351-57.

"Yellow Fever Etiology" (letter), *Journal of the American Medical Association*, XXXV (October 20, 1900), 1039-40.

"Yellow Fever: History and Geographic Distribution," in *Reference Handbook of the Medical Sciences*, 2nd ed. (New York: William Wood and Co., 1904), VIII, 583-90.

Index

DATE DUE

			Printed in USA

HIGHSMITH #45230